Re-Imagining Your Body

through playful exercise

https://www.re-imaginingyourbody.com

Re-Imagining Your Body

through playful exercise

Anthony Stevens

SILENOS BOOKS
Cambridge, England

Cover image: photograph by Maria Pesma
An Evocation of the Apocalypse
10th Festival of Religious Music, Patmos, Greece

ISBN: 978-0-9955939-1-6

Contents

DEDICATION

This is not a book about theatre – but it is deeply rooted in my experience of teaching theatre over very many years. I've learned more from teaching theatre than I have from any other side of my adult life. Above all, I've learned to be always open to new possibilities and therefore not to start with too fixed an idea of where I'm going. I've learned this from being constantly struck and delighted by the creativity of my students. I therefore dedicate this book to all of them.

PREFACE

WORDS BEFORE THE JOURNEY

PREFACE: WORDS BEFORE THE JOURNEY

A book is only truly worth reading if reading it changes you in some way. Otherwise you are just passing the time (though hopefully pleasantly) which would have passed anyway. This may be a small-scale change, such as when you acquire a new skill or discover a new field of knowledge or where you are stimulated to think new thoughts. Or, much more rarely, it may be utterly transformative, the kind of change suggested at the beginning the great Indian epic *The Mahabharata*, when the sage Vyasa says that if you listen carefully to this story, "in the end you will be someone else".

What does *Re-Imagining Your Body* offer you? And how might this change you?

It offers you a journey.

Any journey entails a change of place. But a true journey is much more transformative than that.

Within the very broad field of 'self-help' literature, there are many books that make big promises – promises of career success, an end to anxiety, increased happiness, and such like. These are all *destinations*. Of course, such goals cannot be attained merely by wishing them true and in that sense you undertake a kind of journey here too, in the simple sense that you have to do something. But such journeys are not intrinsically satisfying or fulfilling; they are merely the means to the all-important end. For this reason, such books often stress how simple and quick the journey to the goal is. Hardly worth the name 'journey' at all, in fact.

In the modern world more generally, the journey – taken literally – has been supplanted by travel. Travel is mass produced. What were once the possibilities of new insights and even adventures on the way have been replaced by minor variations in the stock of duty-free shops and occasional anxieties about getting through security on time.

Re-Imagining Your Body

Even so, we all still have a deep-rooted sense of what a true journey is. Konstantinos Kavafis' great poem "Ithaka" explores this sense. It begins (in my own translation from the Greek) like this:

> As you set out for Ithaka
> wish for a long journey, one
> filled with the unforeseen, full of seeing.

The island of Ithaka was the homeland of the Greek hero Odysseus, to which he set sail following the Greek army's capture of Troy. But it took him ten years to get home, with many weird and wonderful adventures on the way which form the main plot of Homer's *Odyssey*. Kavafis takes this as a model of the kind of journey which is, in a strange way, more important than the destination. Nevertheless without that (or without some) destination there could be no journey. The poem ends:

> Keep Ithaka in mind always.
> To arrive there is your destination.
> But don't rush the journey, not in the slightest.
> Better to take many years
> even to arrive there in old age
> rich with all you have gained from the voyage
> not expecting riches from Ithaka.
>
> Ithaka gave you the wonderful journey.
> Without her, you would not have set out.
> But she has nothing more to give you.
>
> And if you find her faded, Ithaka will not have
>   deceived you.
> As wise as you'll have become, with so much behind
>   you,
> You'll have understood by now what Ithakas mean.

By the time you arrive at Ithaka, that is, you will have realized that what Ithaka, your destination, truly promised you was the journey to it.

As I've said, *Re-Imagining Your Body* offers you a journey. 'Ithaka' in this case can be described as a positive transformation of your relationship to your body, one through which you will attain greater presence, poise, confidence... above all greater awareness of and access to your psychophysical potential.

But the journey – that which really matters – is a journey of discovery of the many dimensions of *your body-as-you.*

It's not an intellectual journey, but a practical one. In a sense, it's your body – or rather, it's *you as your body* – that needs to *re*-discover itself, something which cannot possibly happen 'in the mind' alone. But as you'll see, this involves the whole of you. Above all, it requires the full participation of your imagination.

Before you set out, I'll try to clarify a little in the Introduction what 'your body-as-you' means and how the playful exercises in the rest of the book will help you discover it, to provide a kind of map of the journey to come.

INTRODUCTION

YOU ARE YOUR BODY

INTRODUCTION: YOU ARE YOUR BODY

If we want to change something for the better, we may well need to 'work on' it (in the common phrase). We can 'work on' a wide variety of things, such as on our French, on our marriage, on our self-esteem, on our soufflés.... Among these many things, some involve relationships, either with others (as in working on our marriage) or with ourselves (as in working on our self-esteem).

In fact I'm not entirely comfortable with the slightly puritanical phrase "to work on," but let that pass for the moment. Here I want to ask: among the relationships that you can usefully work on, is one *your relationship to your body*?

Not to work *on your body*, mind, but *on your relationship to it*. You can do the former in the gym. The latter can only happen in some sense 'inside you'.

I'll guess that this idea – that it may be a good idea to work on your relationship to your body – probably doesn't strike you as odd. After all, you might be one of the many people who have a less than easygoing relationship with their bodies. But perhaps it should strike you as odd.

You see, *you are your body* – even if you don't fully realize that fact. You don't have a relationship to your body as you might have to another person (which is the trap poor Narcissus fell into when he fell in love with his own image). Nor do you have a relationship to your body as you might have to an object you possess or own (which is a trap that many others fall into). Nor do you even have a relationship to it as you might have to some specific aspect of yourself, such as your self-esteem. Since *you are your body* lock, stock and barrel, to work on your relationship to your body is to work on your relationship to yourself. That's okay, it makes sense. But the key is this: *once you realize – fully realize – that that's what it means, a significant part of the need for you to work on your relationship to your body disappears!*

It's that simple – in theory, anyway. But at the same time it's not so easy to realize, fully realize, in practice (in your everyday life, let's say) that you are your body. I'll outline the underlying reason why this isn't easy a little later in this Introduction, since it's too deep an issue to delve into right at the start. For the moment it's enough to say that we can't easily *think of* ourselves as being our bodies unless we first learn to *experience* ourselves this way, where this is made difficult by a complex of powerful and deep-rooted cultural influences that serve to alienate us from our bodies, to make our bodies seem somehow 'other' than ourselves.

Such experience is the practical goal of this book.

As you progressively achieve not so much the experience that you are your body as the many rich and varied experiences that this consists of, you will find not only that your self-contentment and self-confidence are increased, but also that you discover physical – or better, psychophysical – resources that you never suspected. As you become more at one (literally) with your body, you will find your posture, your poise, your fluidity of movement, your energy level and your physical presence all enhanced (for these are all psychophysical, not merely physical). These are the 'payoffs'. But as I said in the Preface, it's the journey that matters – the encountering of and the deep learning from those many rich and varied experiences.

Re-Imagining Your Body is a book of exercises, along with some reflections upon them, which has the goal of transforming your relationship with your body. It's more a course in self-discovery than in self-improvement. But that's not the most important distinction here. In following this course, you're not going to try to 'improve' your body through *hard work* – you're going to extend your awareness of its reality and potential by re-imagining it through *play*. (This is why, a little earlier, I expressed reservations about the phrase "to work on".) As you'll discover, you will need the playful power of your imagination for this. It's your imagination – which I like to think of as a 'spiritual muscle' – that will bring you fully in touch with the nature of your *body-as-you* and help you discover the riches of truly *being your body*.

YOUR BODY-IN-THE-MIRROR

Right from the start, you must realize that 'you are your body' means much, much more than that *you are the body that others see*. This, your body-for others, is important. But almost certainly you identify it with your body-in-the-mirror, which, for you, is a detached and externalised body. And the body-in-the-mirror is a 'problem body' for far too many people. This fact is worth examining.

Negative body-image is really a problem on two levels. On one obvious level, the body-in-the-mirror falls distressingly short, usually in several ways, of some learnt and internalized ideal. On another, deeper level, the body-in-the-mirror *is an object*. When you look in the mirror you don't see the body you truly *live in,* nor even the body you *live through*; you see the body you have to *live with*. The deeper problem, then, is that whatever a person does to solve the problem on the first level not only doesn't solve it on the second level, but, on the contrary, reinforces it on that second level too. She or he might manage to make some visible improvements, but only at the cost of increasing alienation from her or his body. This is true even for a person who manages to transform their body enough (as an object) to start to like it (as an object).

I'll try to show more fully what this means, and how one might break out of the trap it involves, with the example of an exercise, which I'll describe at some length. This will also give a preliminary idea of how the exercises in this book work and of the broader philosophy behind them. However, there's no need for you really to do the exercise – in fact, it's too advanced to be a starting-point for the programme, so it's best that you don't try to do it; all you need to do here is to follow its logic, to imagine or contemplate doing it. This will be enough for you to understand the point.

'IMAGINARY BODIES'

Suppose, then, that you suffer from some degree of negative body-image and I tell you that I can solve your problem. "Great!" – you say (assuming you believe me) – "Tell me how!" Well, you're going to need to use that spiritual muscle of yours, your imagination, in the following way....

One of the great actors and teachers of acting of the twentieth century was Michael Chekhov. Chekhov developed a kind of 'trick' by which an actor can become the character that they have to play. Once the actor has gained a good idea of the psychology of a character, they should imagine the *kind of body* such a character would 'naturally' have – 'naturally' in the sense of most appropriate to or expressive of that character's psychology. Then, once the actor has imagined the character's body with sufficient clarity and detail, their next step is to imagine it as their very own body. They should imagine, that is, that they are inside the imaginary body of the character, which occupies much the same physical space as their own body, while they just get on with their own lives. After doing this for some time, while keeping a vivid sense of their new body, they find the character's psychology emerging and growing within them, taking them over. Thus they become the character!

This really does work. But apart from that, it's fun – a kind of game. It will help to make the game a bit more concrete with some examples. Following Chekhov's suggestion first: an awkward, slow-witted, rather inert person might be short, thickset, rather flabby, with a relatively large head and short, broad neck, with an upper body evidently burdened by gravity (Chekhov, 78). Alternatively, an energetic, dominating and judgmental person might have a slim, fairly rigid but forward-leaning torso, locked knees when standing, tense, narrow shoulders and a neck that turns briskly, but only in a 'sharp' way, with eyes that tend to flick sideways, being always on the lookout for threats and challenges. Or again, a sensual, self-indulgent but also warm and generous person might have a fairly full but 'well-distributed' figure, with mobile waist, active and expressive arms, and a tendency to tilt the head a little to the side when with others.

'Trying on' such imaginary bodies is a bit like trying on new clothes. Initially, you need simply to stand, to walk a few steps, to sit down... just to get the feel of them. Only gradually do they become *yours*. But you have to be very specific, for real bodies are distinctive in every aspect. It helps in this respect to distinguish between three different, but overlapping, levels:

a) the actual physical qualities of the imaginary body (a short or a long neck, broad or narrow shoulders, a trim or a flabby waist, and so on);

b) the character's physical way of relating to or 'inhabiting' that body (how the head is held, whether the shoulders are pulled back or rounded, whether the feet point outwards as the character walks...);

c) physical mannerisms which seem to 'go with' the specific body, rather like accessories (a tendency to drum the fingers on the thighs, to touch the chin or cheeks, to stand with the weight on the left leg, and such like).

We'll just imagine here that you really did play this 'Imaginary Bodies' game for sufficient time, taking on several contrasting imaginary bodies and, most importantly, experiencing how they made you feel. We'll also assume that you've had fun doing so. Now consider the following proposition:

The body-image, for the majority of people, is an imaginary body.

And it functions in exactly the same way, by 'taking over' one's psychology. So you see...

"But wait," you might well interrupt. "If my body-image is an imaginary body, surely it's the imaginary body that seems to fit most closely with what I feel about myself as a person. In this sense it *expresses* my psychology; it doesn't 'take over' my psychology in a way that transforms it."

I agree – up to a point. But this way of looking at it overlooks the strength of the *feedback* that's involved here, feedback that reinforces and almost certainly also amplifies everything negative in the way you feel about yourself. So you see (to pick up the thread)... instead of all that 'positive thinking,' telling yourself you've got deeper qualities, that you're a really interesting person, worth talking to... etc. etc., why not just imagine the 'new body' that goes with your target self-image and then take it on as yours! For keeps! After all, it's much cheaper than a full-body makeover.

"But if I do this," you ask, "what will happen when I look at myself in the mirror? Looking at imaginary bodies in the mirror wasn't part of your (or rather Chekhov's) game, was it? And I can see why not. Because it might have broken the spell."

I'll agree this far, that you shouldn't pick a 'new body' that's too obviously different from what you've got. So start from what you've got and enhance it. But in case you're thinking that imaginary bodies exist only 'in the mind' – in your imagination, that is – that's not true. A good actor, on stage, can look taller or shorter or thinner or fatter than they appear to be in real life, and something like Chekhov's trick is the way that they do it, even if they're not aware of that fact. Apart from that, your body-image *is* an imaginary body, as I've said, yet it's what you really do see in the mirror; it's not exactly what other people see when they look at you even though you imagine that it is.

Suppose now that I've convinced you that this might just work. Something – a doubt – still holds you back. What is it? Maybe you can't quite put it into words, but you still try:

"Playing this game seems like a lot of fun.... Using the same technique to transform my body-image seems a bit crude by comparison, a bit reductive...."

Exactly! Now we need to get past that little word 'fun'.

The fun of the game lies in discovering your *physical-imaginative potential.* Maybe you had thought that imagination was for day-dreaming or fantasy, things that happen 'in the head' – and therefore don't really happen. But playing this game reveals that your imagination can act within the physical world to transform it. Imagining a different body for yourself transforms your thoughts, your feelings, your desires, your impulses – your psychology, in a word – but the transformation doesn't end there. Your 'new' psychology transforms your real body too – not its given physical characteristics, of course, but the way you relate to and use these, and to that extent it even changes your actual appearance.

So yes, you're right – using this extraordinary power merely to overcome your negative body-image, by locking yourself into one new imaginary body, is crude and reductive.

Do you see what is happening here? You are taking a vital step beyond the *body-as-object*. You are discovering – or recovering – the *body-as-subject*. You are discovering the extraordinarily subtle – and subtly transformable – relationship that exists between your awareness of your body and your sense of self. And along with this you're realizing that your awareness of your body – the body-awareness that truly matters – is much, much more than what you see in the mirror, and your sense of self is much, much more than your idea of how others see you. In short, you have gone beyond the problem of negative body-image.

And that, of course, is to solve it!

Still, apart from the fact that I only asked you to imagine playing this game, which means that you (probably) haven't yet experienced the extraordinary transformative power of imagination in practice, I should also come clean and admit that I'm exaggerating – a little – for in reality such problems are not quite so easily solved. They are anchored too deeply in the socio-cultural mud. Even so, the story I've just outlined should be taken as a kind of parable-version of how the book as a whole works. In summary: *Re-Imagining Your Body* is fundamentally concerned with overcoming the alienation from the body that is so deeply entrenched in Western civilization and that lies at the root of so many of our discontents.

THE WESTERN 'BODY-VIEW'

I began by focusing on body-image problems as familiar territory, but these are really just a symptom of a deeper malaise. To get a better sense of this, imagine two scenes. First, a group of medieval monks flagellating themselves with scourges to 'mortify their flesh'. Next, a group of people 'working out' in a modern gym with weights, treadmills, bicycle machines, rowing machines.... Technological progress apart, it's pretty much the same thing – don't you think?

But perhaps you don't. Those medieval monks, you might object, were expressing a kind of hatred of the body. They wanted to suffer physically for the good of their souls. The gym-goers are prepared to suffer physically for the sake of their bodies. So it's different.

'No pain, no gain' in both situations, but with very different types of (hoped for) payoff? That's true – up to a point. But what I'll call *the new asceticism* is paradoxical. While it idolizes the body even as it makes the body suffer – not only in the gym but through fasting (I mean diet plans), even by putting it under the knife – there is still a kind of 'hatred of the body' involved in it, a hatred of the body as it really, typically, normally, naturally is.

It helps to see things this way (while recognizing, of course, that there are still good reasons for keeping fit). You cannot be so in thrall to the 'ideal body' if you realize that this entails a form of hatred of the real thing, a hatred more culturally entrenched, hence more easily overlooked, than just *your own* dislike of *your own* body.

Up to a point, we can blame capitalism for this. Yes, I mean it! Modern capitalism badly needs your body-dissatisfactions and actively promotes them in all available ways in order to get you to part with your money. Again it helps to think of this in the right way. What you're really being sold is not a range of body-enhancement tools and aids. What you're really being sold is the illusion of power – of power over your body-for-others. But precisely in being sold this, you're being stripped of real power, *the power to truly occupy your body as you.* In a word, you're being *alienated* – not, as in the classic Marxist formulation, from the product of your labour, but from the true sensuous ground of yourself.

Nevertheless it's only up to a point that we can blame capitalism, for capitalism needs to tap into a very deep-rooted and long-standing cultural attitude to the body in order to get away with its mass production of exploitable dissatisfactions. It's easy to see that you're being sold something. It's more difficult to grasp how the body has been reduced to less than itself by a couple of thousand years of Western dualistic thinking. Within Western culture what is rightfully the body's own has been ascribed instead first to the *soul*, second to the *mind*, and third to the *brain* (insofar as this gets distinguished, these days, from the body that serves to carry it around). In all these variations on a theme the body is robbed of its potential fullness of being. Not only that, but ultimately it is robbed of *YOU* – for 'you,' in this world-view, are always defined as something more than your body; supposedly you are more your soul than your body, or more your mind than your body, or more your brain than your body (there's also a pop version in which you're more your personality than your body). Your body, thus, is reduced to something *you have*, and it is difficult to re-conceive it as something *you are*.

Capitalism can only sell you its tantalizing promises in relation to the body you have. It is powerless over the body you are.

HAVING A BODY / BEING A BODY

Now it's time to return to the question that I left hanging earlier: Why is it not easy to realize that *you are your body*?

Suppose you see a beautiful horse in a field. It would be odd if you said, "That horse has a beautiful body!" Instead you say, much more simply, "That's a beautiful horse". But if you see a good-looking human being, you can say "That's a beautiful man/woman," but it seems equally possible and equally appropriate or right to say "S/he has a beautiful body". So what's the difference?

Human beings can think of themselves as *having* bodies and as *being* bodies. You might suppose that these are simply different ways of thinking about the same thing. But that's not true. In one superficial sense the body *I have* and the body *I am* are the same thing – at least, they occupy the same space. But in another, deeper sense they're very different things. The body I have tends more to the status of object. The body I am tends more to the status of subject. Both of these are valid ways of conceiving the body, provided that they're *both* understood to be valid ways. *But within Western culture, the body I have has come to dominate and displace the body I am.*

The fundamental reason that we, as human beings, can think of ourselves as having bodies is that we can also think of ourselves as having minds. But thinking in this way has a tendency to set up – or to assume – a split between body and mind, in the simple sense that they appear to us as different things.

The trap this can and often does lead to is identifying the *mind* with the *self*. It's as though the separation between body and mind that arises, when we think of these as things we have, in turn gives rise to a question: which of these, my body or my mind, is more truly or more fully what I am? (After all, the only alternative is that 'I' am something other than the body or the mind that I have.) But this question should never have arisen. Identifying the mind with the self reduces the body to a kind of 'accessory,' albeit a necessary one. The body is now merely what carries the self around and carries out actions within the world in the interests of that self.

This conception is profoundly wrong and very damaging.

When I truly think of myself as *being* a body, I don't – in fact, I can't – think of myself as simultaneously *being* something else, that is, a mind. Instead, the body that I am contains the mind that I also am. But because of our habit of thinking of a body and a mind as things we 'have,' we may find it difficult to realize this, at least to realize it fully – not just intellectually, but in such a way that we experience it too.

Notice that this is not true the other way round. If I think that I am my mind, my mind does not seem to contain my body in the same way. This is the clue to the difference between body and mind *as concepts*, but not *as things* – for body and mind do not actually exist as different things, but only as aspects of the same thing.

The vast majority of us will readily accept that horses have subjective experiences, as we do, in other words that they are fully sentient creatures rather than automata that merely behave as if they are conscious. The body that the horse so simply *is* clearly contains this subjective, sentient, conscious life. We see the alert vitality, the sensitivity, the 'charged awareness' *of the body*. No problem! But human beings, it seems, are so entranced by the 'little intelligence' of the mind, which appears to them as what is so special about them, that they find it hard to think of themselves as being *embodied* in the full sense that Friedrich Nietzsche so rightly insists that we are. For Nietzsche, the body is in fact all that we are. The body, in his conception, is a 'great intelligence,' one which contains our 'little intelligence' (the mental or spiritual dimension of being human) within it. Most people, he suggests, are unfortunately so enthralled by the capacity of their 'little intelligence' to *say* 'I' that they fail to grasp that the body has a capacity that goes way beyond this – the capacity to *enact* or *perform* 'I' (Nietzsche, 61–2).

Many of the exercises in this book can be thought of as exercises in performing 'I'.

For 'I' am not a consciousness, not even a self-consciousness, that sits somehow 'inside' my body in the way that a driver sits inside a car. 'I' exist, both consciously and self-consciously, as a *self* only in and through my embodied or bodily interaction with the world. 'I' am *in* my body, then, and nowhere else, not as anything distinct from it (a 'soul'... a 'personality'...), but in the *very subjectivity of my flesh* (for this is what I think Nietzsche means by the body's 'great intelligence').

THE SPIRIT OF PLAY

These are big, serious issues. But *play* – don't forget, you're going to re-imagine your body *through play* – is serious too, in two ways. Firstly, it's serious because it has a function or purpose. As most child psychologists will tell you, play is essential to the child's acquisition of a wide range of physical, psychological and social skills. From the child's point of view, however, play is simply fun. It's a bit like sex. Sex is for reproduction. But sex is also for pleasure – or, better, for joy. The joy of sex, we might say, is the trick by which Nature gets us to reproduce. And the fun of play is the trick by which Nature gets the child to acquire all those necessary skills.

But not only the child. We can *all* learn through play at any stage of life.

Here, however, we should go an important step further. Play truly works as a way of acquiring skills when it is *not* done with that purpose. In other words, play truly works as a way of acquiring skills *only* when it is done 'just for fun'. That's not true of sex. Sex can function as a means of reproduction when engaged in joylessly for that purpose alone – as some religions have advocated.

Work, as the opposite of play, is that which we do consciously and deliberately to achieve certain goals; that is, enhancements or ameliorations or transformations of ourselves, our environments or our situations. If we're lucky, we'll get a lot of satisfaction through this too and this may feed back into our work, improving its quality. In principle, however, such satisfaction is incidental, not strictly necessary to the attainment of the goals of work.

But the fun of play is essential.

Still, you must take note of something important here. Young children take their play very seriously. This is the second sense in which play is serious. Such seriousness, through which the world of the game *displaces* the world which is not a game, is a precondition of the (right kind of) fun. (I say 'right kind' because there's an adult way of playing that is too conscious of 'merely playing' and which therefore generates fun of the wrong kind.)

The exercises in this book should be carried out in the spirit of play. They will work much better if you enjoy doing them. This means you need to take them seriously in the sense of giving yourself over to each exercise for its own sake, and this, in turn, will prevent you 'end-gaming' (anticipating the desired result), which tends to be self-defeating. However, it doesn't mean you need to make any conscious effort to forget the goals of the exercises. That should just happen as you give yourself to or enter into the exercise itself.

PLAYFUL EXERCISE

Earlier, I asked you to follow the logic of 'Imaginary Bodies'. As an exercise, 'Imaginary Bodies' makes a demand on your imagination but not on any physical resources such as strength or stamina or flexibility or balance. Please don't get the wrong idea from this. Many of the exercises in this book will make physical demands on you, and they will help you develop and extend your physical resources in the process. They count as true 'physical exercises'. But almost all the exercises will ask you to use your imagination as an essential part of the exercise. This is what makes them 'playful exercises'.

Broadly, we can distinguish three types of, or ways of doing, physical exercise:

MINDLESS EXERCISE is where you can still perform the exercise adequately even if your mind isn't in it, in the sense that it's free to go off wandering somewhere else. You might be on an exercise bike or a treadmill, or doing push-ups, working very hard, while thinking about what you've got to do later at work or what to wear for the next date. This is more likely where the exercise involves repeating the same movements over and over again.

Mindless exercise has its place. But you need to understand its limitation: the fact that it enhances only what we can call the *mechanical* functions of the body.

MINDFUL EXERCISE is where your mind must be 'in it,' in the sense of fully concentrated and focused on what you're doing, for the exercise to be maximally effective. All stretching exercises are like this. So are martial arts. And weight lifting.

By definition, mindless exercise doesn't become more effective when done more mindfully. But there's an important exception to this: when you need to improve your technique (which can apply even to something as natural as walking), then you need to focus mentally on what exactly your body is doing.

Re-Imagining Your Body

Mindful exercise, of course, is good for the 'mind' as well as for the 'body'. It is really a kind of *meditation-in-movement*.

PLAYFUL EXERCISE also requires your mind to be 'in it' in order to be effective. But whereas many properly mindful exercises can be done (badly) in a relatively mindless way, it's simply not possible to carry out playful exercise without the full involvement of your mind. This involvement is not simply concentration and focus, nor even visualization; it's the exercise of your *creative imagination*. A few examples will communicate the kind of thing this means. You might walk while imagining an elastic rope attached to the top of your head and to the sky, which is tending to lift you off the ground, so that your steps must include the effort to stay grounded. You might relax while standing upright by imagining that your body is a skeleton, which therefore cannot have any muscular tension and which stays standing purely because of way the bones are balanced on top of each other. (Feel the wind blow through you!) You might imagine playing in the sea, feeling the resistance of the water as you stir and swish it with different limbs until you feel that you have become the sea, that it's not just all around you but actually flowing through and in you.

Only playful exercises can help you transform your relationship to your body and get much more fully back inside it.

Playful exercises can also have very beneficial effects on a wide variety of physiological functions: balance, flexibility, coordination, energy level, even stamina.... But they are not a universal panacea. For all-round health and fitness it's best to practice them alongside other exercises specifically designed to enhance aerobic capacity and muscle strength, as well as in combination with yoga or *tai chi* or *qigong*. This, by the way, will help you get more out of your playful exercises too. And you should find that you can enhance the effectiveness (and pleasure) of many 'normal' exercises by adding an element of imagination to them.

YOUR BODY-AS-A-WHOLE

Another vital distinction needs to be made here. Your body consists of parts. But it is also a whole – and as a whole it is *more than the sum of its parts*. Some kinds of exercises, especially mindless ones, focus on specific body parts. Playful exercises, in contrast, tend to focus on (or at least consciously to involve) the whole body. Crucially, becoming one with your body, such that you experience it *as you*, simply cannot happen at the level of the part. It cannot even happen at the level at which the whole is just the sum of the parts.

At the end of this Introduction you will find a simple exercise to make you more aware of your-body-as-a-whole.

The majority of exercises in this book require you to 'tune in to' and 'listen to' your body-as-a-whole, whether or not they explicitly refer to the need for such whole body awareness. Hence you should always try to be sensitive to the complex interconnectedness of your body. Above all, do not think of your body as a machine! In a machine, part A impacts part B, part B impacts part C, part C impacts part D, and so on. But your body is much more like a tightly bundled network or web of links, pathways, associations, reflections and echoes. Of course, this is not to say that you can or should forget about the parts. On the contrary, developed whole body awareness is necessary for fully effective use of the parts. You've probably seen those performers who imitate robots. The technique they use is called *isolation* – the isolation of one body part from the rest. Thus they turn themselves into 'machines'. The paradox is that they could not do this without a highly developed awareness of the body-as-a-whole. The same is true, perhaps in a more obvious way, of belly dancers, who also use the technique of isolation.

THE BODY'S SELF-AWARENESS

Through the exercises in this book you will also be training two senses that are not normally given much conscious attention – at least not among those who are not professional performers or athletes. These are your *kinaesthesia* and your *proprioception*. Kinaesthesia is internal awareness of the body's movement. Proprioception is internal awareness of the body of a more general kind, including its placement, balance and condition. There will be no need to think about these things as you perform the exercises (and I won't refer explicitly to them in describing the exercises), but it's useful to understand why they matter.

They matter, above all, because they are *principal ways of being inside your own body.*

Ballet dancers often train using mirrors in which they can check their position, posture and alignment. Some research suggests that the use of mirrors in training can contribute to negative body-image among dancers. This, in turn, raises the question of whether or not mirrors are truly necessary for the technical aspects of such training. Ballet, of course, is a very strict and demanding discipline and it's the case that, for many people, even trained ballet dancers, proprioception and kinaesthesia are insufficiently fine-tuned to ensure the required precision.

But for you, in performing the exercises in this book, it would be *wrong, wrong, wrong !!!* to do any of them looking in a mirror.

Because they require you to *search within*.

Just as in some kinds of 'depth psychology' you can benefit from digging deep into what is usually called your unconscious mind and bringing its contents more into consciousness, so you will benefit from digging deep into your 'unconscious body' to render it more conscious, more aware, more sensitive and more fully 'alive to itself'. No mirror can help you with this.

Through the exercises you will also find that your imagination becomes 'fitter' – that is, sharper and more vivid – though you do nothing to train it.

Here, however, I must give a warning. If you had in fact tried the 'Imaginary Bodies' exercise described earlier, it's possible that you might have imagined having a new and different body in the wrong way. To understand this, try a simple experiment: close your eyes and imagine that you're either much slimmer than you are or much fatter. Take enough time to fully experience this.

Now, having done that, did you: a) *feel that you were inside* a slimmer/fatter body; b) *see yourself as having* a slimmer/fatter body?

This is an interesting experiment because it's quite easy to find yourself 'flicking between' these different perspectives, like flicking between channels. But it's the former perspective that you should aim for, the sense of your body as subject. The latter is the 'problem of the mirror' again, the sense of your body as object.

ORIGINS OF THE EXERCISES

I said earlier that 'Imaginary Bodies' was devised by Michael Chekhov as an aid for actors. In fact, the majority of the exercises in this book are adapted from exercises used in training actors or more generally in drama classes. But here their goal is to develop a richer sense of the *lived body* for anyone at all – anyone at all of whatever age or 'body type'.

I've worked with these kinds of exercises in theatre classes for a very long time. For a very long time I've also had the strong sense that their benefit goes way beyond training actors. But, again for a long time, I did not try to formulate what that wider benefit might be – not until quite recently. Why not? Mainly, I think, because the exercises are such fun. As I've suggested above, the best way to do them is to enjoy doing them without thinking about their purpose. To some extent that applies to showing others how to do them too. When you stop to think about it, however, it's the very fact that they're fun that's the clue to their wider relevance for people in general and not just for actors. If they're fun for trainee actors, they should be fun for others too – and if being fun is essential to their beneficial effects, these effects ought to be available to anyone able to enjoy doing them. They've become thought of as actors' exercises simply because actors are, for professional training purposes, allowed to *play* much more than the rest of us 'grown ups' are.

Nonetheless, it's worth looking just a little more closely at their benefit for actors. According to Michael Chekhov in his book *To the Actor*, the actor needs to achieve *great sensitivity of the body to psychological realities*. He stresses that this cannot be achieved by physical exercises alone, in the sense of exercises that work on the body as a merely 'mechanical' system, for body and mind (or body and soul) must be experienced and lived as one. Whereas in everyday life it may remain possible to think of the physical and the psychological as being distinct realms, or distinct kinds of reality, the actor has to learn how to absorb psychological qualities into their very flesh, even, I would add, into their bones, so that the body of the actor becomes what Chekhov calls a "sensitive membrane" through which thoughts, emotions, feelings and urges freely pass and can therefore be expressed (Chekhov, 2).

One can readily see how this approach will help the actor, since the actor's job is to communicate to audiences the complex, shifting *internal* life of characters via their *external* being and behaviour. But it ought also to be possible to see, in the light of earlier parts of this Introduction, how it challenges the sense of a split between body and mind that permeates Western culture, and how it can help us overcome the alienation from our bodies that follows from this split. It may even be sensed that here is a way to get wholly back inside our bodies.

As far as possible I've indicated the original source of an exercise (or at least where I first came across it), even where I've made significant changes to it. Even so, my knowledge of these origins is far from complete. While some exercises are easy to attribute, anyone who has taught in this field will be aware of the complex process of sharing, recycling, adaptation and evolution of exercises that makes the 'parentage' of many others more obscure. I should also acknowledge here that even those exercises which I consider my own inventions have been stimulated or influenced by the work of others; but it would be too cumbersome, and pointless in the present context, to try to record the details of this.

THE SPIRIT OF EXPERIMENT

Naturally I've been very selective in the choice of exercises. My criteria of selection have been that the exercises included here should
1. promote the goal of bringing you more in touch with your body-as-subject,
2. be doable by any reasonably fit individual, and
3. be doable on your own.

The third of these criteria is the most restrictive, since many actors' exercises and games are designed for pairs or for groups. But there are plenty enough left to make a complete *autocours*. Occasionally, however, I've described an exercise or game that needs more than one participant, in the interest of clarifying a crucial principle.

Working on your own necessarily means that you do not have a teacher or guide to observe you and perhaps 'correct' any 'mistakes'. Is this a problem? Not at all – not, that is, if you adopt the right *spirit of experiment*. In fact, I would argue that there is a benefit in working on your own like this (given the same proviso) – after all, it is *your body* that you are exploring, getting fully in tune with and realizing as *you rather than yours*. If you remain focused on and alert to your own psychophysical reality and open to psychophysical changes, then you cannot make 'mistakes'. Nothing you will learn can be called 'technique,' a word which implies some kind of going beyond your natural endowment; on the contrary, you will be reconnecting with your nature.

Still, I cannot stress strongly enough the need for that spirit of experiment. The great and influential acting teacher Jerzy Grotowski, who revolutionized our ideas of performance in the second half of the twentieth century, insists that exercises should never simply be repeated. They can be varied as necessary as a way of avoiding repetition, but most importantly each exercise should always be approached in a spirit of exploration or research, as if for the first time. There were times, he says, when his group gave up doing exercises entirely, even for as long as eight months, because they realized that the exercises were being done for their own sake, not as a means to further discoveries. When the exercises were resumed, they were experienced in a completely different way (Grotowski, 210).

I am not advocating giving up the exercises for such long periods, of course! I'm saying that you need to find ways to avoid merely repeating the exercises, where 'merely repeating' means letting what is psychophysical become merely physical. In effect, 'merely repeating' implies no longer doing the exercises in the spirit of play, for the spirit of *play* and the spirit of *experiment* are very closely connected.

One simple way to help keep the exercises fresh and exploratory is to keep varying the ones that you do and the sequence in which you do them. But this applies only after you've worked through the book, which is organized as a progressive course. Above all, the division between Parts One, Two and Three of the book should be respected, since each new Part takes you significantly deeper in 're-imagining your body' (see below). However, once you've worked through these three Parts you will be fully free to do whatever exercises you like in whatever order you like.

THE THREE LEVELS

As just noted, the division of the course into three parts is important. These parts can be thought of as 'levels,' with Part Two taking you deeper than Part One, and Part Three taking you deeper than Part Two. In outline, Part One aims to make you aware of the unity of self and body. Part Two aims to transform your sense of your body's being-in-the-world. Part Three aims to develop your sense of what might be called the spiritual expressiveness of the body.

If your goal is simply to improve your poise, your posture, your presence, the fluidity and power of your movement, and such like – that is, all those qualities that flow from your 'being-at-oneness' with your body – then Part One, 'Being Fully Inside Your Body,' will serve you amply. But if you wish to embark upon a real journey of discovery, one which may take you to places you did not initially envisage, then you need Part Two and especially Part Three as well. Part Two, 'Demoting the Conscious Controller,' tries to shift the idea of the body as something that acts in the world in subjection to our will (a conception that separates the body too much from the world) towards an idea of the body as receptive, responsive and finely tuned to the world, and able to tap into and draw from its rich resources. Part Three, 'Metamorphoses,' then shows how exploring the 'Unconscious Body' (by analogy with the Unconscious Mind) can take us beyond our everyday and socially-normative behavioural patterns into the deep spiritual waters of what I call the 'body-as-possibility".

The book also contains two Appendices, for those who wish to follow up the ideas behind the exercises in a more theoretical way. Appendix One provides a brief history of the Western dualistic thinking that lies behind the distorted or lop-sided view of the body that remains so prevalent today. Appendix Two surveys some recent scientific research that may provide an explanation of why and how the exercises in the book work.

For many other supplementary and related materials, visit

https://www.re-imaginingyourbody.com

That's it! You're now ready to start out on a journey of discovery of *your-body-as-you* and of *yourself-as-your-body*. Here, then, to close this Introduction, is the simple exercise I promised you a little earlier, which has the purpose of making you more aware of your body-as-a-whole. Its effect is subtle, but striking.

EXERCISE: CHEST EXPANDER... TORSO OPENER... BODY SMILE

You start 'mechanically' (and, to be honest, boringly) with something all too familiar. Stand with your feet a little more than shoulder width apart. Bring your hands in front of your chest at shoulder height, palms down, finger tips almost touching, with your elbows out to the sides, also at shoulder height. Then swing your arms outwards as far as you can, straightening them at the elbows, **keeping the palms facing downwards.** *Immediately swing them back again, bending the elbows, and... just keep repeating this, over and over (but not for too long, just enough to get a feel for it). This, of course, is a simple mindless exercise, focused on a part of the body. For the time being, all you have to do is remain aware of your body. Don't start thinking of something else (easy though this is with such 'mechanical' exercises).*

And... stop. The next step is to change one detail. From now on, in the way you swing your arms outwards, you must also **turn the palms over** *so that they come to face directly upwards at full extension of your arms. As you* *swing your arms in again, **turn the palms back over** so that they're facing directly downwards when they almost meet in front of your chest. Do this a few times and notice the difference. You should feel that now your chest expands, or 'opens,' much more than it did before, and you naturally raise your head a little higher. In a general (whole body) way, you become 'bigger' and more open, in fact. Try to understand why this is, how something as simple as the direction your palms are facing can make such a huge difference to the way you feel.*

*For the third phase of the exercise you need to use a little imagination. Perform exactly the same repeated movement as you just did (turning the palms over), but this time, on the 'outstroke,' as you feel your chest opening, imagine also that your lower torso, your abdomen, is opening as well. Try to feel this as an 'echo' or 'amplification' of the opening of your chest. You might even feel yourself opening a little at the knees (provided they're not locked, which they shouldn't be) too. Then... smile, just a little, as you continue the exercise, **smile as you open.** You should feel that your smile is a perfectly appropriate, fitting part of the exercise. It's not imposed. A smile is naturally an 'opening' of the face, isn't it? Whereas a frown is a closing of the face. Now imagine the way your whole torso opens on the outstroke as being itself a kind of smile, a smile of the whole body! It's a good feeling.*

Once you've appreciated that good feeling, then, just to see that something real is going on here (for we often need to use the imagination to get at the real), go back to the first way of doing 'chest expander,' with no turning over of the palms. Smile as you do this. You'll find that there's no connection at all between the smile and the movement; it's just like you're thinking of something else!

PART 1

BEING FULLY INSIDE YOUR BODY

PRELIMINARY THOUGHTS

Many of the damaging body-ideals (or, more accurately, body-fantasies) of the modern world circulate and are promoted by means of photographs and videos. Such visual images, flatly lacking in warm, soft fleshiness and all too often looking straight back at you, serve to reinforce the cold dominance of 'the mirror' in modern Western culture.

But one truly vital thing that cannot be photographed and to a significant extent cannot even be videoed is a person's *way of being inside their body*.

To begin to understand what this means, think first of the common saying (or maybe quotation, though I've no idea who first said it), "At twenty you still have the face you were born with, but at forty (or, more likely nowadays, fifty) you have the face you deserve". The idea here is that as you grow older your face comes to express the 'real you' – your character, let's say.

To the extent that there's some truth in this, it's also true of your body – and, for that matter, of your voice.

But how much truth is there in it? Focusing here on the body, we can say that after a certain point in life (quite early, in fact – much earlier than twenty) our bodies are products of *two* things: our genetic inheritance *and our habits*. As we get older, the proportional influence of our habits on our bodies increases. It's important to understand 'habits' here in a broad sense as including not just bad posture or insufficient exercise, but also our habitual ways of thinking about and experiencing our bodies or aspects of them. Psychological habits, in other words, are just as important as physical ones. Among these psychological habits, many have a cultural origin.

Some might argue that a third factor is involved, as we grow older, in giving our bodies the 'shape' and maybe even in a sense the 'feel' that they have: wear and tear. But a great deal of wear and tear is the product of our habits – not all of it, of course, but more than we might imagine.

Insofar as we can distinguish psychological from physical habits (although in an important sense all such habits are psychophysical), the exercises in this book focus more on the kind of psychological habits that commonly underlie our physical habits. We are often much less aware of our bad underlying psychological habits than we are of our bad physical ones. But it's our habits, especially our psychological habits, that constitute for each of us our individual 'way of being inside our body'.

Bad psychological habits, moreover, can be said to cause us *not to be fully inside our body* as a specific 'way of being inside our body'!

True, that's an odd concept. Even so, you may well have noticed that some people seem more inside, or more fully inside, their bodies than others – in the sense of more *at one with* them – but you can't easily explain why. In fact, words are not very good at capturing the sense of this idea – except, perhaps, in the following 'suggestive' formula: living *in* your body is better than living *through* your body, which is better than living *with* your body. If you live through your body, your body is reduced to a medium or instrument of your self. If you live with it, your body is something you just have to 'carry around with you'.

However, we need to be very clear about what living *in* your body really implies, for the phrase is open to misinterpretation. What exactly this idea means will become completely clear only through practising the exercises. But three important points can be usefully made here. Firstly, you cannot be truly 'inside your body' in any sense that also distinguishes you from that body, so you're not inside it as a driver is inside a car. Secondly, when you are dissatisfied with your body-image you cannot be fully 'inside your body,' because you relate to your body as to an image in the mirror. Thirdly, being fully 'inside your body' is always attractive!

As you work through the exercises in Part One you will discover that whether or not a person seems fully inside their body depends on the following factors: 1) What seems to be their natural or normal *body-centre*, and where the impulses that generate their movements seem to come from. 2) The way they relate to and 'inhabit' the space around them. (How a person 'rides' their potential energy is also important, but that will be developed in Part Two.)

THE 'YOU' INSIDE YOUR BODY

Where is the *centre* of your body?

Shouldn't I be more specific about what I mean by 'centre' here? Does it refer to the geometrical mid-point, the centre of gravity, the 'nerve centre' (literally or metaphorically), or some kind of 'most important place'? If the latter, how do we define 'most important'?

But I don't want to be more specific – at least, not yet. The notion of a 'body-centre' is both complex and subtle. It's far better that you discover for yourself what it means, through some exercises.

EXERCISE: IMAGINARY CENTRES

To start this journey of exploration, all you have to do is to imagine different centres in your body, following and expanding on an idea of Michael Chekhov's (Chekhov, 7, 80-4), while taking note of how imagining each of these imaginary centres makes you feel, how it makes you experience yourself, others around you, and even life itself. This is considerably simpler than the 'Imaginary Bodies' exercise outlined in the Introduction (which you were only asked to imagine doing) – but as you'll discover, its ramifications are immense. To do it, you simply focus your attention in a particular part of your body, so that your consciousness seems centred (or focused) in that place – so that YOU seem to be centred at that place.

You'll be exploring possible centres, then – not just one centre. The important thing is how differently each makes you feel. In the end, you'll be able to decide for yourself if your body has a single 'true' centre or not.

The Three Main Centres: Chest, Head, Abdomen

Begin by focusing your attention – a part of your consciousness – in your chest, in the middle of the chest, at about the height of your heart, and deep inside you, that is, not too close to your front or your back.

*Keeping your attention focused in this **chest-centre**, perform the following simple 'everyday' actions, in whatever sequence you like. Walk around, quite slowly, on a flat surface. Stand, with hands on hips. Stretch out an arm to point at something. Walk a bit quicker. Turn around. Lean against a wall. Sit down. Stand up. Add any actions you like, as long as they're simple.*

If you have someone with you, go over to them, look them in the eye, shake hands and say, 'Nice to meet you' – all with your attention still focused in your chest-centre.

Ask yourself, 'How does the chest-centre make me feel?'

Re-Imagining Your Body

*Now focus your attention in your head, more or less in the middle of your head, that is deep inside, but a little more towards the top – in the middle of your brain we might say, but you mustn't think of your brain, only of your head. Keeping your attention focused in this **head-centre**, perform the same sequence of simple everyday actions, including, if possible, 'meeting' someone. Ask yourself, 'How does the head-centre make me feel?'*

*Next, focus your attention in your abdomen, centrally, about 6–8 cm (2½ –3 in) below your navel, and quite deep inside, though a little more towards the front of the body. Then, with your attention focused in this **abdominal-centre**, perform the same series of actions, and ask yourself, 'How does the abdominal-centre make me feel?'*

These three body centres are very different from one another. They make you experience yourself, others, life itself, very differently.

It's always interesting to listen to individual reports of how these different centres have been experienced. Different people have different insights, and some may be able to express very subtle shades of feeling. But the common ground of the experience is roughly the following:

The **chest-centre** makes you feel confident, positive, open – including open to others, in a way that is implicitly generous and warm – and you feel quite powerful, though not in any dominating way.

The **head-centre** makes you feel lighter, not wholly present, somewhat diffident, perhaps even hesitant, a little closed or reserved towards others, with a sense of weakness that is nothing like fatigue.

The **abdominal-centre** makes you feel grounded, stable but in a 'springy' way, powerful, ready for action, confident with others but not really open or generous towards them, perhaps because you might be about to 'use' them in some way.

You might have noticed something else. Different centres can seem more or less appropriate for different tasks. The abdominal-centre is perfect for climbing up stairs, for example, while the chest-centre adds a dimension to the way you point at an object, especially if it's a distant object.

You should keep experimenting with these three centres in order to refine your awareness of both the different feelings they set up in you and their respective appropriateness for different actions. Gradually add more and more different actions to your repertoire here. You can also 'switch on' any particular centre while going about your daily business, while vacuuming, or just walking in the street, or shopping, or while doing conventional exercises, including swimming.

You can also observe other people, asking yourself which of the three main centres seems to be activated within them at any particular time. It may help you here to be aware of an actor's trick and then to watch people *as if* they are using it. Actors can think of the head-centre as their 'thought centre,' the chest-centre as their 'emotional centre' and the abdominal-centre as their 'action centre'. By asking themselves whether, in a particular scene, they're mainly thinking or feeling or doing, they know which centre to activate.

But while this may help you to observe which centre seems to be activated in another person, it's *not* the way you should experience these centres for yourself. It's too reductive. That's why I call it a 'trick'. (Not only that, but it's even a little misleading – particularly in relation to the head centre, as you'll see.)

In fact, your goal is to become more subtle in your exploration of potential body-centres. To do this, you need to experience centres other than the main three. Even so, it's important to think of these three as the *main* centres. We'll see why later. Not only that, but you might already, at this stage, have come to feel that the abdominal-centre and the chest-centre, while they're different from each other, are somehow more closely related to each other than the head-centre is to either. You might have come to feel that the head-centre is not appropriate for any specific tasks in the way that the other two centres are. It's as though the chest-centre and the abdominal-centre are the *two main centres* among the *three main centres*, so to speak. Again, we'll see why this is so later.

The Pelvic Centre and the Gaze Centre

Now, instead of focusing your attention in your abdominal-centre, focus it in your pelvis instead. This is a larger centre – the full size of your pelvic girdle – and a little lower down, the 'ground floor' of your torso. It's also the 'gateway' to your legs, via the hips. Perform the same sequence of simple actions – and any other actions you like.

It feels different. If with the abdominal-centre you are 'ready for action,' with the pelvic centre this feels even more to be the case. You may even start signalling this readiness, possibly with a kind of swagger.

Re-Imagining Your Body

Now compare the different ways the abdominal-centre and the pelvic-centre make you experience your upper body. You need a kind of split-attention for this, focusing your attention in one part of your body while remaining attentive to another part, but it's not especially difficult.

It helps to approach it this way. Forget centres just for a moment. Simply walk, on a flat surface. At first, deliberately walk with your upper body quite stiff, so all your 'walk' is in the lower body. After this, walk with your arms lightly swinging and your shoulders loosely and freely moving in coordination with your legs. You'll experience this more fully in the contrast with the previous stiff walk. But don't exaggerate, and don't walk fast. It should be a very natural walk – which also feels much better than the 'lower body' walk. Now do this natural, full-body walk with your attention focused in the abdominal-centre. There should be no problem with this. The abdominal centre clearly works with this way of walking.

Now try it with your attention focused in the pelvic-centre. This time you will probably feel your upper body start to stiffen up, or, if not exactly that, to lose some of its looseness, if only a little. True, you can make a kind of special effort to keep your arms swinging, but this effort may seem to be somewhat separate – detached – from the pelvic-centre. (Moreover, if you walk fast while focused in your pelvic-centre, the energy and momentum of the walk is more easily transferred to the arms, keeping them swinging – but even in this case you should be able to feel a kind of split.)

The point is this: the abdominal-centre can function as a centre for your whole body in a way that the pelvic centre can't – or, to be more precise, can't always (for sometimes it can). This, of course, is why the abdominal-centre is a *main centre*, more particularly why it's one of the *two* main centres among the three main ones.

This doesn't make the pelvic-centre unimportant, of course. It's *very* important, and we'll return to it later. For the moment, think about this: have you ever wondered about the 'logic' of that adolescent male fashion statement of recent years of wearing jeans that hang down low on the hips, opening up large rear vistas of underpants? Isn't this a way of focusing attention on the pelvic-centre – not just the observer's attention, but the wearer's too?

More generally, how do clothes, and the ways we wear them, contribute to the way we 'centre' our bodies?

Next, compare your head-centre with a different but anatomically close centre, one in your eyes. We might call this the gaze-centre rather than the eyes-centre, because if you focus your attention in your eyes your gaze comes to dominate your being. You are your gaze. You become filled with what you see. Now, this sets up feelings which are in many ways the opposite of those generated by your head-centre. So focus your attention in your eyes and even imagine that your eyes are enormous, occupying much of your body. You now feel bright, alert, sharp – and above all, so oriented towards the outside world, so extroverted that you have been 'turned inside out'! Your head centre, in contrast, makes you introverted and cut off. However, that light, rather 'airy' quality you feel with your head-centre is preserved in the gaze-centre – but combined now with a feeling of 'quickness'. By the way, Chekhov suggests placing a centre in just one of your eyes; this, very differently, will make you become insincere and sneaky (Chekhov, 81).

Now try a little experiment in imagination. Let's say that the head-centre is 'airy'. The gaze-centre is 'airy' too, though not in so vague a way. The abdominal-centre, in contrast, could be called 'earthy,' and the pelvic-centre has a related kind of 'weightiness'. The chest-centre could reasonably be called 'fiery'. True, if you're not angry or passionate about something, it's a slow burning, gently warming 'fieriness'. But that's good enough.

Then can you find a centre corresponding to the fourth element, a 'watery' centre?

Without saying – yet – where I place this centre in myself, I will simply note here that it generates a peaceful, contemplative, perhaps even complacent feeling. Compared to the centres dealt with so far, it is probably the least conducive to action.

Some Other 'In-Body' Body Centres

There are three other actually-in-body body-centres to try before we move on. In each case, try to discover as precisely as you can how these work for you.

1) In the soles of your feet. This gives you a strong connection to the earth and is excellent for scrambling up and down steep hills. Imagine the soles of your feet are like suckers. Try imagining your feet are comparatively much bigger than they really are. But how do you feel when you sit or lie down with your centre kept here?

2) In your throat. I experience this as generating a slight sense of constriction, and with that a somewhat perturbed, even anxious feeling. It's like a 'no man's land' between the head and chest.

Re-Imagining Your Body

3) In the top of your skull. One way to achieve this is first to imagine a string attached to the top of your head exerting a gentle upward pull. Then, in imagination, simply remove the string, leaving your attention focused where the string had been attached. You might well feel a little taller, perhaps slightly superior (though you won't necessarily be 'looking down your nose' at others). It also makes me feel rather grave and business-like, a little austere. For some reason, I imagine myself as a newly appointed head-teacher!

As for the 'watery' centre, I place it just below the sternum, in the soft upper belly area about 10 cm (4 in) above the navel. And I think of it as my 'Buddha-centre'.

'Out of Body' Body Centres

For the next phase, you need to start imagining *body-centres that are outside the body!* (That's why I used the phrase 'actually-in-body body-centres' above.) Since this is odd, it may help to think of it as a game called 'Ball and Chain'. After all, if you really were a prisoner wearing a ball and chain, your experience of your body would be seriously affected by a 'centre' lying (heavily) outside it.

Let's be clear: you're not going to have any 'out of body' experiences by playing this game! Your experiences will all be *in body*. But they will be produced by the way you imagine your centre to be outside your body.

Try imagining the following centres, in this order:

1) 80–100 cm (31–40 in) above your head.
2) 20–30 cm (8–12 in) in front of your nose.
3) 30–40 cm (12–16 in) in front of your belly.
4) Between the shoulder blades, 20 cm (8 in) behind you.
5) About 20 cm (8 in) below and around 10 cm (4 in) to the rear of your anus.

In each case, perform your sequence of simple, everyday actions, observing how you feel – how you experience your body – throughout.

Very interestingly, you really do have to imagine that these centres lie *outside* your body. If, instead, you imagine that your body expands in the appropriate direction and by the appropriate amount (so that, for example, you have a very tall head or a very long nose, as in

'Imaginary Bodies'), it's really not the same thing. Try that as well, to see the difference. When the centre is truly outside you, it exerts a different kind of influence on you. It 'holds' you. Or it 'pulls' you. Or you have to pull it along with you.

Of these five, the second is probably the easiest to get the feel of. With a centre 20–30 cm (8–12 in) in front of your nose, you become inquisitive, prying perhaps, even nosy, continually drawn towards things. I wouldn't be surprised if you experienced yourself as quite thin as well.

With the third, make doubly sure you don't imagine your belly itself to be bigger. If you do that, you will become like an 'oriental potentate,' rather flat-footed, hedonistic and, perhaps, cruel in a petty way. But with this centre properly placed outside you, you may well feel like a lithe and limber wrestler, perfectly balanced, with a kind of shield in front of you protecting your softest, most vulnerable parts – the 'shield,' that is, of your confidence in yourself.

The fourth is very much the opposite of the third. It's not quite like having a 'weight on your shoulders' but it certainly holds you back. It's not easy to move forward, you want to keep stopping. You don't feel timid, you're not 'shy and retiring,' but you certainly lack the ease that confidence gives. There's something problematic, but not with the kind of problem you can think through – you're not centred in your head, after all. What is it, then? The past, perhaps? Something unresolved but also forgotten, only half left behind you?

The fifth centre immediately turns you into a slack, lazy, even gross type of person. One to avoid!

Now, before we go back to the first out-of-body centre, you should have noticed that the four centres discussed so far all create *characters*. In your own explorations, you might experience some of these characters a little differently, but that's no problem – as long as you're not 'forcing' the experience, as long, that is, as your sense of character arises naturally from the game.

It's not my goal to turn you into an actor, but I'd like you to ask: to what extent is a character a physical – a bodily – thing, as well as a psychological thing? (That a character is psychophysical is built into Chekhov's 'Imaginary Bodies' as described in the Introduction.)

As for the first centre, the one up above your head, John Wright claims that using this centre is an excellent way to create a *tragic sense* (Wright, 238–9). I'm not sure about this. Michael Chekhov, who is the inventor (or discoverer) of *imaginary centres*, alludes briefly to placing a centre above your head but he says nothing to link this to tragedy. In fact, Chekhov proposes a quite different way of creating a tragic sense, one which, in my opinion, is more effective. To play a tragic role, he suggests, you should imagine a kind of presence (not a centre) that goes everywhere with you. It can be behind you, in front of you, beside you, over your head, under your feet (like the Ghost in one scene in *Hamlet*) – that doesn't matter. What matters is that this presence should be *more than human*, and your relationship to it must be such that you are *dependent on it* while it is *independent of you* (Chekhov, 124-6).

A centre above your head won't do all that work.

Nonetheless, there is something 'otherworldly' about this centre. Of all the out-of-body body-centres, it is the *most* out of body (this is why I think it's good, or interesting, to start with it) – not because of the greater distance, but because of its placing. If you greet another person ('Hello, how are you?' – handshake and all) while focused in this centre, you do not feel diffident or introverted, as with the head-centre. You do not feel any such easily labelled, common *psychological* feelings. Instead, you feel that while on the one hand you share a world with the person greeted, so that your greeting is sincere and honest, even quite open (though not with the warm and full openness that you get with the chest-centre), on the other hand you, you alone, are *also in another world*, one to which the other person whom you greeted has no access. It's as though you are 'condemned' in some way. But you don't know what you have been condemned to. It may not even be bad!

Note that these five centres, although they lie outside the body, are all aligned with your body's vertical axis of bilateral symmetry. What happens, then, if we place a centre off this axis (like that 'ball and chain')?

To do so, first focus attention in your chest-centre, then, in imagination, shift that centre – keeping it at the same height – to the left or to the right of your actual body, so that it sits about 20, 30 or 40 cm (8, 12 or 16 in) outside you. Walk around and perform some sequence of simple actions, as usual, keeping your attention focused in your laterally displaced centre. Then do the same thing, starting from your abdominal-centre.

It's not quite so easy, is it? In fact, it's disturbing. The easiest movements are to the side, not forwards or backwards. If your centre is to your left, then in moving to your left, you feel yourself being pulled. In moving to your right, you feel that you have to drag your centre with you. Try this by placing centres on each side in turn and then ask yourself whether there is any significant difference in the experience, which may be related to the fact that you're right-handed, or left-handed if that's the case. Then ask yourself if, normally, you tend to favour one side – that is, get pulled towards it – rather than the other. After all, our bilateral symmetry is only approximate. If you are naturally centred 'off-centre' it will probably only be by a small amount, but that might still be a significant habit among the many (psychophysical) habits that make up the person that you are.

If you've not done anything like this before, you'll probably have been struck by how differently you feel as a result of nothing more than imagining different body-centres. Maybe also you'll have been struck by how easy it is to generate different feelings in this way.

Then go on experimenting with different possible centres, both in-body and out-of-body ones. Use your imagination. You'll probably find that some work and some don't. But if a part of your body won't function as a centre, that's significant too.

Before we move on, I need to stress something. Michael Chekhov refers in a general way to 'imaginary centres'. It's true that you use your imagination to 'place' a centre within, or even outside, your body, and it's true that it's often useful to actors to imagine centres other than their own in creating characters. But it's also true that *some* of the centres you've experienced in the work done so far are *real centres*.

What this means will emerge through the next section.

IMPULSE-AWARENESS 1

The impulse awareness aimed at here is not for those suffering from 'impulse control disorder'! The kind of impulse you need to get in touch with is not the compulsive urge to steal something from a shop or to punch someone who gets in your way. More basically, it's 'that which sets a movement in motion' – the initial pulse or 'kick' of energy. It's true that intentions or purposes or desires often lie behind our actions and hence our movements, and these are commonly thought of as the *causes* of our actions and movements. But that can't be wholly correct, for we can have intentions or purposes or desires without actually carrying out the actions and movements they require for fulfilment. An impulse, on the other hand, is something we *feel* as the beginning of a movement even if we immediately block it and nothing shows.

Of any movement we can ask: where, in the body, does it start from?

EXPERIMENT 1: *In a standing position, stretch out an arm. Move only your forefinger up and down, keeping the arm still. You can quite easily feel that the movement of your forefinger doesn't originate at the knuckle that connects it to the rest of your hand, although that's its visual point of origin, seen from outside. You can feel 'something going on' just above that knuckle. Next move your whole hand, but only your hand, up and down. The movement doesn't start from the wrist, even if it looks that way to an observer, for now you can feel 'something going on' in your forearm. Next try to start the movement from the elbow. This time you feel 'something going on' in the upper arm, and probably the shoulder too. Next wave your whole arm up and down from the shoulder. In this case you should be able to feel that 'something going on' down your side, but shifted a little towards the rear of your body.*

All this is simple enough, and not surprising. But it's important to go a stage further. Continue to wave your arm up and down, from the shoulder, but more strongly, in an undulating way, like the flapping of a large wing. Make it as big as you can – imagine your arm to be longer than it is – but without deliberately engaging the lower body. As you do so, ask yourself where the impulse of each up-stroke seems to come from. How 'deep' in your body is it?

You should be able to experience this impulse originating at the base of your spine. (We'll return to the significance of this later.)

We need to ask in a more general way, which parts of the body can be – or rather, can be experienced as being – the sources of impulses?

EXPERIMENT 2: *Again in a standing position, make various 'large' or sweeping movements with one or with both arms. You don't have to stand stiffly to do this; you can let the rest of your body, especially the torso, 'join in,' but only in a minor (following) role; the major (leading) movement must remain in your arms. After this, focus your attention in your* **chest-centre.** *Now make the same kinds of 'large' arm movements again, while imagining that your chest-centre is where the impulses for your arm movements originate. You should experience, quite strikingly, that now your movements feel 'larger' and more powerful than they did before.*

Earlier, you performed a series of natural, everyday movements while keeping your attention focused in your chest-centre. You should now do the same again, while imagining that all these movements are actually generated in the chest-centre.

You will notice that this works better, that is, more easily and more effectively, for some kinds of movements than for others. We'll return to this later. For the moment what matters is simply that it works: not only can you experience it, but the movements become more well-defined and in a sense stronger too.

*Next, run through the same thing – starting with 'large' arm movements, then going on to a series of natural, everyday movements – but this time imagine that the impulses for these movements originate in your **abdominal-centre**. You'll find this experience is different, and this is something we'll return to, but for the moment all that matters is that it works in just as powerful a way.*

*After this, try it with your **head-centre**. But don't try for too long. You'll quickly find that it's impossible!*

The fact that it's impossible with the head-centre tells us something important. It tells us that *something real* is going on – we're not deluding ourselves – when it works with the chest and abdominal centres.

Now, you might have felt that your chest-centre works a little better for generating arm movements while your abdominal-centre works a little better for generating leg movements. But if there's some truth in this, it's not the most important truth. What really matters is that you can generate leg movements from the chest-centre and arm movements from the abdominal centre. Make sure you experience this to the full.

Walk around – it's important that this is on a flat surface – adopting different styles or modes of walking. Try generating these ways of walking in your chest-centre. Try imagining that your legs somehow 'begin' in your chest. Then generate a wide variety of arm movements in your abdominal-centre. Don't force it by actually moving the lower torso more than necessary. Feel it. Here you can try imagining that your arms have 'roots' (going down from the shoulders) in your abdomen.

Re-Imagining Your Body

As you work through each of these, make sure that you experience the wholeness of your body.

It is also important that you *cannot* imagine impulses originating in the other actually-in-body body-centres that you explored earlier – with one crucial exception. It's important for the same reason: it tells us that something real is going on in the case of the chest-centre and the abdominal-centre. (It's important to be clear about this. Chekhov says that any imaginary centre can seem to be the place in which your activity originates (Chekhov, 80). This may be true in a certain, loose sense, but *not* in the sense that you can experience actual impulses, which are physical, originating in any centre.)

The one crucial exception is the **pelvic-centre**. This is a centre we now need to look at closely.

"Sexual intercourse began in nineteen sixty-three," said Philip Larkin in his poem "Annus Mirabilis". Around then, at least, it became something one could more easily talk about. As a variation on this theme, I might say that the pelvis was 'discovered' around the same time, not as something to talk about, but as something to *use expressively*. A little earlier, Elvis Presley had been dubbed 'Elvis the Pelvis' on account of the onstage gyrations and thrusts of the lower torso that scandalized the middle-aged 'squares'. Soon after, in the early Sixties, new styles of dancing spread through the gigs and the discos, dancing that was simultaneously solo and collective, with pairing off allowed but never enforced, seemingly (but not really) without rules. What truly distinguished the new dance from, let's say, the waltz, was not its lack of formalized steps and positions, nor even its complete freedom with respect to whether you had a 'partner' or not, as the all-important fact that *now you could freely move your pelvis*.

Oh, yes, the pelvis played a major role in the 60s revolution!

Still, perhaps there really is nothing new under the sun. Well over two thousand years ago, the Greek philosopher Plato, in a work called *Laws*, condemned a certain kind of dancing as *ou politikon*, which means 'not of the *polis* [city];' he meant that it was inappropriate in a *civilized* world. This was the dancing of the *satyrs* – mythological creatures, part animal, part human – which, in certain festivals, you could dress up as and so 'turn into'. The dancing of the satyrs was almost certainly quite free, a bit wild, with leaping and stomping – and almost certainly it would have made expressive use of the pelvis.

EXPERIMENT 3: *The pelvis, of course, is 'normally' quite restrained. So let's let it 'speak for itself,' step by step. Firstly, stand up straight with your feet quite close together. In this position, how much can you move your pelvis? You can 'waggle' it a little, but not much, and you will find yourself slightly bending your knees to achieve even this. Next, place your feet a little further apart with knees bent, but not too much. Now you can move your pelvis more freely, with a greater range of movements. Then increase the gap between your feet and the degree of bend in your knees even more. Again, you will discover a corresponding increase in the range and facility of pelvic movements. In this way, find the position that gives you the maximum pelvic expressiveness.*

EXERCISE: PELVIC GRAFFITI AND PELVIC PUDDING STIRRING

In this position, try Dymphna Callery's exercise called PELVIC GRAFFITI *(Callery, 30). First imagine a large paint brush attached to the base of your spine (or gripped by your sphincter). Use it to write something – whatever you like – on an imaginary wall behind you. Make the letters as big as possible. (There's no need to keep moving sideways as you do this – you can write the letters one on top of the other.)*

Next substitute a large wooden spoon for the paint brush. Imagine a large bowl of pudding mix directly underneath you. Stir it well – feel the resistance of the mixture as you do so. Because the bowl is underneath you, you now have to use different movements than for PELVIC GRAFFITI*. Together, therefore, these exercises will help you experience the full expressive potential of your pelvis.*

Now imagine certain formal social situations – a cocktail party, for example, or going to the theatre, or queuing in a bank – in which, for a change, everyone stands and moves around in the position you used for PELVIC GRAFFITI and PELVIC PUDDING STIRRING. But don't imagine them using their pelvises in an expressive way.

The incongruity is comical, of course. Such 'civilized' situations might be defined as ones in which we never need the full scope of the pelvis, because a) we *don't need to fight* (notice the 'default' position of wrestlers), b) we're expected not to *engage in sexual activity*, including a certain kind of lower-body sexual gesturing, and c) we have *no cause to dance*.

Now, I wouldn't be surprised if, in imagining those formal social situations with participants in such 'inappropriate' postures, you had thought that there was something 'animal' in the people or in their behaviour, as imagined. Fair enough. After all, I said a little earlier that satyrs were part animal, part human. But they were also *part divine*. That is why we must try to grasp the full significance of – and the connection between – the three things that are ruled out of such formal (civilized) social situations: *fighting, sex and dance*.

Try to think of a kind of continuum or spectrum here. It's a complex one; after all, fighting doesn't 'gradually turn into' sex, does it? Rather, *opposition* is replaced by *communion*. Moreover, for the fighter the pelvis is a source of stability and groundedness, as well as of the energy that flows out from it in kicks, punches and making holds, but in sex the pelvis itself becomes both expressive and a focal point of contact. Then, in dance, communion gives way to *celebration* – but one which involves a wider communion, not the pairing-off kind, but one where you commune with yourself, with the others dancing alongside you, with the music, with the rhythm at the heart of existence, with the meaningfulness of the universe....

For dancing *is divine*. In ancient Indian thought, while the gods needed to *invent* theatre, they (Shiva, to be precise) simply *remembered* the dance (Gupt, 73). Dance, that is, coexists with the gods. Whenever you dance, you partake of – you share in – the divine.

EXERCISE: COME DANCING

So your next exercise is... to dance. Choose your music, then – something that expresses 'you' – but not with too 'mechanical' a beat, please.

In this dance you shouldn't quite let yourself get 'carried away,' for you need also to be an observer of yourself. So observe how the dance can be experienced as originating in – streaming out of – your pelvis. To help in this, imagine that the music itself is playing inside and emanating from your pelvis.

This is a kind of 'freestyle' dance, of course. You can make whatever moves you like. What you're aiming for is this: a sense that while the dance originates in the pelvis, it is not dominated by the pelvis. There should be a feeling of perfect balance and coordination between the pelvis and the rest of your body. This is because the pelvis is truly feeding the rest of your body – feeding its impulses out through all your limbs – while also expressing itself.

EXPERIMENT 4: *To help get the full sense of your pelvis as the source of the dance, try this: dance in a similar way, but leaving the pelvis a bit 'uninvolved' or 'firing on only one cylinder'. You'll have to put more of the dance into your arms and legs. This should feel awkward and weak. But next time you're somewhere with people dancing, see if you can see anyone actually dancing this way.*

Next, do the opposite. Put too much of the dance into your pelvis. Let the impulses generated there tend to express themselves largely there, so they don't naturally travel out through the rest of your body. Of course, there will still have to be some movement of arms and legs, but your body will now seem more mechanical – your pelvis like an engine chugging away inefficiently, shaking the whole rather than sending energy out in any precise way. Again, next time you're in a position to do so, look for someone who really does dance like this.

Earlier (p. 30), I pointed out a difference between the abdominal-centre and the pelvic-centre. This is really a difference between these centres as sources of impulses, although we hadn't got onto that topic at that point. Briefly, the abdominal-centre sends impulses into the upper body more easily than the pelvic-centre does. But now we can see that it's not quite so simple. Perhaps it depends on the energy level involved. If you're walking slowly, then, true enough, it's not so easy to send impulses from the pelvic-centre to the shoulders and arms to sustain the 'whole body' involvement in the walk. The abdominal-centre is better for this. But as we've just seen, in freestyle dancing the ideal is a perfect balance and coordination between the pelvis and the rest of the body, in which the pelvic-centre is fully able to send impulses out through the upper body. No problem. Obviously enough, such a dance has a higher energy level than such a walk. Still, we need to test this more rigorously.

EXPERIMENT 5: *If you're a good swimmer, try using the chest-centre, abdominal-centre and pelvic-centre while swimming, using both breaststroke and crawl. You may feel that the chest-centre feels a little more natural for the crawl, while the abdominal-centre feels a little more natural for the breaststroke, but it's equally – or more – important that both centres work for both styles; that is, you can send impulses from each centre to both arms and legs. (In fact, when swimming in the sea, I prefer the abdominal-centre for the crawl if the sea is calm – it helps me maintain a balance between upper and lower body, so I don't over-exert the former. But if there are waves, I feel I need the extra arm power that the chest-centre gives me.) But if you switch to the pelvic-centre, in breaststroke or crawl, by focusing attention in your whole pelvic girdle, you immediately feel that your arms*

*are cut off from this source of impulses. But in this case it doesn't really help
to increase the energy level – the effect remains.*

So what's really going on here? Notice that in the dance the pelvis
itself is expressing some of its own impulses. That's not all it's doing,
of course; it's also sending impulses out through the rest of the body.
If we want the image of a pelvis expressing *all* its own impulses, we
can go back to PELVIC GRAFFITI or PUDDING STIRRING (p. 39). These
aren't 'normal' (*socially* normal) kinds of movement. Occasionally,
some students even get embarrassed when asked to do them, though
the vast majority experience something more liberating. Even so, it's
not as truly liberating as the dance, where a balance is achieved
between pelvic expressiveness and the expressiveness of the rest of
the body. In dance, it seems that the pelvis easily functions as the
source of impulses to the upper body, as well as to the lower, not only
because of the high energy level involved but also because the pelvis
itself is actively expressive.

However, we need to clarify an important point here.

Remember 'flapping' your arm like a wing (p. 36)? Then, you
should have experienced the impulse as coming from the base of your
spine. That's not the pelvic-centre, but *a particular part of it*.

EXPERIMENT 6: *So do this again, making the movement very large. Ask
yourself, does the impulse arise in any kind of actual motion, however slight,
in the pelvis or not? To test this, flap both arms at the same time, again very
large. This prevents any slight abrupt rocking sideways of the pelvis. Ask the
same question.*

*You should be able to feel the impulse originating at the base of the spine, but
without feeling that the pelvis itself needs to be 'active'.*

*It's very important now to ask where exactly you experience the impulse
originating from, hence where the 'base of your spine' seems to you to be
located. Does the impulse seem to originate at the point at which the spine
emerges from the pelvis (the beginning of the flexible lumbar vertebrae)? Or
does it originate from the part of the spine (the fused sacral vertebrae and
the coccyx) that is embedded in the pelvis?*

*If it's the former, please make an effort of imagination to experience the
latter instead. It may help to think of the end of your spine, the part which
belongs to the pelvis, as a tail. After all, your arms are like wings. But don't*

imagine any tail extending out from your normal body, that is, one going any lower than the base of your pelvic girdle.

Next, try to imagine the impulse not only travelling up your spine and out into your arms, giving the upstroke, but also as firing down and out through your tail too.

It will help here to think about explosions. Explosions always 'go off' in all directions. But there are means of directing the energy of explosions along specific pathways. A gun directs that energy out through the barrel. But in firing the gun, you feel the 'kickback' too.

Think of your impulses as explosions. Your body, of course, is infinitely more sophisticated than any gun in its capacity to channel the energy of those explosions in very varied ways. But, as with a gun, there will also be a 'kickback'. That's what I just asked you to feel going down and out through your 'tail' as you flap your arms upwards.

Now take this one step further. This time, exactly as you begin the upstroke with both arms, also stamp one foot, very firmly. It may take you a few moments to get the coordination right, but once you've done so you should experience the following. The impulse now begins in the pelvis and travels straight down the leg, but as the foot impacts the ground the energy of the impulse is immediately blocked and bounced back (or 'kicked back') up again, where it continues on up the spine and out into the arms. As you continue doing this, you should feel that no real effort is going into the flapping of the arms. It's all going into the stamp. But at the same time you feel your upper and lower body to be very connected.

And in a way, that's what we've been fundamentally concerned with for some time now: the connectedness of the upper body and the lower body. *We can define this more appropriately as the connectedness of the downward-tending energy sources and the upward-tending energy sources in the body.*

In relation to this, it is essential that you do not think of (or imagine, or feel, or experience) your spine as *beginning* only where it emerges (as the lumbar vertebrae) from the pelvis, for this sets up a kind of disconnect between lower body and upper body. Your spine, whose natural vector of energy is upwards, is also rooted in the lower body, to which the pelvis belongs.

The part of your spine that belongs to your pelvis, the sacral vertebrae and coccyx, is in fact like a different centre, a centre in its own right. You *can* send impulses to the arms from this centre, without the pelvis itself becoming expressive, though not so readily for all types of arm movements; when swimming, for example, it works considerably better for breaststroke than for crawl. When you imagine the pelvis as a whole to be your centre, you naturally become more centred in the hips, which are a little 'distant' from the spine, and thus in the downward-tending energy sources. But as we've seen, it's really from here that you can also generate *in the dance* the energy flow in all directions that is your participation in the divine.

THE DIFFERENT 'YOUS' IN YOU

We can now return to the question raised at the end of the first section of Part One: which of the body-centres explored so far *are real rather than (merely) 'imaginary' centres*?

Of course, any particular individual may have a body-centre that is 'real' for her or him, in the sense that s/he tends to be dominated by its influence. But such centres are *habituated centres*. I mean that they come into being as a consequence of habits. When I refer here to *real* centres, I mean *natural centres* – ones you're born with, even if you've lost touch with them.

Your real centres, in this sense, are *those from which impulses can be sent through the whole body*: your chest-centre, then, and your abdominal-centre, and your *dance-centre*. (I shall refer to your pelvic-centre as your dance-centre when it functions to send impulses through the whole body. Otherwise, I'll refer to it simply as the pelvic centre.)

The head-centre – one of the three 'main centres' we started with – isn't among them!

"Ah!" you might say, "That's only because you've put the emphasis on *impulses*, rather than on *thoughts*. But I'm a thinking being too!"

True enough. But *where are you*, when you think? Are you in your head-centre? I doubt it – at least you're not *wholly* there. Conversely, when you engage your head-centre by focusing your attention there, do you seem to yourself to be 'thinking'? Isn't it rather that you feel (yes, *feel* – and not just in the sense of 'believe') that you should be thinking about something but you're not sure what it is?

As a matter of fact, when you think *intensely*, you think with your whole body. All good actors know this, and it's the main reason why it's reductive to think of the head centre as a 'thought centre'. This applies more specifically to the kind of thinking we can call 'problem-solving' – or *heavy thinking*. There's another kind of thinking, which can also be intense (but in a different way), which doesn't engage your whole body. We can call this 'day-dreaming' – or *light thinking*. But when you day-dream, are you centred in your head? No, not a bit. You're 'somewhere else'.

In a way, it's a mistake to think you can ever be *really* centred in your head.

Of course, you know that your head is where your brain is placed. But – contrary to what some neuroscientists and even some philosophers (who really ought to know better) seem to think – *your brain is not you*. How could it be? It's an *organ*. You are an *organism*.

Even so, your head is one of your three main centres, the three we started with. Why is this? Interestingly, you have three main voices too, which are 'focused' in the three main centres, your **head voice**, your **chest voice** and your **abdominal voice**, and your head voice is a bit problematic compared to the other two. The reason is the same. *Your head-centre tends to be disconnected.* 'Disembodied' – in a sense. The *full body* gets left out, or left behind. But this happens. That is, it's a psychological reality for some people – not because they're thinking, not even in the 'light' sense of day-dreaming, but much more deeply because they need, and even in a sense want, to be disconnected in this way. As an aspect of this, they may well over-intellectualize or filter all experiences through rationalization. They may well do so in order to avoid certain emotions and visceral experiences. Your head-centre, you see, is the principal place you go in order *not to be inside your body*.

It's important, though, that your body offers you just such a place!

EXERCISE: THE THREE VOICES

It's relatively difficult to describe voice exercises so I'm avoiding them in this book, but I'll relax my rule here, since if you can experience your three different voices it will help you better understand the above. Each voice is produced by making a certain part of the body resonate. Pitch is also involved, but it's far less important than resonance. Even so, there's no need to think in terms of resonance. You just need to 'focus' your voice in the relevant body part, as if you have a mouth there. If you try this, you must do so standing up. Say, or sing, whatever you like.

For the head voice, only the upper skull or cranium resonates, so make sure you avoid nasal or 'throaty' resonance. This voice can seem 'fluty' and it's a little weak. Even if, in using this voice, you take deep breaths, you cannot then use that breath in a 'full' or 'free' way; that is, the ratio of the number of words spoken to the amount of breath used will be high. It can seem a 'hurried,' somewhat inhibited and possibly even anxious voice. It's OK for explaining something, even with enthusiasm, but it's no good at all for expressing emotion; if you say "I love you" or "I'm very, very angry!" using your head voice, it sounds completely unconvincing, even ridiculous.

The chest voice resonates in the thoracic area. If you place a hand on your chest at about the height of your heart, you should feel some vibration there. Using this voice, the relationship of breathing to expression seems much more balanced; you don't need to 'ration' your breath, hence you can give words their full emotional weight. This voice can seem very calming and reassuring to others – unless, of course, you use it to express anger at them.

For the abdominal voice, you need to produce resonance in the abdomen, which you will not find possible unless you are able to breathe deep down into the belly area (there are exercises in Part Two to help you achieve this if you find it difficult – see especially pp. 127-129). In using this voice you feel as if you are reaching deep down inside your body and pulling the voice up from there. The result is an earthy, maybe gravelly voice, not one you would use in most social situations. To help understand it, think about the animal expression of growling. You can bare your teeth and growl in your throat, but this is very unconvincing. If you can generate the growl in your abdomen it's far more threatening. This doesn't mean that the abdominal voice is always frightening, but you would probably keep just a little distance from someone using it, for it does not have the warmth and potential intimacy of the chest voice.

The majority of people find it very difficult to access their abdominal voice. It's not that they don't have one – everyone does – but that they have lost all contact with it, probably long ago. Some people, though relatively few, even have difficulty finding the full range of their chest voice; it's as though their voice gets trapped in the upper thoracic region, maybe even the throat. Such blockages can have major psychological significance and a branch of psychotherapy (Voice Movement Therapy) focuses on this. Our voice, after all, is both distinctively personal, that is, recognizable, and the principal means by which we *reveal ourselves*. It's not surprising that we learn to 'mask' the full range of our voice and that we then mistake the mask as being all there is.

But everyone can do the head voice. Everyone, moreover, can appreciate its *comic* quality when it's used to try to express emotion. And everyone responds to the idea that *the head voice is like a bird trapped in a cage*. And if you go on to ask yourself what exactly that feeling is, and why it's at least as comical as sad, you will realize, more clearly than you would by simply adopting the head-centre, that it's an experience of being *disconnected from your body*.

At this point, we ought to ask: Are the chest-centre and the abdominal-centre 'equally main' as centres? Note that Chekhov emphasizes the chest-centre as the most useful for an actor who wants to improve his or her 'presence' on stage. In fact he doesn't single out the abdominal-centre for any special mention. Compare this with what the Japanese actor Yoshi Oida says in the wonderful short book on acting, *The Invisible Actor*, that walking around with your energy focused in the upper half of your body is much more tiring than if your energy is focused in the *hara* instead (Oida, 25-6). The Japanese concept of the *hara* corresponds to part of the abdomen, a little below the navel. It is both the centre of gravity of the body and the 'core of the essential self'.

So there seems to be some disagreement here. If he were alive, Chekhov might point out that actors aren't like footballers – they don't cover nine or ten kilometres when on stage (although Oida's point refers as much to everyday life as it does to acting). Moreover, Oida is clearly influenced by the Japanese traditional Noh theatre which has been defined as the 'art of walking'. However, writing in the context of the Western theatrical tradition, Lorna Marshall also stresses the need for actors to be centred in the abdomen, above all to counter a widespread Western tendency to 'upper body acting' in which the actor's whole physicality seems to press upwards and forwards into the head and into speech, in the mistaken belief that this is the 'level' of drama that matters most (Marshall, 15-17). It's a mistake, of course, that reflects a more general overvaluation of the head in Western culture.

The issue for us, however, is not effective acting but something more basic – being *fully* inside one's own body. How, then, can we resolve this issue?

Re-Imagining Your Body

EXERCISE: STARFISH AND (HUMAN) BABY

Lorna Marshall describes an interesting exercise called 'Starfish' (Marshall, 13). Start by lying on your back, though you can do this exercise while standing or lying on your front. The idea is to imagine yourself as a starfish, with five limbs – your two legs, your two arms, and your neck-and-head. These limbs are all more or less the same – as in any symmetrical starfish. So spread your legs and stretch out your arms to the sides, then imagine your neck and head lengthening a lot. In Marshall's exercise, the movements travel outwards through all five limbs simultaneously, but for our purposes you can move one limb at a time – at least initially. There's no need to try to go anywhere. Just contract and expand your limbs, twisting them around, exploring your environment. Remember, all your limbs are the same; in principle, then, moving your neck-head is just like moving an arm or a leg.

Since you're not really a starfish but a human being, you may find this feels a little odd. Never mind! As I'm sure you've already guessed, the next steps are to try it with a sense of your impulses all coming from your chest-centre, then with these impulses all coming from your abdominal-centre, and afterwards to compare the two experiences. (Note: in the way Marshall sets up the exercise, the impulses all come from the abdominal-centre.)

So, which feels more 'natural' – being a starfish from your chest-centre or being a starfish from your abdominal-centre?

Suppose that you *can* answer that question with some confidence (though I'm not at all sure you'll be able to). Does your answer tell us anything about your 'true centre' as a human being?

Probably not. So let's try again.

In the way Marshall sets it up, STARFISH is primarily intended to re-establish connection with your body as a whole. In fact there's another way of doing this – one in which you forget about starfish – which may be more revealing concerning the question of your true 'centre'. Instead of imagining your neck-head getting longer, hence more like your legs and arms, you can imagine your legs and arms getting considerably shorter relative to your torso, hence more like your neck-head. What are you now? A human baby, obviously! One aged, let's say, between eight and twelve months.

It's good if you can watch a baby of this age, before it stands and before it crawls on all fours (though it may do the 'commando crawl'). What you'll see is that the baby's whole torso will seem to be its centre, one full of energy and impulses. As you recreate this in yourself (start by lying on your back), you should experience a very pleasant reconnection with your torso as a unified and dynamic whole. Make sure you let your torso twist and turn. Don't think of the spine as doing this, but the torso as a whole.

Perhaps Chekhov and Oida are both 'wrong,' then... but in a sense that's very close to 'both right'.

In her inspiring book, *The Right to Speak*, Patsy Rodenburg tells you how to find the *centred position* which is essential for voice work. It's simple, at least in principle. You stand with nothing rigid in your body, a kind of well-balanced 'tower' in which the hips are directly above your feet and your head is balanced on top of your spine. Your weight is equally distributed on both feet, your knees are not locked and your shoulders are loose, being neither held back nor slumped forward. To get a full sense of the 'easy balance' of your posture, you let yourself sway a little, forwards and backwards, then to each side, noticing the different muscular tensions that arise in your body as you do so and how they disappear as you return to the centred position. Rodenburg then points out that your true centre is not a specific place or 'point' within you, and more specifically it is not located in the belly area, but it is distributed evenly *through your body as a whole* (Rodenburg, 126). What this tells us is that being centred is, in fact, being fully inside your body.

Hence: *once you have experienced different possible centres, localized ones, in your body, you must go beyond them, 'forget' them (in a sense), you must 'throw them away'.*

If you meet a Buddha, kill the Buddha – said Linji Yixuan. Take this as a general principle. It doesn't only apply to enlightenment (whatever that is) but to all development.

Of course, you can go back – at any time – to your chest-centre, your abdominal-centre, your dance-centre, or to any of the possible IMAGINARY CENTRES, to work in some specific way with them. This is required in later exercises, in fact. You can also ask other sorts of questions, related questions – why, for example, do you feel certain strong emotions in the 'pit of your stomach,' that is, in the area of the solar plexus? Is that a kind of centre too, an 'emotional centre'? But whenever you do something of this kind, related to your *different* possible centres, you must do so in a certain spirit – you must do it order to go beyond it, to 'forget' it, to 'throw the work away' like a ladder which you've used to climb up to a higher level.

I entitled the first section of this work on centres, 'The 'You' Inside Your Body'. But it should be 'The 'You' in You'. What ought to be clear by now is that there are many different kinds of 'You' in You, corresponding to the different possible centres. In fact, the 'You' in You is a shifting, mercurial, chameleon-like thing.

The greater your awareness of this, the better.

Being *balanced* – in a fully psychophysical sense – does not mean remaining constantly in the 'centred position' as described by Rodenburg. That would be both impossible and undesirable. It means *being able easily to return to that position*. And that, in turn, means not getting 'locked into' any particular localized centre.

In relation to this, note that 'bad tensions' (bad tension is useless tension, such as can build up, for example, in the neck and shoulders) are also 'centres' – undesirable ones. If you suffer from such tension, realize that it too is really a 'You' inside You (especially if the problem is chronic) – but one which blocks the natural flow of different, changing 'Yous' which constitutes your *real You*. (We'll explore tension fully in Part Two.)

IMPULSE AWARENESS 2

So far, in dealing with impulses, we've focused largely on the question of where, in the body, the impulse comes from. But it's also important to ask, where does it *go to*?

EXERCISE: IMPULSE LAUNCH PAD

To explore this, first adopt a standing position with your heels touching and your toes pointing outwards, so your feet form an angle of about 60 degrees. Stand tall, with the tips of your fingers (only) gently touching your thighs. Shift your weight onto the balls of your feet so that you're leaning a (very) little forwards. Now turn your head in the same direction as one of your feet – it doesn't matter which. Next, raise your head a little, quite slowly. Think of this as pointing with your chin at something on the floor a few metres (or yards) away from you. This will cause you to lean in that direction too. It's a pose that looks and feels very 'ready for action'.

You are about to make a large movement called a lunge. Suddenly, you take a big step forward with the foot that points in the direction in which your chin is pointing. You don't move the position of your other foot, although the heel may come off the ground a little. You end in a pose in which the leading leg carries all your weight and is bent at the knee (make sure the knee is directly above your foot), while the trailing leg remains straight.

It is very important that you let the impulse to make this lunge 'just happen'. You mustn't merely let yourself overbalance, so that the lunge is a kind of 'correction' – it won't be big enough if done like this. Nor do you tell yourself 'Now I will make the lunge'. If you can just let yourself experience all the potential energy contained in the initial pose, then the impulse will come of its own accord.

The energy released by your lunge is also felt in your arm. If, say, you lunge forward with your right leg, then your right arm takes over and continues the movement. As your right foot hits the ground, preferably with a good, strong sound, your right hand is thrown upwards and forwards, so that it ends in an extended position with the forefinger pointing in the direction in which you lunged.

Do not think of this motion of the arm as a 'knock-on effect'. Your body doesn't work like billiard balls do. Instead, think of – or rather, try to experience – the initial impulse as travelling smoothly up through your body and out into your arm.

Now you can ask the question, 'Where does the impulse terminate?' By performing this movement many times, leading sometimes with the left foot and sometimes with the right, you will find that the initial impulse is quite variable in strength. Sometimes it fizzles out before the arm has become horizontal, leaving the forearm drooping quite loosely from the elbow. It might only just reach the wrist, leaving your hand dangling. It might stop just before the finger, so that your arm is straight out but there's no real sense of 'pointing' in the gesture. It might terminate exactly at the end of your forefinger, giving you a sense of perfect poise and efficiency. Or it might go flying off from the tip of your finger into space! In this case, notice how far it travels, for this is variable too.

Spend time exploring this. It's worth it. But never force it. Never decide in advance how strong the impulse will be. Just let the impulse 'be itself' – it really does have 'a life of its own'. Try to become as sensitive as you can to this.

It is very important to realize that the impulses that originate in our bodies can *go beyond* the bodies in which they originate. It's also very obvious – though we probably have never stopped to think about it in this way. It's how a nail gets hammered into a piece of wood, for example. Look at it this way – it's not the hammer that drives the nail into the wood, it's your impulses. The hammer is just a medium for your impulses when they flow out from your body.

Your impulses are physical, bodily. While in one sense they 'fly (or flow) out' from your body, in another sense they take your body with them – *because they belong to it.*

EXPERIMENT 7: *Kick a ball. Throw a stone into the sea. Imagine – feel – believe, as you do so, that your body itself is flowing out of you, not as an object, but as an actor upon and within the world. Think of a kind of line, a visible arc, of your energy being left in space by the ball or the stone, before it fades away. That line was also you.*

Pick up a mug, to drink from. Move a vase from one place to another. Put flowers in it. Even send a text message with your phone. In each case, do not think of the objects you are handling as separate from you. Think of them as becoming extensions of yourself in the way they receive and carry your impulses onwards, out into the world around you.

Through this you will begin to experience your body as much less "cabined, cribbed and confined". It's very much part of the world, interacting freely with it – not a closed entity, separated off.

In this way we begin to shift focus – from your potential *centres* to your potential *boundaries*. It may seem paradoxical, but in order to be fully inside your body, you need to realize that your body doesn't simply stop at your skin.

YOU AND THE SPACE AROUND YOU 1

Your relationship to the space around you is a complex matter, with several different aspects to it. We've just seen that your impulses, or some of them, can be thought of as flying out into space and, as they do so, extending your body in some sense. But there are other ways in which you can 'occupy more (and sometimes less) space' than your actual body takes up.

Your 'personal space' is usually thought of as a portion – a kind of bubble – of space, with *you* at its centre. You experience it primarily when it's violated, when another person, a stranger perhaps, or a colleague at work, comes too close to you.

Imagine – or recall – that experience. It's very strong. Usually, there's a kind of 'suspended' quality in the feeling too; the way you 'stiffen up' is at least partly a waiting for the violator to retreat, or a hope that that will happen quickly, which is why you don't immediately act on your feeling.

Sometimes you know that you can't act on such a feeling, so you 'switch it off'. This happens on crowded buses or underground trains. You withdraw mentally from the over-bodied public space around you, to create a private space within. On a bus, there's often a window to look out of. On the tube or metro, you may need a book. Above all, avoid all eye-contact! It's not so much that you mustn't recognise the presence of the other as that you mustn't *let the other know* that you've recognised their presence.

What counts as personal space – how much of the space around them a person 'owns' – varies from culture to culture. But there's another sense in which some of the space around you 'belongs to you,' which is defined physically rather than culturally. It's what Rudolf Laban called the *kinesphere* (Newlove and Dalby, 17). Roughly speaking, the boundaries of the kinesphere are as far around you as you can reach with an outstretched hand while keeping your feet in the same position, no steps allowed. It's the sphere of your potential movement. The feet should be placed sufficiently apart to give you stability while allowing maximum freedom of movement. Using one arm at a time, you stretch as far as possible upwards and downwards, while also reaching out as far as possible to the sides, to the front, the back, tracing imaginary lines with your fingers. You stretch and twist your body, and you move downwards into a squatting position, as necessary. This marks out your kinesphere, like drawing it.

There's an *ideal* kinesphere – the space within which a perfectly tuned body can move without changing foot position. A person's *actual* kinesphere will depend not only on how flexible but also how well-balanced they are.

EXERCISE: FINDING YOUR KINESPHERE

Explore your kinesphere as a simple stretching exercise. Make sure your movements remain slow, smooth and steady. It's a good stretching exercise, in fact, because it should engage the whole body throughout – as you draw those imaginary lines always as far away from you as you can, you are necessarily stretching out with one arm, but your torso, your hips, your legs and your feet all have to contribute to the maximising of that distance. And make sure you explore the left side of your kinesphere (top and bottom) with your right hand as well as with your left hand, and vice versa.

As an exercise, this hardly needs much imagination, but once you've done it, you should be able to imagine your kinesphere as always around you.

And in this way you can carry it with you as you walk. Try it.

Once you've got a good sense of that, we can go on to ask an odd question: how might a snail experience its shell – as a 'portable house' or as part of itself? And how do you experience your kinesphere?

A little earlier, I said that you should "draw those imaginary lines always as far away from you as you can". As far away from *you*? But what exactly does that all-important little word "you" refer to here? Might I not have said instead that you should "draw *your boundaries* always as far away from *your centre* as you can"?

At this point, I need to introduce a third concept, which I call your *psychological skin*. This is the 'skin,' the boundary, of your *You*. It's elastic. That is, it's very variable – and it's highly context-sensitive.

EXPERIMENT 8: *Just reach out to pick something up, let's say a glass of water. Try this standing and try it sitting. In each case, first imagine that the glass lies outside your psychological skin, so that your hand has to 'break through' and reach out beyond that boundary of your 'You'. Then perform the same action again, but this time imagine that the glass lies well within your psychological skin. Notice how different the action feels in each case.*

In general, if you're tense and anxious, your psychological skin contracts. It can even seem smaller than your actual body. If you're relaxed and confident, it expands well beyond your real skin. By imagining your psychological skin in different states, you can actually switch such feelings on – as you should have just experienced.

These three things – your personal space, your kinesphere, and your 'psychological skin' – are different things. But they are all aspects of the way you relate to the space around you, in particular to a kind of space which is in some sense 'yours'. Initially, the exercises that follow focus on the kinesphere, for this is the easiest to work on directly. Then, as the exercises go (literally) beyond the kinesphere, in order to *psychologically-extend* it, they start to work on the way you experience (or relate to) your personal space and your 'psychological skin' too.

EXERCISE: FLOWING KINESPHERE PHASE 1 – DRAWING

For this, you don't have to keep your feet planted, as you did for FINDING YOUR KINESPHERE. *You can move freely. Begin simply by making broad movements that take up plenty of the space around you, as you've done before. Recall that you can make these movements seem bigger and stronger by imagining them being generated by impulses from the chest-centre or the abdominal-centre. This time, also think of these impulses as continuing out beyond you, extending you. For the moment, however, don't think of your impulses as flying out far beyond you, but as 'leaving lines' around you.*

If I say, 'Draw shapes in the space around you, as large as you can, with your movements,' you will probably think initially of 'drawing' shapes with your hands. That's fine. But you can do the same thing with other parts of the body too. The legs, obviously (one at a time, if you're standing – but you can lie down too). The head. The shoulders, either together or one at a time. The hips. The buttocks. A knee.... Any of these, can become the 'pencil' that draws the shapes, all as large as possible, in the space around you. Try them all, then combine them, switching from one to another in any way you feel like – but in such a way that the movements keep 'flowing'. Throughout, try to keep imagining the impulses that generate the movements continuing out beyond you, extending you, in the sense of generating the lines.

EXERCISE: FLOWING KINESPHERE PHASE 2 – SELF-SCULPTURE

When you've really got the hang of this – that is, when you can easily keep the movements flowing while continuously shifting the focus of the movement in the body (the 'pencil,' if you like – or the point from which the impulse leaves the body) – go on to imagine that you are doing this inside a stretchy elastic membrane. Feel its resistance. It's never slack. If you stand still and upright with your arms at your sides, it fits you snugly. But as you move, it forms a continuously varying shape. Imagine it to be opaque, not transparent, so you can more easily see, in your mind's eye, the moving sculpture in space that your body is creating. But make sure you fully feel this sculpture too, from the inside. You're no longer drawing two-dimensional shapes in the space around you but sculpting three-dimensional ones – or rather, you are sculpting one three-dimensional shape that keeps evolving, changing, transforming itself. If you think of yourself as stretching, it's as though you're trying to stretch out in all directions at once! Above all, believe this: whatever shape your stretching out gives rise to, it's beautiful – and the way one shape turns into another is also beautiful.

Experience your impulses as flowing into this shape, to keep it evolving.

*It's best to do this with your eyes closed. This helps you feel or sense the **whole body shape** that you are making at every instant, whereas when you were drawing lines at the edges of your kinesphere you were focused primarily on the leading edge or 'pencil'.*

EXERCISE: EXPANDING INTO SPACE 1

Go back to the first phase above, DRAWING your kinesphere. Once again you're going to draw shapes in the space around you, using different parts of your body to do so, all the time keeping your movements flowing. But this time, instead of imagining making shapes around you at the edges of your kinesphere, think of these shapes as being projected far out into the space around you. If you're in a room, entirely fill it with your shapes. If you're outdoors, let your movements seem to flow out to the horizon, up into the sky, even down into the earth. There's no need to 'fling' your movements outwards. Smooth expansive movements work best. To achieve this, don't think so much of your impulses flying far out from you as of the movements themselves continuing into the space around you.

This is a very strong and a very beautiful experience. But how exactly you experience it will depend on your associations. Do you feel like a king or queen – or a god – or, perhaps, a recently born baby that hasn't yet realized where it begins and ends?

The following exercises all develop the principle that the body extends 'beyond itself'.

EXERCISE: ARCHETYPAL MOVEMENT 1 – OPENING AND CLOSING

*This exercise is from Michael Chekhov (Chekhov, 6). Stand upright, feet parallel and quite close together, your arms at your sides. OPEN by spreading your legs wide (move one foot first, then the other – don't jump) while simultaneously raising your arms, with the palms of your hands turned forwards, so your whole body makes an X shape. The movement should be smooth and strong. Stand in this position, feeling yourself opening and expanding, getting bigger and bigger, with a kind of '**inner movement**' that continues after outer movement can go no further. Expand in all directions; let your feet send down roots into the earth.*

Then reverse the procedure, ending where you started.

CLOSE *by first crossing your forearms in front of your chest, fists closed but not tightly clenched. Go down, with a smooth motion, onto one knee. If your right forearm is in front of your left forearm, then bring your right knee to the ground. As you do this, begin to curl your upper body forwards and downwards. Continue this in the kneeling position. Become as closed and as small as you can, but don't force it. When you can't close and shrink any more physically, continue closing and shrinking for a few seconds more in imagination (this is '**inner movement**' again). Shrink, if you can, to a point. Where is that point?*

Then reverse the procedure, ending where you started, in the 'neutral' standing position. Try to come up as smoothly as you can.

Repeat the whole OPENING AND CLOSING *sequence, kneeling on the other knee when closing (and with the other forearm foremost).*

Do the OPENING AND CLOSING *sequence once more, this time imagining the movements flowing out from – then flowing back into – the chest-centre. Try to do this with your eyes closed. Then do it again, but using your abdominal-centre instead. Notice any differences in the ways these different centres make you experience the opening and the closing.*

The next five exercises also involve what we can think of as *archetypal movements*, ones in which the body expresses its capacity in a clear, powerful and expansive way. These are movements that, in a certain sense, go beyond the body. Thus the body goes beyond itself. But that's exactly what the body is so good at! To maximize the sense of this, you need to think of your movements not only as being *mighty* but also as expanding outwards into the space around you, much as you did in EXPANDING INTO SPACE 1. If they are performed in the more usual 'self-contained' way, the exercises lose their value.

EXERCISE: ARCHETYPAL MOVEMENT 2 – WEILDING THOR'S HAMMER

Imagine you're holding a large hammer, at least sledge-hammer size, preferably larger, the handle let's say 120 cm (48 in) long. Obviously you need both hands for this. Feel some weight in the hammer head – but you don't have to imagine the full weight of a real sledge-hammer (since it's all too easy to end up merely pretending that you feel this). Stand with your feet a little apart, the toes pointing slightly outwards. Your hands, holding the hammer shaft, should be just in front to your navel or abdomen, one hand just above and touching the other (this helps your hands to work together, although they would be separated on a real sledge hammer handle). In a moment, you'll take a big step forward with one foot; if that's your right foot, then it's your right hand that should be just above your left hand on the shaft.

Begin the movement by raising the hammer above your head. Raise it a little first, then swing it backwards. Feel the extra effort needed right at the beginning to get the hammer moving. But once it's moving, there's a momentum that you can 'ride'. Through the whole of this, breathe in through your nose.

Then take that big step forward, with one foot, just before the hammer reaches its maximum height. As your foot hits the ground strongly, begin the downstroke. At the same time, breathe out, explosively, through the mouth, making a noise. (Experiment to find the exact point at which you begin the explosive breathing out. Is it a fraction before your foot hits the ground, simultaneous with this, or a fraction after?) As you follow through with the downstroke to strike the hammer on the ground in front of you, feel the way the hammer head accelerates through the swing. Make sure you terminate the swing as the hammer hits its target – don't let your arms follow through further than they would in reality. Imagine the thunderous impact.

For the whole of this, imagine that the movement, and the power behind it, flows out from your chest-centre. But don't let this focus in your chest-centre cause you to lose your sense of the great arc made by the hammer head. It's wrong if you only 'feel' the small arc made by your hands. So imagine that the hammer head is an extension of yourself, of your body. This means that your hands shouldn't move too quickly, especially at first as you're getting the hammer head moving. If your hand movement seems too quick, it's because your focus is in your hands rather than the hammer head.

Return to your starting position, after holding position for a moment (experiencing the 'inner movement' of the blow continuing after the impact), keeping the feel of the hammer in your hands as you lift it back ready to begin another blow. As you do this, feel the movement – and your power – flowing back into your chest-centre.

Both in striking the blow and in returning to initial position, make sure you keep your balance and your poise. This will be easy, too easy, if you don't really extend yourself. By fully extending yourself, however, you are putting your ability to keep your balance to the test. If you overbalance, it means either that you over-extended yourself or that you weren't fully focused on the action.

Strike at least three blows with one foot leading, then at least three blows with the other foot leading. (Don't forget to change the relative position of your hands on the handle when you change your leading foot.)

Try it also using your abdominal-centre. Notice the difference.

EXERCISE: ARCHETYPAL MOVEMENT 3 – LIFTING THE GREAT STONE

The challenge of LIFTING THE GREAT STONE *is different from* WIELDING THOR'S HAMMER *since it takes three distinct movements to accomplish the lift, and you can pause, even (in a sense) 'rest,' between them.*

Stand with the (imaginary) Great Stone just in front of you on the ground. Your feet need to be well apart, set a little wider than the Great Stone itself. Then squat down, bending your legs only as much as necessary to be able to reach and grasp the Stone. Do this quite slowly, purposefully. Breathe in as you squat down, through the nose. Grasp the stone firmly, then stand up by straightening your legs again, nothing more. (Note: although your back will naturally straighten through this movement, it's not doing any of the lifting.) As you do so, breathe out forcefully through the mouth. At the end of this first movement, you are holding the stone, with your arms still straight down, in front of your genital area.

Now you have to raise the Stone to the height of your shoulders. If it were light, you could easily achieve this by raising your hands in a semi-circular arc in front of you, a movement entirely from the elbows. At the end of it, your arms would be fully bent, still close to your sides. But the Stone is far too heavy for that. So you're going to have to start the forwards and upwards movement of your hands by pushing forward as firmly as you can with your pelvis. This needs to be a 'big' movement. You'll need to bend your knees a little to achieve it. As you do this, imagine pushing, almost 'rolling,' the Stone up onto your belly, which should now be protruding as a result of the way you thrust your pelvis forward. Then, in straightening your legs again, your belly will push upwards, helping the Stone on its way. From this point, your arms should be able to take over, heaving the Stone to shoulder height. All this needs to be a single, continuous movement; it will help you greatly if you breathe out forcefully through the mouth as you perform it. So you need to take a good deep breath, through the nose, before you begin. The only other necessary movement here is a simple adjustment: you shift your hands a little more underneath the Stone as it reaches shoulder level, to be able to hold it stably.

The third stage is not too difficult. Obviously it will need an explosive thrust to get the Great Stone high above your head. This can't come from the shoulders alone. You need to find how to involve your whole body in it in order to meet the challenge. An explosive out-breath through the mouth will help. As you breathe out in this way, a kind of 'spring-like' motion should pass up from the feet, as they press suddenly and strongly down into the ground, continuing, through the knees, the pelvis, the torso and into the shoulders and arms. (Keep your feet aligned; it's not a 'clean and jerk'.)

As you lift the Great Stone high, imagine you're lifting it high into the sky. So high that you can leave it there! That is, after a moment just holding it in position, let go of it and walk a few steps away, leaving the Great Stone sky-high – as though you have left a great imprint of your body in the sky.

Do all this (as usual) firstly with your focus in your chest-centre as the source of your movements and your power, and secondly with your focus in your abdominal-centre. Notice the difference.

EXERCISE: ARCHETYPAL MOVEMENT 4 – CYCLOPEAN THROW

The CYCLOPEAN THROW begins in the same way as LIFTING THE GREAT STONE: you imagine a large stone, a boulder, on the ground which you initially raise by bending your legs, grasping it, then straightening your legs again. Now, as before, you can 'rest' for a moment. The next phase, however, is not merely to lift the stone to shoulder height but to swing it up over your head. Fortunately, the boulder you're going to throw is a little less heavy than the Great Stone! But only a little.

The second phase also begins with a forward thrust of the pelvis, sufficiently strong to 'kick-start' the arm swing that will raise the boulder over and just a little behind your head. Through the whole of this phase, breathe in deeply through your nose (so it's not like LIFTING THE GREAT STONE where you breathe out explosively in hoisting the stone to shoulder height). Then, with the boulder high above and just behind your head, you take a single large step forward, just as you did in WIELDING THOR'S HAMMER, and, while breathing out explosively through the mouth, you hurl the boulder as far as you can. As you do this, feel the stone as an extension of yourself, as you did with the hammer. You need to overcome the inertia – the dead-weight – in the stone, so feel its weight and don't let your hands move too quickly. As you release the stone, let your arms follow through, but by moving much more slowly than in the throw itself. As your arms pass through horizontal in front of you, let your body sway a little, shifting your weight to your back foot. Finally bring your front foot back to starting position, as your arms come fully down. Through all this, do not take your eyes off the stone as it flies through the air, extending you way out into space.

Imagine you are Polyphemus, the Cyclops, hurling rocks into the sea trying to capsize the ship of the escaping Odysseus. (There's no need to imagine, though, that you've only got one eye!) Hurl a rock leading with your right foot, then hurl one leading with your left foot.

Once again, do this initially with a sense of your movements and your power emanating from your chest-centre. Then switch to the abdominal-centre and notice the difference.

EXERCISE: ARCHETYPAL MOVEMENT 5 – BRIDGING THE HORIZONS

This is an exercise in which the archetypal movement of pulling turns into the archetypal movement of pushing, then pushing turns back into pulling, and so on, all very rhythmically.

Stand with your feet well apart – wider even than for PELVIC GRAFFITI AND PUDDING STIRRING (p. 39) – and with your knees bent. Note how far you can lean to one side or the other, not just with the upper body but also by shifting your weight onto one foot or the other, simultaneously bending the knee all the more while letting the other leg straighten. It's important to maintain such whole body movement throughout.

Stretch as far as you can to the right and stretch both arms out as far as you can in the same direction. Then begin pulling something from the right-side horizon. The pulling is focused in your hands, of course, which will seem as if holding something (a thick rope, perhaps), but as your hands move to a position in front of your navel your whole body will shift position too, fully involved as it is in the effort of pulling. With your hands at this mid-point, you change orientation. Your pelvis is still turned to the right although your weight has now shifted more onto the left foot, so you rotate your pelvis to face more to the left as you 'slide' it a little to the right, and simultaneously you shift your weight more onto the right foot. Now you start to push something with your hands, palms outwards, fingers upwards, towards the left-side horizon, as far as you possibly can.

Re-Imagining Your Body

The whole movement, including the shift from pulling to pushing, should be very smooth. Practice it a few times without putting much effort into the pulling or the pushing, to get the feel of this smoothness, and of the 'rocking' motion of your pelvis at the mid-point. It's essential to feel how pulling can turn smoothly and naturally into pushing.

The pushing must now turn back into pulling equally naturally and smoothly. You push as far as you can to the left horizon, then you simply start pulling something back towards you. Imagine that your upper body is quite elastic. Your arms have stretched out a long way and now they naturally start to contract back. At the end of the push, moreover, your palms also turn downwards as though your hands are taking hold of something.

The two crucial things in this exercise are, firstly, to maintain a very smooth and rhythmical flow from pulling to pushing to pulling to pushing to... and, secondly, to maintain the feeling that you are 'bridging' the horizons, pulling something all the way from one horizon and then pushing it far out to the opposite horizon. Ideally, this is an exercise for outdoors. If you're in a room, don't think of the walls as your horizons or the movement won't be psychologically 'big' enough. Try to imagine the horizons outside.

But what are you pulling and pushing? Try imagining that it's your breath. In fact, you should be breathing in (through the nose or the mouth) whenever you're pulling, and breathing out (through the mouth) whenever you're pushing. So now you're taking in your breath from one horizon and expelling it to the opposite horizon. You could even be the wind!

As you try this, you may experience the temptation to go faster. Give way to it! But make sure the movement remains big throughout. In fact, as you push fully outwards, you can let your rear foot come off the ground, pressing it hard down again to begin the pulling inwards. And you will need to take quite deep breaths. But not too deep. You will probably find that the nature of the movement causes you to take in a breath which fills your ribcage, but not one deep enough to fill the belly area as well. This is not 'shallow,' that is, merely upper thoracic breathing; it's deep enough to sustain quite vigorous movements, should you want to keep going. But it's not so deep that you're likely to make yourself dizzy, something that can happen when you expel too much carbon dioxide.

If you do feel dizzy, of course, just stop. Sit or lie down. Take a deep breath and hold it for a while. Then breathe deeply but also slowly.

Imagining pulling in and pushing out your breath like this sets up a natural focus in the chest-centre. There's no need to make yourself think of this centre as the source of your movements and power, for in a way you're already doing this simply through your attention to the breath. There's no need to attempt the exercise while focusing on your abdominal-centre either. (You can do this, but only if you slow down sufficiently to allow you to breathe deeply into the abdomen.)

But note that before you started thinking that what you were pulling and pushing was your breath, while you were just getting the movement right, you were probably quite focused in your pelvic-centre. Or was it your dance-centre?

EXERCISE ARCHETYPAL MOVEMENT 6 – RINGING THE COSMIC BELL

BRIDGING THE HORIZONS works on the horizontal axis, but RINGING THE COSMIC BELL works on the vertical axis. Imagine a great bell high in the sky, up among the stars. There's a rope hanging down from it. With your feet apart, slightly wider than your shoulder joints, you grasp the rope (it's thick) with both hands in front of your chest or a little higher. You begin to pull it downwards, not just with the hands - right from the beginning it needs to be a bigger, whole-body movement, bending the knees to lower the torso too. High up, the great bell only swings a little to one side on this first down-pull, not enough to sound it but enough to pull you upwards as it swings back. Just let this happen. Feel the weight of the bell, keep a firm grasp on the rope and let it extend you upwards, 'opening you out' as it does so. You can now begin the second down-pull from a higher starting position, so it's a longer, stronger pull. You're overcoming the inertia in the bell, so this time you can bend your knees more and let the arms follow through further. Keep your torso fairly straight; above all, make sure you don't bend your head over your hands where it would hit the rope. Now, since this time you've swung the bell further, as it swings back the rope will pull you higher, more strongly.

As you continue like this, you set up a rhythmic, undulating movement through your body - it's exactly like a wave passing through you - in which, at the bottom, your hands almost reach the floor and your knees are well bent (but keep your feet fully flat on the floor), and at the top, your hands go high above your head and you rise up on tiptoe. The great cosmic bell is now ringing! Try to imagine the sound. It fills the universe - but not by being loud!

Re-Imagining Your Body

The crucial thing is to experience yourself as pulling on the downstroke and as being pulled on the upstroke. To experience both to the full you must feel the great weight of the bell vividly in your imagination. If you find yourself overbalancing at the top of the upstroke, it's because the bell-rope isn't real enough in your imagination to hold you steady.

You should be breathing in the following way. Breathe in through the nose throughout the upstroke. It's as though this in-breath happens naturally; air flows in as your body opens out. Breathe deeply into the belly. Feel the breath flowing deeply downwards as a kind of counter-action to the way the rope rises upwards high into the sky. Breathe out – again through the nose – through the downstroke. In pulling downwards, your body is contracting and this helps push the air out of you. Still, it's very smooth; firm but also easy. There's nothing explosive at the start of the out-breath (which is why you can keep breathing through the nose). This is because the upstroke turns naturally back into the downstroke as the great bell swings back again. There's energy – it's your energy to start with, of course – now in the bell too. Once the full, expansive movement is established you don't have to force it. Just 'ride' it. And keep it slow. If you go too fast, the movement will not seem so powerful.

Feel the rope pulling upwards high into the sky. Pull the rope downwards as though you are pulling it towards the centre of the earth.

Perform RINGING THE COSMIC BELL by focusing firstly on your chest-centre and secondly on your abdominal-centre, in each case as the source of your power and your movements. Notice the difference.

EXERCISE: THE OAK WITHIN THE ACORN

Now you're ready for the important *downsizing principle.* Often we need to make large, expansive, even archetypal movements in the first place in order to experience our body in a certain significant way. But after we've done this, it becomes much easier to experience the same thing in making smaller, more everyday movements too.

You've experienced a wide range of large, expansive movements in the preceding exercises, so let's 'downsize' this experience by seeking it in smaller movements too. The idea is to experience these *as if they're much bigger.*

First, simply walk four or five metres (or yards), but imagine you're walking to the far horizon. Alternatively, while walking, imagine that your steps are very big (although in fact they are normal size). Stretch one hand upwards, imagining it's going high into the sky. Sit down, imagining your body lowering itself towards the centre of the earth. Stand up, imagining your body moving up into the sky above you. Pick up any small object, imagining that the movement is much bigger than it really is. Even a movement as slight as turning your head can be thought of as 'much bigger' in this way.

Do this kind of thing often. Get into the habit of it – not all the time, of course, but regularly. It's also a good idea to apply it to certain other kinds of physical exercises too, especially stretching exercises. This will enhance their effectiveness. But for the purpose of 're-imagining your body' the most important thing is to apply the principle to your normal, everyday movements.

But why? Well, if you were an actor, you might be following Yoshi Oida's advice. If you want your movements to seem significant – that is, to draw attention to them – onstage, you certainly mustn't think to yourself, "I must make 'significant' movements". That's abstract and meaningless. Instead, you should imagine your movements as being bigger than they are, that's all (Oida, 37). You don't actually make bigger movements. You *imagine* doing so. Presumably, then, your movements are really the 'same size'. So how is it that they seem more 'significant,' more able to draw the audience's attention?

Because your imagination transforms the way you relate to the space around you. This is something the audience can 'see'.

It's an aspect of your presence that people can 'see' – or sense – in real life too.

To be able to understand this more completely, we now need to take account of the fact that there's yet another aspect to the way you relate to the space around you. You can easily grasp it by imagining two different situations, in each case a person coming into a room. In the first, it's a newly appointed CEO entering her spacious, luxurious office for the first time. In the second, it's a thief entering someone else's living room – also (I suppose) for the first time.

To what extent do you feel *at home* in the space around you (especially when it's not a part of your home)? This is very variable, because it no longer refers to any portion of space that's defined solely in relation to your body. In part, it's defined architecturally or by features of the landscape. Above all, it's a potentially social space – that's to say, a space that you may find yourself sharing with other people. But not necessarily sharing equally.

Re-Imagining Your Body

To what extent do you feel you 'own' any such space (and in what precise sense of 'own')? To what extent do you feel that you control it – control the things, and the people, within it? Do you feel free within it or constrained? These are really all versions of the same question: to what extent do you feel at home in it?

In our everyday lives we frequently need to adjust our behaviour so that it fits the space we find ourselves in: a church, an art gallery, our own kitchen with a friend visiting, a bank, the street, a park... and so on. These adjustments are largely unconscious. They're basically psychological changes. Change in behaviour follows from a change in one's relationship to the space. On some level we're aware of this relationship; we must be, though typically we are unaware that we're aware of it – this is the sense in which the adjustments are largely 'unconscious'. But we can easily raise this into full awareness. This is important because we need to be *socially sensitive* to any potentially shared spaces. Although we can use the exercises above to expand into the space around us, to make fuller and freer use of it, at the same time we mustn't do this in a way that dominates others.

Imagine a person who talks too loudly. He's talking to a companion maybe a metre (or yard) and a half away, but as loudly as would be justified if the companion were ten or fifteen metres (or yards) away. This could be in a closed space, say a train carriage, or an open space, like a beach. Either way, it's a public space. Really, the loud person is occupying too much – more than their fair share – of that public space. Vocalizations, including speech, are the products of impulses. This person's vocal impulses are flying out from his body – *extending his body* – in all directions. It's one way of dominating that space and, of course, of dominating the others in it.

There are many other ways in which a person can dominate a public space. They might just stand insensitively, but not unawarely, in your way. They might try to occupy the most 'commanding,' i.e. powerful, position within it. Dominating a space is not good. You can only ever dominate a space which is not yours to dominate, for if you 'own' a space (in a psychological rather than any literal sense), you never need to dominate it. Dominating a space is a kind of 'land grab'.

However, if you truly grasp the principle involved in 'expanding into the space around you' by imagining your movements to be bigger and more expansive than they are, you will realize that there's no real risk of dominating a space in this way.

It will help here to think a little about acting (once again). You might wonder how an actor applies the principle of imagining their movements to be bigger when they're playing, for example, a very shy, introverted, retiring character – the kind of person who shrinks into themselves in public situations and whose movements become consequently smaller. To answer this, we need to distinguish sharply between the *what* and the *how* of acting. If you have to act weakness (the what), you still have to act it strongly (the how). Imagine you're an extremely shy person in a public place. Your steps are small, weak, very tentative, tending sideways rather than directly forwards. You might try acting this initially in a 'literal' way, thinking of your steps as being small, weak and hesitant. You might then act it again, making exactly the same kinds of steps, but this time imagining that your moves are bigger than they are. Doing this, you would easily see that the principle works in such a case too. But not only that. The second performance would probably seem more convincing to an audience. That is, it would seem even weaker! The *character*, that's to say, would seem weaker, not the *performance* – which is a way of saying that the performance would be stronger.

I'm not suggesting, of course, that you need to find a way to 'act yourself,' as an actor acts a character. Not in the least. I'm saying that if you make a kind of habit of imagining your movements to be bigger than they are, in the way described (that is, without actually making them any bigger), the feeling of this will gradually seep into you and this will transform the way you relate to the space around you, increasing your 'presence'. This will happen naturally. You won't have to 'turn anything on' or make any kind of conscious effort of imagination when you find yourself in certain public situations.

On the contrary: you'll be free just to *be yourself.*

MOVEMENT PHRASES

By a 'movement phrase' I basically mean a connected series of movements with a distinct beginning, middle and end.

We refer to a certain type of event as a 'movement'. But very often this 'movement' is made up of more than one movement. Just think of picking up a cup of coffee, taking a sip, and setting the cup down again. It's easy to think of this as constituting a single movement – because the beginning and the end are very clear.

There's a limit to this, of course. The first half of a football match has a clear beginning and end, but the forty-five minutes of action in between don't constitute a single movement, not even for a single player. There are too many obvious other beginnings and ends in between for that.

EXPERIMENT 9: *Extend one arm to your side to about shoulder height and immediately lower it again. Think of this as a single movement. Now do it again, but with a little pause before you lower your arm. Probably, it still seems to be a single movement. Do it again, with a longer pause. Keep on like this until you find the point at which it becomes impossible to think of – or more precisely, to experience – the raising and the lowering as part of the same movement. Through this you'll appreciate that a pause can either be a part of a movement or the end of it.*

Often enough, a movement contains two main parts, with the second being a kind of *reversal* of the first. That's the case with raising and lowering your arm, before the pause becomes long enough to break it into two distinct movements. It's the case with picking up a cup of coffee and setting it down (where taking a sip is like a 'pause' that belongs to the movement rather than ends it).

Think of OPENING AND CLOSING (pp. 56-57). Once you've opened physically, you stay (that is, you pause) in this position continuing to open psychologically, before you return to your starting position. The same when you close. The pauses, here, can be quite long, but they shouldn't break the whole thing into two separate movements. You should try to experience the OPENING as a single movement which includes the 'return to neutral'. And you should try to experience the CLOSING in the same way. This applies to WIELDING THOR'S HAMMER and CYCLOPEAN THROW as well. The return to initial position is part of the *movement phrase* that is the exercise.

Why is this? Think of a golfer using a wood or a long iron, so that their swing needs to be expansive and powerful. A good golf swing is a very connected, coordinated whole-body movement. In fact, it's an excellent movement to think about and even to study in order to understand how movements seem to 'flow through' the body. It's also very beautiful, when done well, for exactly that reason: the way everything flows. The other side of this coin is that even the slightest flaw in technique can 'deform' the movement, making it aesthetically weaker. Now, the whole swing is very obviously a single movement, however complex its component parts. At the end of the swing, with the club at the top of the follow through, the golfer will pause for a moment or two, perfectly balanced, watching the arc of the ball flying deep into the distance, which is a great example of the body extending itself out into space by means of its impulses. But what happens next?

Imagine two different possibilities. In the first, the golfer simply drops the club straight down, not all the way down but by bringing their hands to chest height. Simultaneously they straighten (untwist) their body, fairly quickly. Let's call this the 'semi-collapse' (a total collapse would involve dropping the club all the way down, its head hitting the ground). In the second, the golfer lets the club swing back through the same arc as the follow-through to the strike, but in smooth slow motion. Only the second half of the original swing is reversed in this way, of course; as this happens, the body also 'uncoils' itself quite slowly. Note how this also mirrors the initial backswing. Let's call this the 'controlled unwind'. It's a good idea here to mime each of these (provided you've got good sense of a golf swing), to get the feel of them.

Each of these 'finishes' has a different significance. The semi-collapse is a kind of *rejection* of the shot. It's obviously not a continuation of the same movement, and this serves to negate that movement. The controlled-unwind, on the other hand, *is* a continuation of the same movement. It says that that movement was worth completing; in other words, it's an *affirmation* of the shot.

This example should help reveal something crucial. A *movement phrase* isn't just a movement with a clear beginning and end; *it's one where the relationship between the beginning and the end of the movement has both significance (meaning) and aesthetic value (beauty).*

Notice, then, that a movement phrase is highly likely to include a psychological component. Think of OPENING again. You open fully physically, then you continue to open psychologically (it's as though the movement continues within you), then you return to initial position. This is all one phrase. But if, after opening fully physically, your mind were to wander and you were to think, for example, of something someone said that upset you, the movement phrase would be broken.

A movement only constitutes a clear movement phrase *for an observer* if it is first a clear movement phrase *for the person who moves.*

Think about RINGING THE COSMIC BELL (pp. 63-64). It seems wrong to think of the downstroke and the upstroke as separate movement phrases, because they're too obviously connected. It also seems that we have a choice here. Should we think of downstroke-upstroke or of upstroke-downstroke as constituting the movement phrase in this case?

Try both. Try to feel the difference.

Which feels more 'complete' to you? Is your being pulled best felt as a response (the response *of the universe*, let's say) to your pulling? Or is your pulling best felt as a response (*your* response) to your being pulled? Which seems to come first, the universe – or you?

In general, you should try to become as sensitive as you can to your movement phrasing. A vital component of this phrasing is *tempo*. How fast do you move, and how do you vary the speed of your movements within the individual movement phrase? Think here of the golf swing again, in the movement phrase that includes a controlled unwind. It's very important, isn't it, that while the swing itself is very fast, its part-reversal in the controlled unwind goes into slow motion. If it didn't, it wouldn't seem so controlled, and if it didn't seem controlled, it wouldn't seem satisfied.

EXERCISE: EXPANDING INTO SPACE 2

Now repeat EXPANDING INTO SPACE (p. 56), but this time you should pay close attention to your movement phrasing. Although you aim throughout to keep your movements flowing as the 'leading role' is passed on from one part of your body to another, you should still be able to observe the beginnings and ends of particular movement phrases within the overall flow.

As you do this, experiment with varying the tempo of your movements. Don't change tempo arbitrarily but instinctively, that is in ways that seem 'right' for the movements that you're making. For the sake of 'flow,' your shifts of tempo shouldn't be too abrupt either. But you can still easily achieve a wide range of different tempos.

Observe how changing tempo contributes to movement phrasing – above all, how it contributes to the sense of completeness (this is an aesthetic value here) of individual phrases.

By now you should be 'dancing' – if you weren't already when you first tried this exercise. This is not the kind of dance discussed earlier in relation to your *dance-centre* (COME DANCING, p. 40), though of course there's some overlap with that. It's a dance form for the theatre rather than the club or party. It's the so-called 'modern dance' that, very roughly, originates with Isadora Duncan, reaches maturity in major choreographers like Martha Graham, and feeds through to more recent dance styles like that of Pina Bausch. This kind of modern dance 'works outwards' from the natural tendencies and potential of the human body, though of course it also extends these, whereas classical ballet imposes its own aesthetic norms on the human body, often quite unnaturally.

Now, you may not be next in line for a role with the Ballet Rambert or the Nederlands Dans Theater. But that's not the point. What makes your movement like this kind of dance is not your 'trained dancer's body' – *it's entirely your awareness of and sensitivity to movement phrasing.*

You see, it doesn't actually matter if you're a bit inflexible and even 'awkward' here. If you're aware of the way your body 'speaks,' you can dance in this style. I once saw the Merce Cunningham Dance Company perform with Merce Cunningham himself performing a short solo – in his early seventies. His movement was limited, quite restricted, but he was still gripping to watch, very obviously a true dancer.

Because he was so totally inside his body!

You see, as you observe your movement phrasing, you're not like an observer of yourself *from the outside.* Why not? Because although your movement phrasing is intrinsically very visual, you yourself can only 'see' it through the way you *feel* it. If you try to 'see' your movement phrases (let's say in your mind's eye) without feeling them, you will become mannered, pretentious, graceless – and you will probably appear narcissistic.

Put differently, a true movement phrase can't be 'constructed in the mirror' – including the mirror that you carry inside you!

There's a simple reason for this. All aesthetically pleasing movements must begin from deep within you, so that an observer doesn't see merely the *end result* of the impulse but the *whole impulse expressing itself.*

We might add to this the principle, "What is felt in the heart is ten; what appears in movement seven," which Zeami cites in his treatise *A Mirror Held to the Flower* (Zeami, 75). Zeami (1363-1443) is one of the great figures of world theatre, responsible, along with his father Kan'ami, for the creation of Noh. What he means here is that movement should always be restrained in relation to the inner life it expresses, at least in performance. We can put it as a paradox: if the heart feels ten and the movement expresses all ten, then the movement expresses *less* than if the heart feels ten and the movement expresses 'only' seven. To this we might add: if the movement expresses (or tries to express) more than is felt in the heart, it expresses nothing at all.

Re-Imagining Your Body

Now recall the important *downsizing principle* (p. 64) that something that you best discover initially through making large expansive movements can afterwards be transferred to smaller 'everyday' movements.

Have you ever noticed that in the theatre, very simple actions performed onstage can become very watchable? What lies behind this?

EXERCISE: THE 'HALF-DANCE' OF EVERYDAY LIFE

Perform some ordinary, everyday actions, a wide variety of them. Shaving, for example (your face or your legs); washing your face or your hands; opening a door, going through it, closing it behind you; putting on shoes; vacuuming; going to a window to look out of it; picking up a book and starting to read it; slicing an onion; cutting your nails; painting a wall or a door frame; stroking the cat on your lap or the dog sitting beside you; taking items from supermarket shelves.... And so on and so on.

As you perform such actions, pay close attention to the movement phrasing – initially to the way certain movement phrases have more or less clear beginnings and ends, and then to how you quite naturally vary tempo in performing them. You'll notice that many of your everyday actions are focused in your hands. You'll need to be very aware of the 'phrasing' of your hand and finger movements, of course, but don't concentrate exclusively on this; other parts of your body will be involved too, if in a more 'secondary' role, and you must always maintain your sense of the movement as a whole.

You need to spend time doing this. It's better not to do it for too long each time, but do it often – make it a kind of habit. Gradually you'll refine your sense of your movement phrasing in this everyday movement context too. Of any particular movement phrase, ask yourself if it's clear and well-defined, or vague and messy. If it's vague and messy, can it be made clearer, more precisely defined? You can only answer this question by trying to make the movement phrase clearer. Some actions may seem to be intrinsically less well-defined than others, but you'll only be sure of this if you first try to make them as well-defined as possible.

In the beginning, it may be more difficult to feel your everyday movement phasing from within, as against observing it as it were 'from without' (i.e. in your 'mind's eye'), than it was with your larger, expansive dance-like movements. For this reason, you can resort – but only for a time – to Yoshi

Oida's suggestion that you perform certain everyday actions while imagining you're being watched by an audience (Oida, 18-19). Never do this with large expansive movements though! And do it here only as a temporary measure, something to go beyond. Your goal is to become much more aware of your everyday movement phrasing but with a natural rather than a self-conscious awareness. If you really were being watched, you should not seem to the observer to be aware of being watched, and certainly not to be performing for the observer. On the contrary, you should seem totally absorbed in whatever it is that you're doing.

Your full goal, in fact, is to become not just aware of your movement phrasing as being as crisp, clear and well-defined as possible, but also aware of the completeness of your movement phrases as having aesthetic value. This certainly does not mean that you need to exaggerate any aspect of them. You are not dancing now, for dance is always a going beyond the everyday, but whatever you are doing is as watchable and as beautiful in its own right as dance. Try to feel that there is a kind of 'going beyond' – a small miracle – in even the most mundane action.

YOU AND THE SPACE AROUND YOU 2

In the previous 'You and the Space Around You' Section (pp. 52-67), space was treated as being... well, *spatial*. Space was, in a sense, conceived as empty, and your goal, very simply put, was to fill more of it, both physically and psychologically. Your relationship to space was thus seen in *quantitative* terms ('less,' 'more'). Now you're going to explore and extend the *quality* of your relationship to space. To do this, you need more imaginative ways of conceiving of space as the medium in and through which you move. You will need to 'fill' the previously empty space with certain imaginary qualities, which you then respond and relate to.

The four exercises that follow are all taken with relatively little adaptation from Michael Chekhov, though I've simplified some of them a little (see Chekhov, 8-13 for Chekhov's own descriptions). They are truly extraordinary exercises, both fascinating and exhilarating to perform. In performing them, you should also discover just how potent a force your imagination can be in endowing your movements with different qualities.

For each of the four exercises, you start by making a range of large expansive movements, leading with varying parts of the body, just as in EXPANDING INTO SPACE 1 & 2 (pp. 56, 70). These large expansive movements should also 'flow' – though the quality of that flow will be different in each case. Then you reduce the size and expansiveness of your movements (while still maintaining your flow), until they become ordinary everyday movements. (Yes, it's that 'downsizing principle' again.) For this phase of each exercise, aim to conclude by performing the same set of basic everyday movements, not necessarily in the same order: walking; sitting down, changing posture when sitting, standing up; climbing up then down two or three steps; picking up, handling, putting down a small object....

Firstly, your movements will *mould* the space around you; secondly, they will *float* through it; thirdly, they will *fly* through it; fourthly, they will *radiate* out through that space. *Moulding, floating, flying, radiating....* These are the four qualities your movements, both the expansive and the everyday ones, will take on as a result of your imagining the space around you to be something more than merely 'spatial'. At the end, you will also 'let go' of your sense of movement... as you will see.

EXERCISE: MOULDING

For MOULDING, *begin by imagining that the air around you is thick and resistant, so that your movements need to be strong and powerful to pass through it. Probably they'll tend to become a little slower too. Imagine that you're standing deep in water – that's the kind of resistance you need to feel. But whereas water is perfectly fluid and keeps closing all around you – or, to put it differently, the shapes your movements make in the water are immediately lost – the resistant space around you preserves these shapes. As you keep moving, naturally you won't be able to keep a sense of all the shapes your body has made in the space around you, but for each movement phrase, feel it to be 'left there' for a few moments after you complete it.*

EXERCISE: FLOATING

For FLOATING, *begin by imagining that the air around you is buoying you up, that your body floats upon it. Once you've got this sense, you need to extend it. You're not just floating upwards, but sideways, downwards – in all directions, in fact. After all, that's how a fish 'floats,' isn't it? Not on the surface but within a three-dimensional medium that seems to 'cradle' it in each dimension simultaneously! It's quite easy to get a feeling of your arms floating through space as they move but you must also get this sense for your head, your torso, your hips, your legs....*

EXERCISE: FLYING

For FLYING, begin simply by imagining that you're very high up, up in the sky, and that you're weightless. Don't imitate any kind of 'fake flying' movement, as if your arms were wings (you're not pretending to be a bird), but simply feel that you can change direction and speed very easily, by means of the slightest of shifts in your centre of gravity – yes, you still have one of those even though you're weightless! Explore the different kinds of flying movements (again without imitating a bird) – swooping, soaring, gliding....

EXERCISE: RADIATING

For RADIATING, begin by imagining that your movements send radiation – powerful waves of energy, your energy – out in the direction in which you make the movement. Radiate in many different directions like this, using different parts of your body to radiate from. Then feel yourself to be radiating out from the whole body in all directions simultaneously. After this, aim for a continuous shifting between uni-directional and omni-directional radiation, where these shifts follow from the nature of your movements. Let yourself pause often in your movements, come to a halt even, but always continuing to radiate through the pause. If you pause after swinging the head and torso to the right, for example, continuing radiating out in that direction from the head and torso. If you pause in a more neutral standing position, continue radiating outwards in all directions. If you sit down, continue radiating downwards, in the direction, that is, of your sitting down. Lastly, at the end of any pause, feel yourself starting to radiate out in the direction in which you're going to move a fraction of a second before you actually do so.

I can describe in (maybe boring) detail the precise nature of any mechanical movement. But I cannot describe in detail the different qualities of movement you're aiming to achieve through these exercises. I can only suggest it. The rest – the discovery – is up to you. Experiment – play around – with these exercises. If you're open to your own imagination, if you let it work for you, you'll discover for yourself what MOULDING, FLOATING, FLYING and RADIATING really feel like. They will probably feel something like this....

> MOULDING will give you a strong sense of *definition and exerted power.*
> FLOATING will give you a strong sense of *ease, relaxation and calm.*

Re-Imagining Your Body

FLYING will give you a strong sense of *exhilaration and joy*.
RADIATING will give you a strong sense of *presence and power in
reserve*.

*Do the four exercises together, in this sequence, with no break between them.
Go straight from moulding space with everyday movements to floating
expansive movements, and so on.*

At the end of RADIATING, *just stand there, freely radiating out in all
directions, but primarily in front of you and in the direction in which you're
looking. Look around you, to the left, the right, high up, low down. Do this
very naturally, with small adjustments in your posture. Think now of the
way you're* RADIATING *as giving yourself – giving your power – to the scene
before you. It's particularly effective if you can do this out of doors, in a
natural landscape.*

EXERCISE: RECEIVING

*But the whole process should not end with such 'giving yourself'. On the
contrary, you should gradually let yourself become increasingly aware of the
scene before you and all around you; not just what you see, but also what you
hear, what you feel (wind perhaps, or a draught from an open window), what
you smell. Don't let any self-awareness interfere with this. Notice the details
of the world beyond or apart from you. Let all this start entering into you, so
that it is no longer beyond or apart from you.*

As you do this, your giving gradually turns into RECEIVING.

*In receiving the scene before you, nothing in it should seem to you to be
trivial, nothing about it is so minor that it can be taken for granted.
Everything in it and everything about it is extraordinary and wonderful.*

Receive it all as a great gift.

*As you do so, you will experience a great inner stillness. You will understand
that even though your external movements ceased some time before, your
inner movement continued – for as long as you were radiating. Now, your
inner being – your soul, if you like – is perfectly still – as it almost never is in
everyday life.*

You are now pure possibility.

INNER MOVEMENT

If I were pressed to choose just one idea or principle from all those in this book as being the most important, it might well be this one – *inner movement*. We've already come across it, for example in the OPENING and CLOSING exercises, and it's closely associated with the RADIATING exercise just described. We'll come back to inner movement a great deal in what follows, because it is so central to the mind-body relationship.

Just about everyone has experienced inner movement at some points in their lives. In perhaps the most obvious situation, recall being very tired while sitting on a chair but needing, for whatever reason, to get up. First you need to gather all your reserves of energy; as you do this, it's as though you start the process of standing up before you start the process of standing up! The same is true when you're very tired and you badly need to sit down. The relief you feel on just having sat down is just like the act of sitting down continuing.

EXERCISE: INNER RUNNING (OR WALKING)

Still, we need to develop a stronger and more refined sense of inner movement than this, one that does not depend on being very tired. The simplest, most effective exercise I know for beginning to build this sense is Lorna Marshall's 'Running Inside' (Marshall, 132-3). You start by running as fast as you can for fifteen seconds or so, then you freeze for about eight seconds, aware of your stillness. There should be no unnecessary rigidity in the freeze. Then you run again, then freeze, then run again, then freeze.... On the third freeze, you aim to keep the sense - the feeling - of your running continuing inside you, so that when you start running again, you simply 'pick up' this inner movement by re-connecting with it. Then you freeze again, maintaining the sense of your inner running, as before. This time, however, when you start moving again, you can run more slowly, or even walk, while experiencing your inner running as continuing to be very fast.

I find that this exercise works well if students are simply asked to walk very fast, rather than run. What is achieved in this case is not such a dynamic sense of inner movement, but it is still strong enough to impress people that inner movement is a psychological reality.

The exercise is also an excellent way of demonstrating the point behind Zeami's statement, introduced earlier (p. 71): "What is felt in the heart is ten; what appears in movement seven". It can also be associated with the Japanese concept of *zanshin*, which can be translated both as 'continuing body' and as 'continuing mind' (for *shin* is a rich concept that means your centre or core or heart or spirit). In *Kyudo*, for example, the action or 'movement' of the archer is not completed at the moment of the arrow's release. It continues *inside the archer* through to the point at which the arrow finds the target, and even after. Something similar can be observed when a good golfer strikes the ball, as I discussed earlier in a different context (pp. 68-69).

If you think that 'inner movement' exists only in imagination, then please take note of an important observation made by the famous and influential movement analyst and teacher Rudolph Laban. If a dancer, A, has to lift another dancer, B, high in the air, B can become lighter, hence easier for A to lift, if she simultaneously imagines lifting her own centre of gravity upwards. Conversely, if she moves her centre downwards she becomes much harder to lift (Newlove and Dalby, 122).

EXERCISE: KEEP YOUR COOL

The following exercise is great fun – and very tiring. It's fun to watch too. John Wright, who as far as I'm aware invented it, calls it "The Running and Stopping Game" and uses it as preparation for clowning because, among other things, the stopping is a 'drop' (an important clowning technique) that debunks the significance of the running (Wright, 188). My purpose here is quite different and the exercise is adapted accordingly.

Run around madly, crazily, for about ten seconds, then stop abruptly. The moment you stop, you must behave in a cool, calm, relaxed and even 'fresh' way, doing whatever you want but as if you had never run around in your life! (In Wright's game, differently, you must do as little as possible when you stop running so that your underlying or habitual attitude is thrown into relief.) Continue this for fifteen seconds or so. Then repeat – over and over. Each time it will become more difficult for you to behave as if you had not just been running madly around, since you will naturally become increasingly exhausted. I think five 'cycles' is enough!

On one level, your problem seems 'purely physical'. That is, how do you mask the fact that you're out of breath, flushed and maybe even sweating? But you soon discover that this isn't enough. In order to appear as someone who was not just running madly around, you need to mask the masking too, which is much more difficult. The problem is how to adopt a certain manner – a cool, calm, relaxed manner – and you find that the highly energized and activated state of your body won't let you do this.

The trick here is to invert the principle involved in RUNNING INSIDE. *Instead of deliberately sustaining your sense of inner running, you should try to maintain a sense of inner stillness even when you are running. Then, when you stop, you re-connect with this inner stillness. (Wright would not want you to do this. He would want you to run 'as if your life depended on it'. This is because his purpose is to make it increasingly hard for you to adopt any habitual attitude on stopping and thus to 'strip you' of the persona which goes with that attitude.)*

You will discover that maintaining an inner stillness is considerably harder to do than sustaining a sense of inner running when you are still. But it is possible – and it's the only way to solve the problem posed by KEEP YOUR COOL.

Stillness, we might say, is kind of movement (in much the way that zero is a number). Thus the principle of inner movement includes inner stillness. More broadly, there is *inner tempo* – which can coincide or contrast with outer tempo. The expressive value of contrasting inner and outer tempo was well understood by Michael Chekhov (Chekhov, 75-6). However, the usual way of setting up such contrasts involves a kind of 'disconnect' between body and mind. For example, a person is waiting for someone at a prearranged place, but it will soon be too late for them to carry out what they had planned. The waiting person's outer tempo may be slow, with little movement, but their inner tempo may be agitated, their thoughts racing. Or a person may be rushing to finish a manual task such as building a brick wall, while imagining lying on the beach tomorrow, the first day of the summer holiday. We would not normally think of the inner tempo in such cases as being a form of *inner movement*, at least in the sense that 'inner running' is inner movement – but perhaps we should.

The 'disconnect' between body and mind in the above examples is really just the other side of the coin of the *interactive unity* of body and mind. This implies that, for example, outer calm and inner agitation are not simply different things occurring independently of each other. The outer calm is affected by and appears differently to any observer because of the inner agitation, and the inner agitation is affected by and experienced differently by the person because of the outer calm. It's not that the inner state is 'more true' or 'more real' than the outer one. Both belong to the same complex truth or reality.

In a general way, it's no harder to have slow inner and quick outer tempos than it is to have quick inner and slow outer tempos. So why is KEEP YOUR COOL more difficult than INNER RUNNING? The example I used above to demonstrate a quick outer tempo suggests the answer to this. Bricklaying is fairly repetitive and therefore rhythmical as an action. Running around madly with frequent changes of direction, hence also frequent changes of pace, is not. Inner stillness is much easier to maintain when the dynamic outer movement is also strongly rhythmical. Think of running here (as in athletics, not 'running around'). A sprinter always needs to 'sprint inside'. But a long distance runner needs 'inner stillness' – except at those hard times of extra effort.

It may seem a simplistic way of putting it but it's as though we have an 'inner body' inside the outer (flesh and bone) body. This 'inner body,' moreover, is like a bridge between the psychological mind and the physiological body. In Appendix 2 we will see that this idea is not so simplistic after all!

START THE DAY SEQUENCE

To conclude Part One, here is a great way to start the day – or to start *some* days, when you feel like it (since I'm not recommending any strict regime here, but an open-ended exploration). There's nothing new in it. It's a specific sequence of some of the exercises you've encountered already. It will make you feel positive, confident and generally just really good!

Phase One: *Fill the space around you by making free, large, expansive movements, using the whole of your body to do so and continuously shifting the leading part. Make sure your movements flow. As you do this, you can draw shapes at the edges of your kinesphere (p. 55), you can create a moving, evolving sculpture (pp. 55-56), or you can send your movements far out into the space around you (p. 56). Move from one to the other of these just as you feel like. At the same time, sometimes place the focus of your attention in your chest-centre and sometimes in your abdominal-centre, again just as you feel like. In these ways you keep renewing the way you experience your movements and your body.*

Phase Two: *Perform* OPENING AND CLOSING *(pp. 56-57), then* WIELDING THOR'S HAMMER *(pp. 57-59), then* LIFTING THE GREAT STONE *(pp. 59-60), then* CYCLOPEAN THROW *(pp. 60-61), then* BRIDGING THE HORIZONS *(pp. 61-63), then, lastly,* RINGING THE COSMIC BELL *(pp. 63-64). Perform each of these the number of times – or if it's a repeated rhythmic movement, sustain it for the length of time – that feels right to you. But make sure that for* WIELDING THOR'S HAMMER *and* CYCLOPEAN THROW *you lead with the left foot and with the right foot an equal number of times. You can vary the order of these exercises if you like. In all of these exercises, make the movements as large as you can, so that they extend your body into space, but keep good balance and a strong sense of the clarity of the movement phrase. Keeping attention focused in your chest-centre is the 'default mode' for each of these, but every so often vary it by focusing attention in your abdominal-centre instead.*

Phase Three: *In exactly the way described in the preceding section, go through the* MOULDING, FLOATING, FLYING *and* RADIATING *exercises (pp. 74-75). End with* RECEIVING *(p. 76). In this case, receive the new day as the greatest of gifts. It will become yours – yet at the same time you will realize that it is so much greater than you. Before the new day, in other words, you are humble, with the humility that befits all receiving. But you are also extended and enhanced.*

PART TWO

DEMOTING THE 'CONSCIOUS CONTROLLER'

PRELIMINARY THOUGHTS

We commonly make a distinction between *involuntary* and *voluntary* actions. Involuntary actions are those we make 'in spite of ourselves,' such as starting in fright, yawning or having a fit of the giggles. Voluntary actions seem to be the results of our choices. They are, at some level, *willed*. However, the concept of the will is difficult both philosophically and scientifically – philosophically because it's not at all clear that 'willing an act' contains or implies an 'act of willing' (and if willing is not an act, then what is it?), and scientifically because we have no real idea, as yet, of how the will might operate, or even if it exists, at the level of physical brain activity. Nonetheless we seem to need the distinction between involuntary and voluntary actions, since it appears to us that there really is an important difference between them.

Even so, it's not difficult to complicate the distinction. Think of driving a car while you're deep in thought about something else. For much of the time you'll be on some kind of 'automatic pilot,' slowing down, stopping, speeding up, adjusting your direction and such like, without needing to think about it. But these all remain choices. It's as though you leave it to the 'computer in your brain' to make such choices for you, leaving 'you' free to think about something else. If you come to a junction where you need to think, even momentarily, about which road to take, then what you normally think of as your 'will' gets activated. If a sudden hazard appears causing you to brake sharply, the act of braking may seem to have been initiated automatically by your 'brain-computer,' but it is accompanied by such an instantaneous re-focussing of your attention on the road scene, giving you the apparent option of consciously making decisions, that the braking itself might, after all, have been more 'deliberately' decided. You can't quite be sure.

A better description of the above – one that does not separate 'you' from yourself – must include the recognition that consciousness is multi-layered. Here I'll distinguish just two levels of consciousness, though probably there are more. When you are driving 'on automatic pilot' you are, of course, fully conscious of everything relevant to your driving. But you are not conscious of being conscious of this. If you need to think about which road to take or if a hazard appears, then your consciousness shifts up a gear to the level at which you are *conscious of being conscious* (or 'aware of being conscious' if you prefer to vary the terms here). Strictly speaking, it's not that you notice things on this higher level, for you notice them on the lower level too; it's that you notice them in such a way that you might be able later to recall them. But when you've been driving on 'automatic pilot' for a while, you may well suddenly realize this and, as you do so, you also realize that you can't remember what you've seen or what you've done. It's sometimes even a kind of surprise to you that you are still on the right route.

Butoh dancers, whose kind of dance typically involves much improvisation, often cannot remember what they have danced. People who have been in trance or semi-trance states, or who have been hypnotized, often cannot remember what they have experienced or what they have done. This is not because their minds have been 'somewhere else,' as in the example of driving a car. Yet there is an important similarity between these states of mind: the absence of a self-consciously controlling 'You' or self.

Western culture tends to be suspicious of or even anxious about those mental states where your 'You' seems 'absent from the scene'. By your 'You' here I really mean your 'consciousness of being conscious,' which is what allows you to think of yourself as making decisions and therefore as being *in control*. In such a cultural context, even the experience of driving 'on automatic pilot,' when you catch yourself doing it (or rather, when you catch yourself *just having done it*, since it ceases with the 'catching'), can be a little troubling, as though you're not quite sure that you were driving safely. But you almost certainly were.

By the 'conscious controller,' then, I mean your sense of *a self that's in overall control of your actions*. Such a 'self' is not discovered by pure introspection, although, as I've said, it rests on your 'consciousness of being conscious' – it is culturally constructed. The other side of the coin of this sense of self is *an instrumental view of the body*, which is equally culturally constructed. The body, in this view, is simply the means by which you – 'you' as distinct from your body – get things done in the world. 'You,' on the other hand, are some conscious, willing, planning, deciding, controlling subjectivity which just happens to have to be embodied.

To understand this fully, we would need to situate the concept historically as *Western Dualism Version 3.1*. Other cultures did not and do not see things this way. To develop this point here would take me too far from my present purpose, but I'll do so in Appendix 1. What matters right now is that, up to a point, you can discover the cultural relativity of the instrumental view of the body in a practical way, by learning how to go beyond it. Many of the exercises that follow have the goal of helping you 'demote the conscious controller' so that you can go past that instrumental view of the body. Why? Because it's a view that alienates you from your body. And that's not good.

By the way, the goal is to *demote* the conscious controller, not to *dismiss* it altogether. It has its uses, after all. Nor is this something that can be achieved quickly. As you work through this section, be patient. First, it's necessary to look closely at some basic concepts and the realities behind them. We'll start with *tension*.

TENSION AS WASTED ENERGY

Often in Part One, I emphasized the need for your movements to *flow*. A major enemy of the flow of movement is *tension*. Many people suffer from it, more than they need to.

Tension is physical. It's basically a kind of 'tightening'. It may well have a psychological origin, but it manifests itself in the body. If you're tense, you may be more or less aware of being tense, more or less aware, that is, of its physical impact. The more aware you are of tension, the more you feel a tightness, a constriction and blockage of some sort, probably associated with certain body areas but not necessarily with specific body parts. In more severe forms it can cause real pain, including headaches (where the pain is referred from the site of tension), but my focus here is on its more common manifestation where it generates 'mere' discomfort. If, on the other hand, your tension sits in the background of your consciousness, which it can, especially if you have become habituated to it, the less you notice those feelings of discomfort or lack of ease. Nonetheless the tightness, constriction and blockage are all still there. And they may well be apparent to others.

What is the opposite of tension? *Relaxation*, of course. If you're tense, you need to relax. You need to exchange 'tightness' for 'looseness'. But while there's a truth here, it's also too simple; it leaves out far too much that also matters. Hence it's a little misleading. In order to go beyond the over-simplification and to see the bigger picture we'll need to relate tension and relaxation to two other important concepts: *energy* and (less familiarly) *neutrality*.

Re-Imagining Your Body

Let's begin by looking more closely at what tension is – and the same, a little later, for relaxation. The first, very important point is that although I began by saying that people 'suffer' from tension, tension isn't intrinsically bad. In fact, some tension is necessary – without it, we'd collapse on the floor.

EXPERIMENT 10: *Try performing some simple actions, but in slow motion – walking, for example, sitting down, standing up again. Make the motion as slow as you possibly can, provided that the action remains recognisable. Doing this, you will become aware (maybe uncomfortably) of tensions arising in different parts of your body. The point is that these tensions also arise, but more briefly and less intensely, as you perform the actions at normal speed, but you tend to remain unaware of them – precisely because they form a natural and necessary part of the natural action.*

Tension is *bad* only when it's unnecessary, or useless.

But what precisely is tension?

Some basic physics: if a string is attached at either end to two pegs on a board, then tightened, it acquires tension. If the string is tightened further, its tension increases. Tension here is defined as the *pull* that the string exerts on each peg. But these two pulls are equal and opposite, so they cancel each other out. Nothing happens. No movement takes place. But there's still a force – some kind of *energy* – at work, or rather (strictly speaking) *not at work*, since nothing is moved (for in physics the definition of work involves moving something). What is there is properly called *potential* energy, then, or *stored* energy.

It's very important to understand the relation of tension to energy in your own body.

You can easily model the tension of the string in your body by cupping the fingers of your two hands together with your elbows turned out horizontally, then pulling as hard as you can. Your fingers are strong enough to prevent the combined outward forces pulling your hands apart, so nothing happens – no 'work' (defined as the displacement of something) is done. But it's obvious that if you continue pulling hard like this, you'll get tired. So you must be *using up* energy.

Tension in your body is not, or not simply, *stored* energy. Unnecessary tensions tend to be *wasted* energy.

And looking at it this way should immediately raise a question. Is relaxation the only way to deal with bad tension? Might it not be possible instead to tap directly into the energy that is being wasted and to channel it differently, more effectively?

If you stand for some time holding one arm out horizontally at shoulder height, after a while your arm will get tired. In this case, the muscular tension serves to counteract the downward pull of gravity. Although your arm stays still, it's clear that your body is working to counteract the downward movement that would take place without that work. (Holding your arm out straight like this really is 'work' – in the precise sense of moving something! Literally, you are moving your arm. But you are moving your arm just enough in the opposite direction to its natural movement downwards, as it is pulled by gravity, that no movement appears!) Many of the tensions you become aware of by sitting down or standing up in slow motion are of this kind.

It's different, though, when your body 'works' *to counteract itself* (rather than some external force) – for in this case it may not be 'working' at all, or at least not working efficiently. But it's still using up energy – and wasting it. This may involve pressing your upper and lower jaws together, or tightening certain neck muscles to support a head that's pushed too far forward. The former may well accompany intense concentration, but it doesn't actually help you concentrate. The latter may be a consequence of poor posture, or of 'upper body straining' to communicate – something which is really very counterproductive. In cases such as these, you gain no benefit whatsoever from your tension.

BUT TENSION CAN BE 'EXPRESSIVE'...

Having set up a working definition of 'bad' tension, I want now to take a little detour. I want to point out that something rather like (but not) bad tension may be useful in those performing arts in which the body needs to be expressive. This will help complete the picture even if its relevance to everyday life is indirect. Most importantly, it will illustrate the very close relationship between tension and energy.

In the theatre, *tension as internal counteraction* may be a good thing. If a performer mimes drawing an imaginary long bow in readiness to shoot an imaginary arrow, it helps the image greatly if s/he pushes *forward* from the pelvis and below, especially with the leading knee (which in the stage image can even be bent for this purpose, although in archery both legs would remain straight), while pulling *back* the imaginary bowstring and, with it, the upper torso.

Re-Imagining Your Body

This sets up a tension of opposition between upper and lower bodies (which would be completely wrong for really shooting an arrow). The audience sees the energy which is expressed in this way and 'reads' it as the energy required to draw the bow; the lower body, that's to say, stands in for the resistance in the wood of the bow. But the principle involved here is not limited to 'giving life' to mimed, purely imaginary, objects. It's an effective trick, when onstage, to pick up a small, light, real object while imagining that it weighs much more than it does. This causes you to set up a counter-tension, let's say in your left leg and foot as you pick up a small glass of whisky in your right hand, as would happen if you were picking up an object weighing two or three kilos (4½–7 pounds). As a result, the audience sees a much sharper, more energized and therefore more compelling image. More generally, in adopting certain stances or postures onstage, whether in dance and physical theatre or even in more naturalistic 'psychological theatre,' it may help to oppose one part of your body to another, making them push (or pull) in opposite directions, as this can make you seem much more 'full of life'.

In general, 'stage life' requires more energy than everyday life, though this extra energy should not appear (at least not obviously) as extra energy to the audience. What grips or involves or captivates an audience is always energy (even in the stillest moments), but the audience doesn't usually realize this. The most important point here, however, is not that there's a difference in energy level between 'stage life' and everyday life. It's that any expressive tensions adopted by the performer are adopted only for as long as necessary. *Bad* tensions in everyday life, in the form of unnecessary oppositions or counteractions within the body, usually creep up on us unawares. They are not chosen, at least not consciously.

This is what makes it so difficult for our 'conscious controller' to do something about them.

It's also worth noticing that tension can exist 'in the air'. There might be tension between individuals or an atmosphere might be tense. (I'll have more to say about atmospheres later.)

EXPERIMENT 11: *Simply imagine that the atmosphere around you is tense. It's easier if you imagine a specific situation giving rise to the tense atmosphere – waiting for election results, a penalty shoot-out in a cup final, an air-raid siren announcing the approach of enemy aircraft – it doesn't matter what, provided it generates an atmosphere of tension, so just imagine the situation that you personally find easiest to imagine. Then, once you've managed to imagine the tension 'in the air,' notice what happens to your body, how it automatically tunes into this atmosphere. Your breathing may tighten, and with it your chest; you may feel your upper arms 'pulling in' a little; if your imagination is strong enough, you may even feel a kind of 'knotting' in your abdomen.*

Now ask yourself: *what is the relation between tension and fear?* (Fear, by the way, has many different forms – including some where we don't even know we're afraid!)

And here we should notice a rather odd thing. Tension can include that essential element of fear and yet be enjoyable! In such a case, however, it's usually called *suspense* and it arises via a fiction of some kind, such as in an Alfred Hitchcock movie. Suspense, we might say, is a mild form of *anxiety* (which is often associated with tension). So what is it that makes suspense enjoyable, given that anxiety is a particularly unpleasant experience? As an answer, it's not enough to say that, deep down, you know you're perfectly safe because the tension-generating situation is fictional, not real. Nor is it enough to say that you've 'switched off' your controlling, responsible self, having placed yourself temporarily in the trusted hands of the filmmaker. Such explanations are not complete because they don't show how a state we normally think of as negative can be experienced in a positive way.

Could it be that we experience suspense as somehow *energizing*?

Of course, none of this means that bad tension is not bad after all. Energy is precious, almost a synonym for life itself (as in *vitality* and *liveliness*), and should not be wasted. Even so, you can still see any bad tensions you experience in a relatively positive light as being a kind of 'message' to you, as telling you something about yourself. It helps here to remember what I said in Part One: bad tensions, in the neck and shoulders, for example, are also body '*centres*' – undesirable ones. "If you suffer from such tension," I said, "realize that it too is really a 'You' inside You – but one which blocks the natural flow of different, changing '*Yous*' which constitutes your *real You*" (p. 50).

It's quite striking, moreover, how you can dispel bad tension in the shoulders and neck simply by putting your conscious focus in your chest-centre – at least if the tension is not too severe. And you can acquire a pleasant looseness of the whole upper body by adopting the abdominal-centre. But these are temporary fixes rather than permanent solutions. Even so, they hint at something important: the ultimate solution to the problem of bad tension is for you to be fully inside your own body in that truly centred, evenly distributed way. (This, by the way, is very much the idea behind the Alexander Technique.)

SO JUST RELAX!

The opposite of tension, as we all know, is *relaxation*. We also all know that it's not always easy to relax.

'To relax' is a verb. Hence you can tell someone, or you can tell yourself: Relax! Then is relaxation something that we *do*? Well, for as long as relaxation is something that you can or need to *do*, you cannot be fully relaxed. Relaxation as such only arises where any 'doing' it becomes 'no longer doing (or needing to do) it'. Of course, you might be lucky enough to find yourself relaxed without having done or had to do anything to achieve this. Lucky you! But for most people most of the time the issue is how to 'switch relaxation on' – or is it how to 'switch tension off'?

There's a deep problem here, which is the main focus of Part Two. If we believe that we have some kind of *controlling, conscious self* (the 'conscious controller' within us) which makes choices and decisions, and pursues plans of action, then it is this self that, presumably, issues the 'instructions' to our bodies to relax. But relaxation *as a state*, which is the goal, involves putting that controlling, conscious self aside – 'turning it off,' as it were. So what 'part' of us, what kind of agency within us, accomplishes this?

To put it a little differently: when we try to relax, we can only succeed by stopping trying to relax. We seem to know this when we say *'Just* relax!' rather than simply 'Relax!' But, of course, it doesn't help.

Fortunately there are many different relaxation techniques and methods out there. You need to find the ones which work for you. My purpose here is a little different. It's to go beyond our usual idea of relaxation.

Often, we think of relaxation (in the sense of something that we do) in such a way that it seems we can't do anything else while we're trying to do it! So we lie in the Yoga 'Corpse Position' (called *Savasana*), flat on our backs, or in the classic Alexander Technique position (which is actually less stressful for the upper and lower spine), supine but with the knees raised and the head resting on a small cushion or a book. And we... relax. Now, this can be pleasant in itself, for as long as we do it, but that's not its primary purpose. Rather, the idea is to attain a state of (greater) relaxation which is then carried over into whatever activities we move on to afterwards – and for as long as possible. So we *do* 'relaxing' in order to *be* (more) 'relaxed' when we go on to do something else.

Why can't we 'just relax' while getting on with that something else?

Of course, we also think of relaxation as a *state* – a state of body-mind that we can be in as we perform varied actions – standing, walking, running, dancing, washing up, vacuuming.... The problem is getting into this state. Lying on our back seems to help us attain a relaxed state because it temporarily 'calls off' what we may tend to experience or think of as the daily contest with gravity. (We'll see a different solution to this 'problem,' which involves thinking very differently of gravity, later.) With your body supported by the floor, little or no muscular tension remains necessary. Being relaxed when you are walking or washing up, on the other hand, means that some muscular tensions do exist in your body – but only the necessary ones. To be relaxed in this case, you – your body, that is – must be able to distinguish precisely and accurately between necessary and unnecessary tensions. This isn't always easy, especially when the unnecessary tensions have become habitual.

If we could distinguish precisely between necessary and unnecessary tensions, surely we could relax – or be relaxed – at any time, whatever we were doing. Could it be that simple – and, in another way, that difficult?

What I'm describing here, in fact, is better called *neutrality*.

I should stress that I'm not against relaxation exercises – far from it – not even the ones where you lie flat on your back. But the two relaxation exercises introduced here are really steps on the way to *neutrality*. They involve finding how to be relaxed while doing something else – standing first, and then walking – by engaging your imagination.

EXERCISE: STANDING/FLOATING/FLYING SKELETON

This is an exercise – freely and extensively adapted from one given by Kristin Linklater (Linklater, 33) – which helps you attain a state of true relaxation while standing. Begin by standing with your feet parallel and fairly close together, directly below the ball joints of your hips. Make sure your knees are

Re-Imagining Your Body

not locked. Close your eyes. Now 'centre yourself' by firstly rocking slightly forwards and backwards from the feet. Your weight will shift from the balls of the feet to the heels and back again. Note the slight muscular tensions that arise in each case. Come to rest with your weight equally on the heels and the balls of the feet, hence without any such tensions. (You need to become aware of these tensions first in order to fully experience their absence.) Now rock forwards and backwards, just a little, from the pelvis or hips (not the waist). Again note the tensions this causes. Come to rest in a position without any such tensions. Lastly, push your head slightly forwards, then slightly backwards, once again noting the resulting tensions, so that you can find the head position which feels most tension-free.

With your eyes still closed (they should be closed throughout the exercise, in fact), begin to imagine yourself as a skeleton. Start with the feet – try to experience your feet as bones and nothing else – a complex set of bones, but don't worry about anatomical correctness. Then 'see' your ankles as bones. Move on to the shin bones, then the knees, the thigh bones and the pelvis. Your whole lower body is now skeletal. Focus next on the spine, making sure you locate its lower part fully within the pelvis. See (feel) it curving naturally upwards. See (experience) the ribs, then the collar bones and shoulder blades. Turn your arms to bones, moving your focus downwards, ending with the fingers. Then imagine your head as a skull. Finally, imagine your whole body as a standing skeleton. (Make sure you don't see yourself in this way from an imaginary position outside yourself. Stay 'inside' your body.)

It's now impossible for there to be any tensions in your body, for you have no muscles! So how do you manage to stay standing up? It's simple: your skeleton is perfectly balanced – the different bones and structures simply sit on top of each other.

After some moments standing like this, preferably feeling the wind passing through you (it's very good to do this out of doors), you let your whole upper body 'collapse'. Your skeleton is articulated, so it doesn't fall apart, strewing bones all over the floor. What happens is that the upper body just 'rolls down,' but as rapidly as possible. Nothing restrains it. It's a kind of free fall, but not a falling forwards, only downwards; the upper body doesn't keel over like a tree trunk but 'flows' downwards like a waterfall. Quite simply, as it falls, your skull should remain as close to the rest of you as possible.

You will be able to experience this 'waterfall effect' if you are truly relaxed. It helps if you let your knees flex just a little, so your head can fall as far as possible.

But why doesn't the 'collapse' of the upper body take the lower body with it? Well, you should imagine something like a butcher's large meat hook attached under your tailbone (the coccyx). Imagine this in place at the moment it becomes necessary to hold your lower body in its initial position – it will give you a great sense of stability. With this image, you can remain completely relaxed throughout, for none of the work of holding the new position is yours. But don't let the image of the (meat) hook make you lose the sense of yourself as a (meat-less) skeleton – so re-establish this sense as soon as you've reached the new stable position.

After a few moments, you start to roll up to your original standing position, while remaining as relaxed as you can throughout. This is the most difficult part of the exercise. The spinal roll up is slow, the opposite of the prior collapse not just in the direction of its 'flow' but in tempo too. This slowness must seem to you a wholly relaxed slowness and the slowness must feel like a pure expression of your 'relaxedness'. You will need a strong image to help you here.

The image of being pulled up, puppet-like, by a string or strings is sometimes suggested to help achieve a relaxed roll up. But it's wrong. Any string pulling you needs to be attached to a different place at each moment – if it's not, various unnecessary tensions arise. A much better image is the way sunlight 'pulls' up a plant. Some plants emerge from the ground in a curled over position, and as they grow upwards they also uncurl and open towards the light. This is a very pleasant image to work with but I find it works better in other, different exercises which include a spinal roll up, in which the feet are placed a little further apart, beneath the shoulders or a little wider, giving a stronger sense of being 'planted'. But try it. Don't worry about 'mixing metaphors' (you're a skeleton and a plant!), for the imagination is very good at this and unconcerned with matters of 'proper style'. Alternatively, imagine that your spine is a hollow tube (that's not far wrong, of course) which is gradually filling with water. As the water level rises, it 'erects,' uncurls and straightens the spine.

Whatever image works best for you, make sure you don't lose your sense of yourself as a skeleton. And, as you roll up, check that no unnecessary tensions arise, especially in the lower abdomen. If they do, simply cast them out – like little demons!

Near the top of the roll up, your head – or rather your skull – will still be dropped forward with your neck relaxed. As you begin to raise it too, change the image you've been using to achieve the slow, smooth, relaxed roll up. Your skull is hollow, of course, since you're a skeleton, but imagine that it's also sealed, hence watertight. This makes it buoyant, a kind of float – and now you're out in the deep blue sea. So let your skull float upwards (it's as though you don't need to use your neck muscles at all). As it does so, feel that as your skull comes to float easily on the surface of the ocean, with the water reaching to about eye level, the rest of your skeleton is held suspended beneath it and by it. Now your skeleton is completely weightless. Feel the pull upwards from your skull cancelling out the downward pull of gravity. Feel the ocean flowing through you, between and around all the other bones of your body, gently 'stirring' them.

An alternative to imagining your skull as a floating buoy at sea is to imagine it as a helium-filled balloon floating up into the sky and trailing the rest of your skeleton with it. What's great about this image is the way you feel yourself getting taller and taller. Even by floating the head up you should be surprised at how long you can seem to yourself to go on 'unfolding' and growing upwards. With your eyes still closed you should reach a point at which you cannot quite be sure if what is happening is that your physical body is somehow continuing to 'roll up' or whether this has been replaced by a kind of effortless 'stretching upwards of the spirit'! As you enjoy this feeling try to imagine that all the articulations of your skeleton, especially between the vertebrae, are opening and filling with light.

After this, go back to the beginning. Turn yourself into a skeleton step by step, starting with the feet. Repeat the exercise. It's best to perform the whole sequence three times, the first two ending with 'floating' and the third with 'flying' the head up.

When you've discovered and explored how powerful this exercise is, you should realize: *You can use the skeleton image to relax at other times,* even, for example, when sitting working at a computer. Whatever you're doing, if it's not too physically demanding, you can imagine yourself as a skeleton; as your muscles 'drop away,' all the muscular tension goes with them.

Lastly – but only when your body has fully internalized this exercise as a result of practising it many times – see how slowly you can do the 'roll up' while remaining fully relaxed. Aim to build up to four or five minutes for this, but make sure the rolling up is smooth and continuous (though it will barely be visible to an observer). Be especially alert to little unnecessary tensions that appear, especially in the lower abdomen, simply casting them out as before. And make sure you maintain the sense of your head floating upwards, although this will now be a much slower movement.

EXERCISE: WATER BAG

This exercise helps you to be fully relaxed while walking. Stand straight, feet about shoulder width apart, with your eyes closed. Imagine that your body is nothing more than a skin filled full with water. You retain your outer shape perfectly, but you contain no bones, no muscles, no nerve fibres, no internal organs. Now sway a little, very little, from side to side. Then twist a little, very little, left and right, from the hips. Feel how this affects the water inside you. You're full of water, so it doesn't slosh around inside you. Instead, the water in you seems to continue the movement you've just made, after that movement ceases, if only for a fraction of a second, with a kind of 'fluid momentum' that presses gently onward in the same direction. As you reverse a movement, by starting a new movement in the opposite direction, it's as though you first have to capture that ongoing momentum and to coax it gently into the new pathway. You understand that you can't force this. Your body will follow your will, but only if you attend closely to its internal needs, respecting them fully.

Open your eyes but retain this feeling. Take a few easy, slow steps forward, then stop. Do the same again. Feel how the water inside you continues the movement for you, how it 'takes over'. The slower you walk, the more you'll be aware of swaying side to side – feel how the water inside you contributes to this too. Increase the tempo of your walk, but not too much, and notice what happens as you stop. Stop gently, not abruptly. Experiment: move in different directions, sideways, backwards... whatever you want, but always gently. Then add a few simple actions such as sitting down (but not on a low chair), standing up again, picking up an object, and so on – but nothing strenuous – all the while maintaining the sense that the water inside you subtly 'presses on' with the movement after you stop moving.

Through this, you'll become like a neutral observer of yourself. You still have to 'will' – that is, to initiate – a movement, but once this movement has begun it, or your water-filled body, takes on a life of its own, which you simply have to observe, to feel, to appreciate. And you never need to *force* your body into action; to get it moving needs only the slightest 'nudge'.

No doubt you'll have noticed the *opposition* between these two exercises, STANDING/FLOATING/FLYING SKELTON and WATER BAG. In the former, you're a skeleton, nothing other than hard, dry bones, while in the latter, you have no bones at all, you are entirely liquid. *The common factor is the absence of muscles.* So, in the next section, let's look more at what muscles 'stand for,' not just what they do.

LETTING GO THE 'CONTROLLING' SELF

Butoh is a form of avant-garde dance originating in Japan after the Second World War. I'll have more to say about it in Part Three. For the present, here is a *Butoh*-related exercise. Its goal is not to promote relaxation, but I include it here because of the light it throws on the previous exercises.

EXERCISE: BONY RUNNING / SQUISHY RUNNING

Just run around, freely, easily, energetically, playfully. (If you don't have much room to really run around in, you can perform the exercise as a kind of 'dancing around' instead.) As you do so, imagine a) that you're a skeleton running around, then b) that you're a liquid-filled skin, with nothing hard inside, running around. Alternate these perspectives as and when you feel like it. Notice how your movement changes. Notice also how your feelings change.

This is great fun. It's especially fun to do in a group because you don't need to be so focused on yourself and your own body that you can't or shouldn't be aware of others. In fact you learn from watching others and there's a kind of feedback set up between individuals which can stimulate new ideas. But you should never merely imitate. The primary impulses must always come from within, as they are stimulated by your imagination of your body state.

But what's the point?

The essential starting-point for *Butoh* is for the performer to leave behind her or his *socially-conditioned* body, and this exercise contributes to that process. But beyond that, it has a deeper significance. Experiencing the contrast between these two images of the body, one as a skeleton, the other as a liquid-filled bag, is a first step towards a *transformation of your relationship to movement*. To understand this, we need to leave behind some of our cultural preconceptions.

Perhaps oddly, while Butoh has spread throughout the world, its origins and practice in Japan are associated with a 'physical system' called *Noguchi Taiso* which remains relatively little known in the West. As a physical system, *Noguchi Taiso* involves exercises, but its core is a way of imagining the body. To Noguchi Michizo, the founder of the system, the human body is best seen as a kind of liquid-filled leather bag in which the organs, muscles and bones are all floating (Kasai (1999), 1). With this image, we lose the 'western' sense of movement which is rooted in the anatomical relationship of bones, muscles and tendons. We lose, that is, the sense that movement depends on a *system of levers*. The 'problem' with that system of levers is that it is *subject to the will*. Put differently: *the crane needs an operator.*

It is sometimes said that *Noguchi Taiso* promotes 'passive movement'. This is probably a misleading formulation, but the system does reject the kind of 'active movement' which seems to need that crane operator to initiate it. It is profoundly *anti-mechanical*, because mechanisms or machines are intrinsically distinct from their operators. To Noguchi Michizo, the muscles are not means to exert a pull, via the tendons, on the bones. They are like *ears* – ears for listening to the word of god, the *god of gravity* (Kasai (1999), 1).

In this system, gravity is not an enemy. But it is very powerful.

Notice how this shifts the emphasis from the internal to the external. In the western view, our movements originate *within us*, in our willed choices. In *Noguchi Taiso*, movement is a kind of easy, unforced response to the environment, even a kind of 'echo' of it.

It's simple to find a prosaic explanation of the value of *Noguchi Taiso: willed movement, via mechanical means, is often more than required, if only to make sure that it's enough.* (This, of course, is something we're typically unconscious of, but if we sensitize ourselves to it we will be very struck by it.) But responsive movement, fully attuned to the demands made on it by the environment, can be perfectly minimal. Hence less tense.

But I think the principle behind *Noguchi Taiso* goes even deeper, for it involves the idea of *receiving* impulses, energy, even strength *from the outside.*

According to a different Noguchi, Noguchi Hiroyuki, certain traditional Japanese poses, called *kata*, put great emphasis on the bones. Yes, we're back with the bones, the body as skeleton. The *kata* of sitting, called *seiza*, he says, "is an attempt to negate all awareness of the flesh, for flesh [muscle] reflects human intention in excess" (Noguchi, 13). It is a pose, therefore, of perfect *receptivity*. The *kata* of *Kyudo*, from the Japanese art of archery, is even more interesting:

> In the standing position, the legs are spread wide apart so that the knees are positioned directly below the elbows when both arms are extended and spread to the sides at the height of the shoulders; the feet point maximally outward.... [A]nyone taking this stance will know exactly how it feels to stand on one's bones. The stance also makes it very difficult to tense the muscles in the arms. Therefore the bow cannot be pulled by muscular tension in the arms; the archer must "receive" something into himself in order to pull the bow (Noguchi, 14).

Here I must leave this as a highly suggestive idea, without further comment, for that is beyond my competence.

Fascinatingly, while early Greek medicine became interested in the function of muscles at much the same time as Greek sculpture started to depict them, early Chinese medicine and art overlooked muscles altogether. In his wonderfully thought-provoking book called *The Expressiveness of the Body and the Divergence of Greek and Chinese Medicine*, Shigehisa Kuriyama argues that the Greek fascination with muscles (which of course had major influence on the European Renaissance) reflects "the emergence of a particular conception of personhood". The very concepts of muscles and of the autonomous will are interconnected, such that "[i]nterest in the muscularity of the body was inseparable from a preoccupation with the agency of the self" (Kuriyama, 144).

I've touched on these deep things to suggest that sometimes it may be desirable to switch off that conscious, controlling self – the 'conscious controller' that initiates actions by willing them, which I've referred to metaphorically as the 'crane operator' who directs the mechanical system of levers. It seems to me that what we may be *really* trying to achieve when we try to relax is exactly this, but mostly we don't realize it. The Western idea that the body, in particular in its capacity for movement and action, is a servant of the will is very deep rooted. Given this, the problem we have in discarding the idea is that, without the 'conscious controller,' we seem to be left with a vacuum. If movement and action do not follow our wills, where do they come from? We can't imagine, so any answer to this seems 'mystical'. But perhaps it isn't really. Perhaps that's just the way we experience a kind of failure of our own world view. In what follows, I'll try to go beyond this rather negative sense of the problem and to suggest ways in which we can 'tune' or 'tap' into some other sources of movement and action – but only after we've come more fully to terms with the idea of *neutrality*.

In order to better understand neutrality, we need to get back to our familiar friend, tension, and its close cousin, energy. There's a widely used concept in theatre training, which generates an integrated sequence of exercises, often called 'States of Tension' but sometimes it's called 'Energy States' instead. The States of Tension exist in different versions, having taken on a strong life of their own after originating – very probably – in the work of Jacques Lecoq. They are used mainly in actor training, although they may have value in rehearsal too. For performers, each state of tension or energy is transferable to many different situations, while the same situation can be performed in different states, generating different effects. For reasons that will become clear, I'm going to call this...

THE TENSION-ENERGY CYCLE

And my purpose here is unrelated to performance; it's to provide a kind of 'map' of the body-mind's 'archetypal journey' – a journey through different energy and tension levels – in its complex and shifting dual-relationship both to itself and to the external world. This is important above all for gaining a clear idea of what neutrality is. I have defined the states accordingly. Naturally this journey is best experienced, so you should try to enact each state in sequence. To try it for yourself you'll need a fairly empty space, but it doesn't have to be that large – except perhaps for State Seven.

EXERCISE: STATES OF TENSION-ENERGY

STATE ONE. *You are* EXHAUSTED. *Start with the sense of a great weight pulling you down. It's your weight. You can hardly walk, but you must, for you have a destination to reach - perhaps just as far as that chair over there, but even so it's like completing a marathon. Every step is a struggle. Not surprisingly, you are very conscious of your body. You notice that your body-consciousness is focused in the area of the knees, probably including the lower thighs and maybe the upper calves too. You also have a strong awareness of your feet, of your weight pushing them down into the ground and of the difficulty of lifting them. Thus you have a focus inside your body as well as one outside it - your destination. Which is stronger, the inner or the outer focus? Which seems to occupy your attention the most? It must be the one inside your body, for if it weren't, there'd be no great problem getting to your destination.*

Re-Imagining Your Body

STATE TWO. *You have now arrived, rested a little (imagine this!) and you find that you have gained some energy. You are in an art gallery, looking at paintings. You keep taking a few steps, stopping and looking. Each time you stop, you put all your weight on one leg. Commonly enough, you then transfer it to the other leg. In fact, your hips seem always in motion. As you walk, your hips swing up and down in an exaggerated way. No doubt you think this looks 'cool'. You're in the gallery looking at pictures, which are outside you (and all around you, so you keep turning), but you're not looking at them closely or intently, or at any one picture for long. Your primary or dominant focus – the greater part of your attention – is really inside you (as it was in* EXHAUSTION*), in your hips (higher than the knees, then), as you keep generating the message, 'Hey, look at me! Better than the pictures, huh?' Notice also the tilt of your head, and the way your arms loosely swing a little; you may even notice an interesting relationship between your chin and your hips. This state is sometimes called* THE HIPSTER *and sometimes* THE CALIFORNIAN.

STATE THREE. *You become* DISTRACTED. *It's as though you remember that you have forgotten something, but you don't remember what. Should you be going somewhere? If so, is it over there, to the left, or straight ahead, or over there, to the right? You go a few steps in one direction, you stop, you seem briefly to think about it, then you go a few steps – maybe only one or two, maybe as many as four or five – in a different direction. Often, when you stop, your head turns in a new direction before your body follows it. Or sometimes your torso turns before your hips and legs do. To an outsider, you seem full of doubt, constantly changing your mind. Your movement is fragmented, broken, tentative, but there's seems to be more energy behind it than when you were looking at pictures (or rather, when you were not really looking at pictures). But this energy, in the form of your impulses, keeps being withdrawn. It's all stop-start, or start-stop. To yourself, you seem over-focused inside your head (higher up than your hips, then), a little trapped there – if you could only remember what it is that you should be doing in relation to the outside world, you could get out of your head!*

STATE FOUR. *This state is* NEUTRALITY. *For the moment I will simply note that it is a transitional state between the first three and the next three. We need to complete the cycle first, in order to understand this state.*

STATE FIVE. *For some reason, a strange question pops into your head:* IS THERE A BOMB IN THE ROOM? *Well, there could be, couldn't there? Anything's possible. If there is, you should look for it. Come to think of it, maybe you should look for it anyway – look for a possible bomb, that is – to find out if* *there is one in the room. So you search. Your search is quite urgent, but it's not as urgent as it would be if you knew for sure that there was a bomb in the room. A part of you is aware that you might very well be paranoid and, after all, you don't want to draw too much attention to yourself. You're still in that art gallery, you see. You make a fairly urgent but discreet search, then. Your energy level has clearly gone up a gear and now your primary focus is very much outside you, but there's still a little self-consciousness in you. It's no longer focused in any particular part of your body, however, as it was before; it's more like there's a part of you looking at yourself from the outside, making sure you're not revealing too much of your inner state.*

STATE SIX. *In the course of your search, you come across something that definitely shouldn't be there: Yes, THERE IS A BOMB IN THE ROOM! As it dawns on you that you have absolutely no training in bomb disposal, you understand that it's time to get out of there fast! For some reason you can't take your eyes off the bomb, so you back away. That, of course, limits your speed of movement. In State Five, you were being pulled towards a possible something. Now you're being pushed away from an actual something. You move as fast as you can while moving backwards, taking your energy level up another gear, only to discover, by means of your hands alone (you still can't take your eyes off the bomb), that all the doors are locked! And there are no windows! Your primary focus is still very much on that bomb, but some internal body-consciousness is rapidly increasing in you, in the abdomen and pit of your stomach. It's fear.*

STATE SEVEN. *What else is there to do now except PANIC? You run madly up and down, in all directions. You're neither obviously pushed nor pulled, but both (not just alternately, sometimes simultaneously! (that's called freezing)), nor is your focus now clearly on the bomb as a located object. Physically, you're 'all over the place,' and in a way that's true mentally too. There's no internal focus either – the blind activity of your panic is 'expressing your fear outwards,' not giving it any chance to build up inside you. It's as though you've gone on to some kind of mad automatic pilot in which you're both acutely conscious and oddly unconscious at the same time. (Apart from any freezes, which never last more than a second or two, this is 'pure energy' – but completely undirected.)*

STATE EIGHT. *You hear an ominous click. This is it! Your whole body freezes and goes rigid. Every hair on your head, and anywhere else on you for that matter, stands up straight. Your eyes stare wildly. Maybe your mouth is wide open with the tongue stretched out so that you look exactly like a cartoon cat that's just been electrocuted. You are in RIGOR MORTIS. (This is* *'pure tension' – all inside you.) But you're not dead! That click was actually the bomb failing to explode! Gradually you grasp this delicious fact. An enormous feeling of relief spreads though you, unlocking all your muscles. You smile broadly. It's time to walk away.*

It's no wonder that now you feel absolutely EXHAUSTED!

Within this cycle, the different states of tension or energy form complementary pairs, like this: EXHAUSTED (1) goes with PANIC (7), THE HIPSTER (2) with THERE IS A BOMB! (6), DISTRACTED (3) with IS THERE A BOMB? (5), and NEUTRALITY (4) with RIGOR MORTIS (8). Diagrammatically:

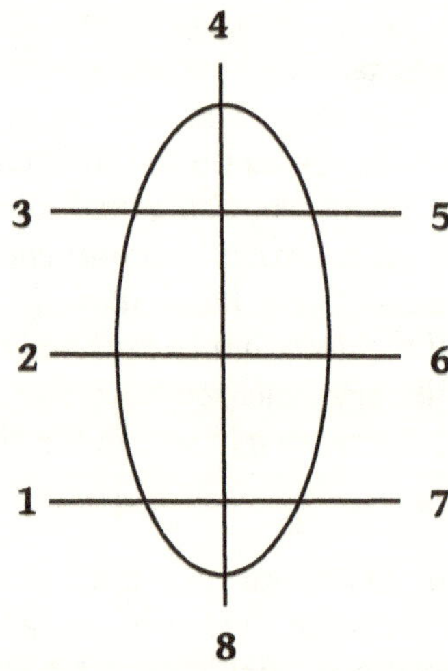

I'm not going to discuss here the significance of the complementarity of States 1 with 7, 2 with 6, or 3 with 5. I'm only concerned with that between 4 and 8.

UNDERSTANDING NEUTRALITY

NEUTRALITY is opposite State 8, RIGOR MORTIS, a state of *total tension*. Neutrality, in fact, is a relaxed state, but it is not total relaxation (which is nowhere in the cycle). Rather, it is a state in which only necessary tensions exist. But necessary for what?

Before we answer that, let's take note of the way the *internal* focus rises through the body from State 1, where it's more or less in the knees, to State 2, where it's in the hips, to state 3, where it's in the head. By this logic, any internal focus in State 4 cannot be localized – there's nowhere left for it to go (at least by going upwards). So it must pervade the whole body. Note, in relation to this, however, that the *secondary* self-consciousness of the outward-directed State 5 is 'like looking at yourself from the outside,' as described above. In NEUTRALITY, you are focused *in* your body, your body as a whole, but in a way that also allows perfect awareness of the outside world.

NEUTRALITY arises at the precise point of this *turning outwards* to the world. In theatre training, neutrality is approached in a very practical way through active exercises. But it could well be described by the Japanese phrase *mizu no kokuro*. This is usually translated as 'a mind like still water,' but it implies a wholly calm and therefore wholly *responsive* inner being.

Note also the rising energy throughout the Cycle – though it is sometimes funnelled into *tension* rather than *work*. (Don't confuse the hard work of State One with energy. In EXHAUSTION, it feels like you have to work so hard because your energy level is so low.) So NEUTRALITY arises at a certain energy level. But none of its energy is wasted.

Notice then that States 1, 2, 3, 5 and 6 all involve some mixture of tension and what I'll call 'working energy' (while States 7 and 8 are pure energy and pure tension respectively). In each of these States there's a task or goal of some kind, but not all the energy that is expressed (for remember, tension can be expressive) contributes to accomplishing that task or goal. But in State 4 it does. This is basically why no task or goal is specified for NEUTRALITY – *because it could be more or less anything at all.*

A good name (in the context of theatre work) for State 4 is THE STAGE MANAGER. The idea is that the Stage Manager just gets on with the job, efficiently and unobtrusively. In a certain sense, s/he is 'invisible'. To take this idea a step further, in the Japanese Noh theatre a Stage Assistant (*kōken*) may come on stage during the performance to put in place or remove a stage property of some kind, or to adjust the principal actor's costume. This must be done in the most neutral ('invisible') way, and only experienced actors are allowed to perform such a role.

There's a kind of paradox here. A person functioning perfectly 'in neutral' is strangely watchable – because it is actually very rare for a person to be able to perform or act in such a way that s/he *expresses nothing at all!* All the other states of tension/energy *express something*, consciously or unconsciously, deliberately or involuntarily. They may express a mood, a character, a situation, even a 'story'. But neutrality is 'expressively empty'. If you can imagine both a) a (good) mechanic efficiently and single-mindedly changing a car engine part and b) a (good) priest performing the sacrament, *and you can see what they have in common*, then you will understand neutrality.

One aspect of neutrality is the *absence of evident character*. If, in the way the mechanic and the priest perform their functions, they reveal some aspect of their characters or personalities, then they are not performing 'in neutral'. In the case of the mechanic, this may well not matter, for it is still possible for the job to be done well. But the same does not hold for the priest, whose 'job' in this case is to be the conduit between the divine and the human, invisible as a person like the rest of us.

Neutrality is not simply an 'internal' state, that of the absence of all unnecessary (including any 'expressive') tensions. It is also, necessarily, *an attitude towards the world*. This is its fundamental difference from relaxation, which can be thought of as being a purely internal state. Neutrality is a kind of *receptive emptiness* and it is always *turned outwards*.

In relation to this it is notable that the great Polish actor-trainer Jerzy Grotowski stopped using yoga among the psycho-physical systems that he explored as potentially useful in his work. Why? Because yoga promotes only introverted concentration, concentration that is 'turned inwards'. It is anti-expressive in the way it generates the kind of 'rest' that ends rather than facilitates action (Grotowski, 208). This is not to imply that you can only be in neutral if you're doing something task-like, in the sense that the mechanic and the priest are performing certain actions. In Jacques Lecoq's most fundamental neutrality exercise, WAKING FOR THE FIRST TIME (Lecoq, 40), you are required simply (!) to discover the world around you, not to do anything to it. This exercise is fundamental because it reveals neutrality to be an attitude towards the world. If you have the right kind of *openness* to the world, or 'receptive emptiness,' then your inner state will automatically be free of any unnecessary tensions.

TAKING IT IN

The following very powerful exercise, as used in theatre training, is usually carried out while wearing a neutral mask. It is also observed by others who learn from watching it. Neither of these things matters here.

EXERCISE: WAKING FOR THE FIRST TIME

Lie on the floor in a foetal position, with closed eyes. Relax completely, emptying your mind as much as possible. Imagine that you are in a profound dreamless sleep.

Stay like this as long as you want.

Then wake. This is the very first time you have woken, so everything is completely new to you. Explore it, discover it... take it all in.

And... that's all! It's a very simple exercise, but it's also one in which certain 'mistakes' are commonly made. I put those scare quotes around 'mistakes' because, in the context of the drama class where attention can be drawn to them, such mistakes are really very useful as learning aides. In the present context, however, it's better that I warn you of them in advance. There's a disadvantage in this, since it trespasses on what you might discover for yourself, but there's too much risk you might not realize that they're mistakes.

The first mistake is concentrating on your own body, as though you need to discover this. For example, I often see students start playing with their fingers and toes. I wonder why this is. Whatever the reason, it's wrong. It's the world around you that you have to discover as if for the first time. Why treat your own body as if it's part of that world around you, which implies that it's somehow distinct from *you*?

The second mistake is trying to manipulate objects too much, as though you want to know how they work. But this is jumping the gun. Surely if you are really experiencing the world around you for the very first time, you will be so struck by its *sensual* richness that you won't get on so quickly to a more 'intellectual' engagement with it.

The third mistake is to over-use the senses of vision and touch, important though these obviously are. It's relatively rare to see students being struck by sounds or smells, let alone tastes! There are two possible reasons for this. Either vision and touch really are our dominant senses or it's easier to demonstrate their function to an audience. If the reason is the latter, the exercise is being approached in completely the wrong way.

Relatedly, all too often I see a student seem to 'run out of ideas' such that, after a moment or two's hesitation, they turn to look at me as though asking to be released. But there is *so much to discover* out there that you should never have to tell yourself what to do next. In other words, there's no need for the 'conscious controller' here.

Still, the worst mistake is the first one. If you fully understand the reason why, it will help you do the exercise properly. So suppose you sit manipulating your toes with your hands to see how much they move. What do you *really* discover? Nothing at all, because you already knew it. *Your body knew it – and your body is you* (but exploring your own body like this splits you in two). Now suppose you're experiencing the texture of a brick wall with your hands and maybe with your cheeks too. Or suppose you are watching dust particles dancing in a ray of sunlight. In these cases *you really do discover something* as if for the first time. There are many things like this that you've never really noticed, or if you did, the memory now lies so long forgotten that it's as if they had never been known.

In this exercise, done properly, there is no need to pretend.

Now recall RECEIVING (p. 76). I introduced this towards the end of Part One with these words: "Gradually let yourself become increasingly aware of the scene before you, not just what you see, but also what you hear, what you feel, what you smell. Notice the details. *Let all this start entering into you.*" RECEIVING is closely related to neutrality, and specifically to WAKING FOR THE FIRST TIME. But there's also a difference. In RECEIVING, you naturally become aware of different things at different times, but all the things you become aware of tend to form or at least suggest a totality. In WAKING FOR THE FIRST TIME, each new sense impression tends to distract you from the previous one and it seems much harder to gain a sense of the totality of the world around you. (This is all the more so if you wear a neutral mask, by the way, because the mask cuts out peripheral vision, such that your gaze is more easily 'captured' by specific things.) In this way, WAKING FOR THE FIRST TIME feels a little more energized than RECEIVING, and this is reflected in the way you actively move around.

In the following exercises, however, you'll be able to focus on one thing and to let that one thing enter into you so completely that it will *take you over.* (These exercises are also based on Lecoq's work on neutrality (Lecoq, 44).)

EXERCISE: BECOMING THE SEA

Firstly, you will become the sea. Start by imagining the sea in front of you. It's blue or turquoise, clear and not too cold – very inviting. In imagination, you go into it. Feel the water level increasing from the ankles, to the calves, to the knees, to the thighs.... Then, when you are deep enough in, but with your feet still on the soft sea bed, you start playing. You swirl and swish the water with your arms and hands... you move your legs, your hips, your upper body in whatever way you like, simply enjoying the feeling of resistance of the water, but also the way it 'lets you through'. Feel the resistance of the water all the time, in all your movements and with all the immersed parts of your body.

Notice now some waves. They're not very big, just strong enough to push and pull you gently, and to lift you up and drop you down lightly. Your own movements, playing in the sea, now become combined with the way the sea is moving you. Can you still tell the difference? If you can, just keep playing in the sea. There will come a point at which you no longer have a will to initiate your own movements and all your movements will be the movement of the sea itself. You will have become the sea. You cannot choose this moment (you left the 'conscious controller' on the beach), you can only become aware that it has happened. Don't stop now! Instead, let the waves moving through you get gradually bigger and stronger. Let go of yourself completely, just go with the sea, with yourself as the sea.

And don't stop suddenly. Reverse the process. First, let the waves get smaller and smaller, then, at a certain point, find yourself again, playing in the sea. Then just walk out of it, feeling the water level going down your body as you do so.

(If you like, see your 'conscious controller' relaxing on a beach towel. This should make you smile, since it's not what conscious controllers usually do!)

EXERCISE: BECOMING THE WIND

Next, you will become the wind. Imagine that it's a windy day, very windy. It helps in this exercise to imagine a gusty wind which keeps changing direction, maybe even setting up little whirlwinds. Initially you have to fight against the wind in order to go wherever you want to go, or just to prevent yourself being blown over. At a certain point, however, but not too soon, you just 'give up'. At this point you become the wind. Rather than blowing you, it is blowing through you.

This exercise is a little more difficult than becoming the sea. The reason is that it's all too easy consciously or deliberately to choose that moment of giving up. But you can't truly 'become the wind' by an act of will. As with becoming the sea, you really want to be 'surprised' by the moment at which the energy of the element you are in becomes your own energy. To help achieve this, while you are being blown around but still resisting as much as possible, try to empty your mind. Above all, don't make any decisions on behalf of the wind as to what it will do next. You have to feel the wind as something other than yourself before it can take you over.

Once again, when you've become and been the wind for a while, don't just stop. Instead, let the wind drop gradually. This will force you, at a certain point, to 'find yourself again' (like finding something in the street, by accident).

For our purposes, these two exercises are enough. However, it's also possible, but a little harder, to BECOME FIRE.

You imagine you're stepping – but hardly able to put a foot down – through a burning field. The flames you imagine should not be high, they're threatening only to your feet – which means you're forced to do something like an 'anti-gravity dance'. At a certain point, as you've probably guessed, you become the flames.

Can you imagine how you might *become earth*? After all, you've seen how to become the other three elements, water, air and fire. What kind of *energy* would you be acquiring if you could 'become earth'? (Don't jump to the conclusion that earth moves too slowly for you to become it. The exercise called EMBRACE – BECOME – DANCE in Part Three (p. 162) will provide you with a way to become earth – or anything else you want.)

In these BECOMING exercises you become the sea or you become the wind by *taking in the energy* of the sea or the wind. It's crucial, of course, that the energy of the wind is different from the energy of the sea, for each has a specific quality or 'shape'. Now let's look more closely at this idea.

THE *FLOW* OF ENERGY

Tension isn't the only thing that can stop energy flowing. It may be that we just don't seem to have enough energy. Nonetheless, often, when we feel energy-less, it's not that we really don't have any energy or even that we don't have much energy – it's that we're not in touch or in tune with our energy. We're somehow alienated from it, cut off from it. We don't know how to tap into it. Why does this occur? And how can we avoid or overcome it?

Obviously I'm not talking here about the kind of low-energy that can be caused by an underlying medical problem. If you suffer from chronic or frequent low-energy levels, you should consult a doctor. I'm talking about the kind of feeling of low energy that's a normal part of being healthy, a bit like 'getting out of bed on the wrong side'.

Relatedly, sometimes a specific physical task seems to take a lot of effort and sometimes it doesn't. In physics, energy is defined as the capacity for doing work. Well, sometimes a task just feels like hard work and other times it feels easy. But presumably we're not really using up more of our energy to accomplish the task in the former case, however much it may feel that way. We seem to be struggling to find the necessary energy.

When we feel energetic, it is also a feeling of ease, of lightness, of relative effortlessness. Our energy seems to *flow* freely. This little and lovely word – *flow* – encapsulates a great deal that, over millennia, human beings have deemed to be positive. *Flow* is good. Anything that blocks flow is bad. To a great extent, ancient medical systems rest on these two complementary observations.

In Chinese medicine, *qi*, or *chi*, is the vital energy, or simply the *vitality*, that flows through the meridians. If it is blocked, or unbalanced, sickness occurs. In yoga, *prana* is the life-force that promotes health if it is abundant and leads to sickness if it is depleted. To the Ancient Greeks, *pneuma* once denoted a similar idea.

All three concepts, *qi, prana* and *pneuma*, are closely associated with breath, the *breath of life*. The famous words of Zhuangzi, "*Qi* brought together is life; *qi* dispersed is death," make perfect sense if *qi* is simply translated as breath. But a yogi will stress that our normal, unconscious breathing does not increase *prana*. *Prana* enters into us only with the conscious breath; hence it cannot be the same thing as breath itself. Even so, its original meaning – *constant motion* – perfectly mirrors the role of breath in life. As for the Greek *pneuma*, the concept became Christianized as *spirit*, but before that it meant breath. Its association with breathing is reflected in the derivative English words *pneumonia*, a disease of the lung, and *pneumatic*, which means inflated with or worked by air – whereas the corresponding Modern Greek word, *pneumatiko*, is best translated as 'spiritual' (though often its sense is closer to 'intellectual'). The word 'spirit,' too, comes from the Latin for breath and breathing, an etymology that can still be felt, to greater or lesser degree, in our words *expire*, *inspire, aspire, conspire*, though not now in *perspire* – although in certain breathing exercises later you'll be asked to breathe out through the pores of your skin!

In *The Expressiveness of the Body and the Divergence of Greek and Chinese Medicine* (the fascinating book that I mentioned earlier), Kuriyama shows how, in the 5th century BCE, a momentous change took place in the evolution of Greek thought, one that laid the groundwork for modern medicine to evolve. This was when the concept of *pneuma* was *internalized*. This, Kuriyama says, "redefined the nature of the body" (Kuriyama, 262). Prior to it, *pneuma* meant *wind*, an external force or influence. The human body – and with it the human being – was conceived as a site which was traversed by such external forces and influences; thoughts, emotions, states of mind, states of health, and fits of madness were not conceived as arising *within* the human being but as entering from *without*. But with the internalization of *pneuma*, "instead of tracking the airs that shaped human life from without, doctors became increasingly captivated by the notion of breaths shaping and animating human beings from within" (Kuriyama, 260).

Prana, however, continues to be conceived as a vital energy that pervades the universe – one draws it in from outside. *Qi* too is usually thought of in a similar way as a life-force that is all around us and which we can draw on.

This momentous shift in Greek thought laid the groundwork for what became, many centuries later, the concept of the autonomous individual.

I'm going to suggest that one powerful way to help attain the *flow* of energy inside you is to think of energy as *flowing in from outside*. You will need to *imagine* this, of course – but this doesn't mean that the idea is fanciful. While it doesn't correspond to the Western scientific view of how energy is generated within the body (although this too relies on prior intake from outside of both food and oxygen), you should take this alternative view very seriously. I'm not saying believe it. I'm saying imagine it as if you believe it!

Apart from that, the Western concept of the autonomous self-contained individual is in some ways a trap, for it's the concept – or better, the set of concepts – that puts the 'conscious controller' in its commanding position.

Of course, in the Western world-view the human body, and with it the human being, has not become thought of as perfectly sealed off from external influence and affect. Far from it. We are well aware of many malign external 'powers,' such as infectious or contagious diseases and the many forms of pollution of the environment that can affect our health. Stress, as the source of internal tension, is also something that we think of as originating externally – something we find ourselves 'under'. We should see, then, that an extraordinary imbalance has arisen in our attitudes. What we nowadays see as the external influences that might affect us are almost entirely bad for us. For the health conscious among us, it may even seem that the only possible positive input from outside is through nutrition; but this, of course, requires avoiding all the possible negative input from the same source.

So what is left that is *out there* that is good for us?

Fresh air!

This imbalance has a baneful effect. It puts nearly all the onus on *us* to be responsible for what is positive in life. All we need to do is tap into our *inner resources*. Step in the self-help industry!

This is why it may be beneficial *to think of energy as something we draw in from outside*. When we feel energy-less, we generally fail to find an energy source within ourselves... (it may be difficult to admit, but we fail). So let's try to find one outside ourselves instead... (in other words, let's just ask for help).

As a matter of fact, actors and dancers are usually quite familiar with this idea, even if they haven't formulated it in full. For performers, energy often seems to flow up into them from through the floor, and a performer's feet need to be sensitive instruments for tapping into the energy of the ground, ultimately the energy of the earth itself. If they feel flat and energy-less, they can use this to quickly become fully energized.

EXERCISE: GRAPE PRESSERS' STOMP

This is an exercise that helps you contact and draw up into yourself the energy of the earth.

Firstly, pre-energize your body in the following way. Stand in a 'centred' position with your feet a little wider apart than your shoulder joints. Breathe slowly and deeply into your lower abdomen (some people find this difficult; if you're one of them, see pp. 127-129 for two exercises to help you learn to do it) through your nostrils, making sure that you don't raise your shoulders. As you do so imagine that you are drawing the breath in through the soles of your feet. Breathe out equally slowly and as smoothly as you can through the mouth, which should be not quite closed, feeling the gentle pressure of the out-breath playing on your lips. Imagine you're making a candle flame flicker strongly but without blowing it out. It's vital that you don't let your chest collapse forcing the breath out quickly, for this will lose all the energy you've drawn in. The out-breath should be as relaxed as possible, with no feeling of tightness in the chest. Think of the in-breath as drawing energy in through the feet, while the out-breath merely expels the 'dead air,' leaving all the energy still inside you. Four or five deep breaths of this kind should be enough, but it's up to you if you want more.

GRAPE PRESSERS' STOMP follows a simple left–right, left–right step sequence to a 1,2,3 / 1,2,3 / 1,2,3 rhythm. The stomp itself is always on the count of 1, hence it alternates between the left and the right foot. To make the stomp, the knee is lifted high and the whole sole of the foot is made to strike the ground producing a strong sound. The steps on the counts of 2 and 3 are much lighter, more delicate, and only the ball of the foot touches the ground. Be conscious of the impulse for all the steps, not just the much stronger stomp, coming from the pelvis. Lastly and crucially, keep the upper body completely lose and relaxed. Now just 'get into it'!

At first, you will have to work. However, the goal is to reach a point at which this sense of having to work disappears; you should start to feel as if the earth is pushing its energy up into you, rather than you pushing your energy down into the earth. This involves the kickback principle which we've met before (p. 43). What happens is a sudden reversal of perspective; your focus shifts 'automatically' to your relaxed upper body, whereas initially – and probably for some time – it had been in your working lower body. When this happens, it feels as though your upper body is receiving energy from below. The literal truth, of course, is that this is still your energy, the energy you're expending with your lower body being reflected (or kicked) back upwards, but it doesn't feel that way, because you no longer seem to be working. So it feels as though the earth is feeding energy into you, and – paradoxically (for all the time you are moving energetically) – you can simply store this energy up inside you!

You can't consciously 'turn on' this reversal of perspective. You have to wait for it, but you also have to be ready for it and open to it. The key here is to remain completely relaxed in your upper body. What happens, in fact, is a kind of trance or semi-trance. That's nothing to be worried about. On the contrary, it's entirely desirable. (HINT: Don't keep counting "one, two, three, one two, three..." in your head. Let your body take over and do the counting unconsciously, which it will do easily. Keep your mind as empty as you can. This will help you get into a trance-like state.)

Part Two: Demoting the 'Conscious Controller'

Western culture tends to be anxious about trance or troubled by what it sees as such 'abnormal' mental states. Why is this? Basically, it's because trance appears as a disturbing loss of self-control. What we're really worried about is *what exactly it is* that takes over when the 'conscious controller' relinquishes control. Other non-western cultures are not at all so worried about this probably because they don't invest so much of selfhood in the conscious, controlling ego.

If the basic idea that I'm proposing here – that we should think of energy as something we can draw in from outside us – still seems odd to you, here's an easy way to make it seem more sensible and more familiar.

EXPERIMENT 12: *Lie down somewhere or sit in a fully relaxed way, close your eyes – and simply listen to some music. Nothing too relaxing or soothing, but it doesn't have to be the kind of music that makes you want to dance or that sets your foot tapping. In fact, a lot of classical music is very good for this experiment.*

As you listen, think of the music as being energy. *That's not hard. Music is energy – energy with a very precise shape and structure. This energy enters into you, it flows through you, and it energizes you. And it comes from outside.*

You can intensify this feeling by imagining that the music is playing inside you. *In fact, this is a great way to experience music. Since all music is experienced in the body, it's also simple to imagine it arising inside you. As you do this, notice which parts of your body seem 'occupied' by different pitches, tones and timbres, as well as by different rhythms. A relatively complex piece of classical music will seem to 'move around' inside you in an extraordinary and invigorating way – like a spiritual massage!*

In doing this, note, you let yourself be *possessed*. No problem. There's no more reason to be anxious about possession states than there is about trance. After all, you're possessed, aren't you, whenever you get a fit of the giggles, or whenever someone's laughter makes you smile or laugh along too, or even when you yawn because you half-notice someone over there yawning. Obviously there's no need here to call in the exorcist. In all such cases it's simply as though the 'conscious controller' is the driver who's just got out of the car to relieve himself behind a bush!

Re-Imagining Your Body

EXERCISE: TUNING IN

Now think about *atmosphere*, or *atmospheres*. I introduced this idea earlier, in relation to tension. There we saw that simply imagining a tense atmosphere can produce some of the effects of tension in our bodies. Real atmospheres are external, outside us, and they can have a very powerful ('possessing') effect upon us. As Michael Chekhov points out, an atmosphere doesn't necessarily take us over completely; an atheist, he points out, remains sceptical in an atmosphere of religious awe (Chekhov, 51). But the external atmosphere still makes itself felt and enters into us to some degree. In an extreme case, such as a man feeling deep grief while at a festive party, the subjective feeling may be strong enough to block out the 'objective feeling' of the atmosphere. But this is like an exception that proves the rule. For the most part, atmospheres solicit and even urge you to 'join in' with them.

Think of an atmosphere as being a kind of *energy-field* in the air.

Chekhov recommends that the actor should observe and try to be as sensitive as possible to a wide variety of atmospheres – real-life atmospheres, initially, ones which are actually experienced. Without this, the process of *imagining* different atmospheres may be abstract or over-generalized. But if you can imagine an atmosphere with sufficient clarity and specificity, then the imaginary atmosphere can have just as much effect upon you as the real thing. And the more this is achieved, Chekhov says, the more capable you will become of imagining an atmosphere without the concrete details of a specific situation: all you have to do is imagine that the air around you is full of that atmosphere, much as it might be full of light or smoke or noise or a smell (Chekhov, 56). In other words, the atmosphere is real in itself, like a material 'thing'.

Try imagining (really imagining – not just 'thinking of') the following situations with their accompanying atmospheres: a very informal ('wild') party; a very formal one (say at an ambassador's residence); a cup final football match; a funeral procession in the rain; a street accident; a school examination; a hospital casualty department on a Saturday night; a simple wedding in a registry office; a wedding in Westminster Abbey; a political demonstration.... In each case the atmosphere is a kind of energy-field in the air which you plug into, or better, tune into. After this, if you like, you can try more directly imagining the atmospheres denoted by nouns such as awe, gaiety, solemnity, expectation, concern, efficiency, righteousness, and so on. (You'll find that it's not so easy.)

If you think about it, atmospheres are not dissimilar to music, though they lack the linear, developmental structure that music has. They exist 'in the air' and they enter into you, 'taking you over'.

This brings me to the key point. In one sense a piece of music like Wagner's *Ride of the Valkyries* is more 'energetic' than, say, Bach's *Air on a G String*. In a similar way, the atmosphere of a party in which people are dancing freely, even wildly, is more 'energetic' than the atmosphere, say, of a company board meeting at which a crucial decision has to be made. However, at least up to a point, it's a good idea not to think of the amount of energy being expressed or used up, but rather of the precise form or 'shape' that that energy takes. Looked at this way, the energy of the *Air* is restrained, sauntering and languidly stretching, while the energy of the *Ride* is pulsating and urgent. Similarly, the energy of the board meeting may be sharply focused, intense and ruthlessly calculating, but with a surface polish, while the energy of the party is frenetic, hyper-active and even, in a strange way, a little 'desperate'.

But can energy be described using words like 'sauntering,' 'calculating' or 'desperate'? Well, what I'm trying to do here is shift the emphasis from the *quantity* to the *quality* of energy. So the question is, is it legitimate to think of energy as taking on distinct and varied qualities? If it is, the problem we face may be how to describe these different qualities. In other words, the problem may be with language and not with the concept in itself.

I would argue, in fact, that energy must take a certain distinctive 'shape'. There's no such thing as 'pure energy' – except perhaps at the moment of the Big Bang – because energy can only be expressed *through something*. The quality of energy is really the quality of the 'shape' it takes in the 'medium' through which it is expressed.

By sensitizing yourself to the quality of energy – to the endlessly variable 'shapes' it can take – you become able to see that energy is all around you. In a powerful sense, it's what everything is 'made of'. You as well.

EXERCISE: SHAMANIC SEEING

Start by looking at plants – flowers, grasses, shrubs, bushes, trees – above all, trees – of all kinds. Each one is an energy-shape. See each plant as a physical expression of energy. To do this, you have to see the extraordinary, endlessly varied shapes of trunks, stems, branches and leaves as a kind of record in space of the process of the plant's growth through time.

If that way of putting it seems a little too abstract, try this instead: see the tree or the plant as a dancer – a dancer caught in a moment of time, as if in a still photograph.

When I first started practising this, the effect was very strong indeed. It still is! Instead of seeing a tree as an object which you also know, intellectually, to be alive, you see it as being full of life. Put a little differently, you see the *tree spirit* in the tree (and as a corollary of this, you become hyper-aware of the astonishing variety of tree-being). I think this is the *Ur-human* (what used to be called 'primitive') way of seeing things like trees. Each tree and bush and plant acquires a vivid presence, as strong as that of another person, but also of a very different kind. Moreover, it's easy to extend this way of seeing to the inanimate forms of rocks and hills and lakes and clouds as well. In doing this, you will come to understand fully the Shamanic world-view in which everything in nature is alive and has a spirit.

It might help to introduce a synonym for 'spirit' here. All you have to do is see the *flow* in things: flow – which is simultaneously energized and easy and shapely. As you do this, you translate *the static into the dynamic* and *space into time*.

Maybe surprisingly, maybe not, you can move on to see artificial, that is, man-made objects in the same way: motor cars, items of furniture, street lamps, gates.... You can see such shapes as dynamic too, as 'flowing' in certain directions, at certain speeds, with certain qualities. This, of course, is not the record of a growth process, but it is analogous – the energy in the object is that which is inherent in the design process. While with a tree you somehow see its growth as happening 'all at once,' with an artificial object you need to see the dynamics of drawing or moulding the shapes as continuing within that shape.

And why shouldn't a motor car also have a 'spirit'?

We'll leave animals out here. Partly, the energy-shapes of animals are too obvious and clear, but above all, animals are too important and we'll need to come back to them later, in Part Three. Go on instead to look at human bodies as 'energy-shapes'. You'll see how varied these particular energy-shapes can be. You might even be surprised – an obese body might suddenly seem very powerful to you, or it might seem surprisingly delicate. You'll certainly leave behind the narrow, culturally-conditioned idea of what is 'attractive' and what is not.

Energy is all around you, then. But can you take it in? Can you draw on it? If so, how? It's important to realize that in seeing, say, a pine tree as an energy shape, your body doesn't immediately or spontaneously absorb any of that energy in the way that it does with music or with an atmosphere. There's an important reason for this: you can only be intensely aware of the pine-tree-spirit as *other than you*. The senses of *presence* and of *otherness* are two sides of a coin here, so much so that in the experience *you lose all consciousness of yourself*. You become *empty*. Your focus on something outside and beyond you is so intense that you automatically become neutral in the strong sense of 'receptively empty'. The moment you become self-aware (or for that matter, the moment any extraneous thought enters your head), you lose the intensity of the experience.

Nonetheless *something deep in you responds*. This is a very delicate matter, hard to express in words.

Imagine you are watching a dancer. The dancer may well be making moves that your own body is incapable of, either in its current or in any foreseeable condition! Yet somehow deep in your body you feel that you know *what those moves feel like to make*. That is to say, somehow the dance of the dancer is *mirrored in your own body*. I stress that this happens 'deep' inside your body, for it's not as though you feel the stretching or the bending as such; it's more like you *sense the possibility* of such movement. Put differently, your aesthetic response to the dance, both the pleasure you receive from it and your sense of its meaning, is not confined to visual appreciation. What you *see* feeds into something else that, deep down, is truly *felt*.

Possibly so-called 'mirror neurons' are involved in this. A mirror neuron is a neuron that fires both when you perform an action yourself and when you see someone else perform it. For the time being, however, and not surprisingly, neuroscience has no clear grasp of the functional role of mirror neurons.

As I write this, I'm sitting at my desk under a pergola on the Aegean island of Patmos. In the garden in front of me I can see a healthy three metre-high yucca and a healthy two and a half metre-high olive tree. I choose these plants from among others in the scene because of the strong contrast between them, a contrast enhanced by the slight breeze this morning that sends ripples and small waves through the sensitive silver-grey-green foliage of the olive, but which leaves the rigid, bright green yucca unaffected.

Re-Imagining Your Body

First I see the yucca as a dancer, by translating the static into the dynamic, space into time. Then I see the olive tree as a dancer, in the same way. In each case, something deep inside me seems to respond. It's as though the 'movement in stillness' I see in the tree sets up the resonance of some possible *inner movement* in me. It's as though something deep inside me *feels* what it is to be a yucca or what it is to be an olive tree, and it's very different in each case. If this were not true, I would not recognize the *spirit* in the tree – for spirit is nothing more, nor less, than what – at a very deep level – I have in common with the tree, although the tree spirit is simultaneously intensely other to me, as I stressed before. (Does this apply to the 'spirit' of the motor car too? I leave that entirely up to you!)

Baloney? Of course – from one point of view.

Still, in Part Three you will be asked to *be a tree* (it's a classic drama school exercise, in fact). You won't get very far with that if you don't have some idea of what I'm talking about here.

And in any case, throughout this book I'm asking you to use your imagination. That's very difficult if you limit yourself to that 'one point of view' in which such ideas are so obviously wrong!

We need to go one step further here. *Inner movement*, as described in Part One (pp. 77-80), is energy. It could be described as a kind of pre-activation of the possibility of movement. But by now you should be realizing that inner movement is not only the kind of thing you feel in INNER RUNNING (OR WALKING). When I suggested listening to music as though it is playing inside you, this was also to generate inner movement. A lively atmosphere generates inner movement. When you are simply keen to get on with doing something there is a kind of inner movement. An emotion is a kind of inner movement – as the term suggests. Something inside pushes or pulls you in specific directions. Grief drags you down. Joy makes you soar upwards. Rage pushes you vigorously forwards towards its object. Envy pulls you slowly sideways towards its object. Love makes you seem to expand and open out, as though to envelop the loved one. Humiliation makes you shrink and shrivel. And so on.

These are not metaphors!

Inner movement, in short, is common, a normal and natural part of being the organism that you are. You need to sensitize yourself to its presence *as a form of movement*, for that is to be always on the point of actualizing it as outer movement.

When you feel energy-less, you experience an absence of inner movement, but not in the form of inner calm, more in the form of inner listlessness. You become inert.

BREATH AS ENERGY

Having learnt to think of and hopefully experience energy differently, as flowing in qualitatively distinctive ways, we can now return to the relatively 'simple' matter of its quantity, or intensity – and to the simplest way of *drawing energy in from outside*, which is by *breathing*. But first I need to make what I think is a particularly important point. Initially it's a point about performance, but it leads on to a more general, and crucial, point about the breath.

I have a favourite 'demonstration-exercise' in teaching theatre, which I always use near the beginning of a course. I'll describe it here because it is revealing. I ask for two volunteers. I tell them to stand about four metres (or yards) apart and to have a normal conversation with each other. They can talk about anything they want, and they should 'forget' that they're being watched. The rest of the group just watches, sitting on the floor, around three metres away. I let this run for a short while, then I tell the pair to do the same thing again. But this time, I ask those watching to imagine that the voices of the speakers are physical objects that come out of their mouths, something like smallish balls, and that these balls are subject to gravity; therefore they follow a kind of arc from the mouth to the floor. Then, after the second 'perfectly normal' conversation has run for a short time, I ask anyone watching to get up and show us the places at which each voice-object 'hit the floor'.

Perhaps it's remarkable (I'm not sure), but everyone always seems to know exactly what I mean by this. Comments as to where the voice-object 'fell' are always readily forthcoming. There may be some small disagreement about where a 'ball' hits the floor, but usually a consensus is very quickly established, although it's also notable that people tend to be sure of their judgement in this matter – they seem to know where the ball hit the floor, as though they really did see it!

Crucially, in this first phase of the exercise, *no voice ball ever reaches the other person* in the conversation. It is always 'seen' to hit the ground somewhere in between the speakers, maybe a metre, maybe even less, maybe as much as two metres, in front of the one who is speaking. Very occasionally, it almost reaches. I then simply note how odd this is, since it's clear that those having a conversation can hear each other, just as the audience can hear what they're saying.

For the second phase of the exercise, I ask the speakers to imagine that the person they are talking to is standing about a metre and a half further away than s/he really is, and to talk to that person in their imaginary (more distant), rather than their real, position. This time, when those watching are asked where a voice-object hit the floor, it usually appears to them that it reaches the other person. (It doesn't have to reach the other person at ear-level, by the way, only to fully cross the physical space between the speakers.)

So what's going on here? Well, theatre isn't a simple 'imitation of action' (as Aristotle called it long ago). The *act of watching* is an intrinsic part of theatre too and it's a powerful, transformative act. We see something which is 'staged' differently than we would see the very same thing in real life. As I said above, I'm struck by how readily, even 'naturally,' people understand this exercise. This seems to be because they intuitively understand the difference between theatre and life that arises as a result of the act of watching. When, in the first phase of the exercise, they see the 'ball' as having landed short, often well short, of its target, they are really pointing to a *lack of energy* in the scene. There is enough energy in the scene for the real-life purpose of having a conversation, since the speakers hear each other's words, but there is insufficient energy *from the point of view of the spectator*. Because of this, the scene seems flat and uncompelling. (The explanation of this is that the speakers do not 'fill' the space in which they are performing, a space which implicitly includes the audience, although they are fully audible within it; they fill only the interpersonal space between them, which in theatre is not enough.) But once the energy level is increased, by the simple expedient of each speaker speaking 'past' the other person as if to a person at a greater distance, the energy level becomes enough to involve, to 'pull in,' the audience – with an involvement, note, that has nothing whatsoever to do with the interest of what is being said.

This is why I said earlier that the energy level of the stage needs to be greater than the energy level of real (or at least of ordinary) life (p. 90).

So what exactly is it that happens when a person speaks 'past' someone else, as described? Well, fairly obviously, they speak louder than they did before. But what exactly does this involve?

EXPERIMENT 13: *To test it, try saying "One, two, three, four" over and over, starting softly but getting noticeably louder each time (while keeping pitch and tempo fairly constant), and, as you do so, observe as closely as you can what changes occur in your body.*

As you speak louder, the most obvious things you will notice are that you open your mouth more, that you seem to engage muscles a little further down your torso, and that you use more breath. But you probably won't feel the increasing pressure of air on the vocal cords that is the direct cause of increasing loudness.

It's the role of 'more breath' that really matters here. Very broadly speaking, we can distinguish between increasing 'muscular input' and increasing breath as twin means to speak more loudly. The former serves to express the breath more forcefully and from deeper in the lungs while the latter increases the amount of breath that is used, as it were, 'per word'. But we mustn't suppose that the latter is simply conditional upon the former, that is, that more breath is needed only because the extra muscular effort uses the available breath up more quickly. This is because there's a difference between *projection* and *shouting*. If you simply increase the muscle power involved in vocal production, you quickly end up shouting. In order to project, you must increase the amount of breath you use while simultaneously minimizing the extra muscular effort involved (and without letting the voice become 'breathy,' which is a kind of wasting of the breath).

All of which leads me to the point I want to make: *breath is energy*. You can experience this truth by projecting rather than shouting, and understanding the principle is the key to effective projection. Increased muscular effort is obviously an expenditure of energy, but increased breath can increase loudness without so much extra muscular effort.

That's all very well, you may say, and it may well be something that every actor should understand... but what's it got to do with me?

Potentially a lot.

The point is this: if stage life needs more energy than real (ordinary) life, by the same token it needs *more breath*. But you too can benefit from *more breath*, even if you don't go on to use it in the way an actor would. Everyone can benefit from learning to breathe deeply into the abdominal, rather than merely the upper thoracic region of the body. Everyone can benefit from the *extra energy* this immediately makes available.

An objection might be made at this point. Since your lungs don't descend into your abdomen, how do you breathe into that region? Well, fairly obviously, what's involved here is breathing as deeply and fully into your lungs as possible by engaging muscles in the abdominal region. The problem is, you can't do it if you think of it this way! At least, you can't do it easily. It's much more effective if you *imagine* actually breathing into the abdomen. And if you do it properly you will see, and of course feel, your abdomen expand – so you'll have to let go of any habit you may have of holding your abdomen in.

You can engage that 'spiritual muscle' called your imagination in other relevant ways here too. That's the great thing about the imagination – once you release it, it goes where *it* pleases. There's no 'conscious controller' of your imagination because your imagination needs to wander, just like the archetypal character of *The Fool* in the Tarot pack. In a sense, it needs to be 'silly'.

So lie on the floor (with raised knees if you like) and breathe deeply into your abdomen by imagining that you are breathing in through your anus. That's very 'silly,' isn't it? But it works! It really helps you breathe more deeply into your abdomen.

MORE SILLY BREATHING

In the famous early Seventies TV comedy show, *Monty Python's Flying Circus*, a celebrated sketch involved the 'Ministry for Silly Walks'. I think a Ministry for Silly Breathing would be a very good idea! And while we're on the subject, what about a Ministry for 'Silly Meditation'? After all, there's a 'Zen Comedy Club' – you must have heard the one about the sound of one hand clapping. But I digress....

Do I?

Enlightenment is a joke. Seriously.

(It doesn't work if you see it coming.)

EXERCISE: BREATHING IN THROUGH...

So contemplate your navel – for breathing through, I mean. And then the soles of your feet. All three – anus, navel and soles – are good for breathing through into the abdomen. Experiment with them to find how they work in different, but familiar positions, standing, sitting and lying down. In all cases breathe in slowly and... (in mere reality, of course, through the nose).

Breathing in through the anus, the navel or the soles of your feet (while really breathing in through the nose) is a bit like placing those 'imaginary centres' we began this journey with. They're not experienced as 'centres' in the present case, but you need to focus your body-consciousness in a similar way.

EXERCISE: BREATHING IN TO...

Now, in an equally imaginative way, you can breathe into (as distinct from in through) different parts of your body. You're already doing this, in fact, by breathing into your abdomen. So go a step further and breathe into your pelvic floor, or, what's nearly but not quite the same thing, into your groins. Both of these are best done by lying on your back with your feet raised on a chair so that your legs form a right-angle at the knees (but with nothing placed under your head). Take your time with this.

Where else can you 'breathe into'? More or less anywhere, in fact, though you won't necessarily see or feel the part move in the marked or obvious way that you should with your abdomen. You can breathe into a thigh (one at a time), into the lower back, into a shoulder, into your skull, even into your little finger. Experiment with this, adopting different physical positions, including 'odd' ones, to help you breathe into the target area. You can also breathe into different parts of your body while you are stretching (while you're holding the stretch, that is) or when in certain yoga poses. In such cases, you may find you can only breathe into certain parts of your body – but that's fine, it's an insight into the nature of the stretch or the asana, and a kind of deeper involvement in it.

You should find that there are two different types of body parts that you can breathe into – those you can actually stretch by breathing into them, provided that you adopt the right position first, and those that you can't. You can stretch your lower back, for example, by breathing into it, but not your thigh or little finger. To experience such a stretch, stand with your feet fairly close together, then bend fully forward from the waist; either a) place your right hand on your left shoulder and your left hand on your right shoulder, as though holding yourself fairly tightly, or b) grip your hands behind you back and raise your arms as high as you can behind your back, keeping them straight. Now breathe deeply and slowly into the lumbar region. You will feel your whole lower back pleasantly stretching.

Experiment with finding physical positions which allow you to stretch the maximum number of areas of your body by breathing into those areas. You may need to be inventive with the positions you adopt. In the end, you should find you can stretch any part of the torso like this in a focused way, that is, in a way that isolates that part.

You can relieve pain and discomfort in this way, at least up to a point. The really 'silly' thing is, though, that you can do this even in those areas which you *can't* stretch by breathing into them!

WASTE DISPOSAL

I've talked about breathing in, but not yet about breathing out – which is a little odd, since you can't have one without the other.

Here are a couple of 'rules' (well, suggestions) for breathing out, when you're practising deep breathing. Firstly, breathe out more slowly than you breathe in – though you're also breathing in slowly, of course. Breathe out up to twice as slowly as you breathe in – but there's no need to be exact. However, you must stay fully relaxed through the out-breath, with no tensing of muscles to hold the breath back unnaturally. Secondly, breathe out either through the nose or through the mouth, but in the latter case with the mouth almost closed so that you feel the pressure from your breath on your lips, releasing enough air to continuously agitate but not to extinguish an imaginary candle flame. Breathing out through the lips like this is a good way, in fact, to make the out-breath last longer than the in-breath without tensing any of your normal respiratory muscles.

As we saw earlier with the preliminary stage of GRAPE PRESSERS' STOMP (pp. 113-114), you can think of your breathing as drawing energy in through the in-breath, while the out-breath expels 'dead air' – or waste gases – leaving all the energy inside you. This can be applied to all 'deep breathing' where you are taking in more oxygen than your level of physical activity at that moment requires. It's good to imagine breathing in through the soles of your feet in this case, since the earth is a source of energy. But you can also breathe energy in through your navel area, as though a limitless source of energy exists in the air around you. Breathing it in through the abdomen takes it directly where it can be stored.

Whether you imagine it entering into you through the soles of your feet or through your navel, imagine that the energy is flowing into you as a *clear stream*, like pure water.

Imagine that the 'dead air' comes out of you as *white steam*. As you breathe out through the nose, imagine the waste gases coming out as white steam through all the pores of your skin.

EXERCISE: ENERGY PUMP 1 & 2

Many people find it difficult to breathe deeply into the abdominal area, at least initially. This is sad, because breathing into the abdomen makes you feel fully alive by placing you much more fully inside your body. Here are two exercises which work well to encourage and facilitate abdominal breathing. Take your time trying to master them because the 'little details' matter.

For each, stand with your feet at shoulder width or even a little further apart. The feet can point slightly outwards, but not too much. You should feel very stable and grounded, with chest and shoulders open. Throughout, you will breathe both in and out through the nostrils, but before starting you need to discover how to 'focus' your breath. First, try focusing your breath at the nostril apertures (as when sniffing); next focus it high up but still inside the nose; then in the area of the palate (but not the soft-palette which, if your breathing is strong, can generate a kind of 'nasal snore'); and lastly in the oro-pharynx (this is where the respiratory tract 'turns downwards,' at the very back of the oral cavity – it is just above the pharynx which is in turn just above the larynx). You'll discover that your breath feels and sounds different in each case. For Energy Pump the focus you want is the last, in the oro-pharynx. You should hear a distinctive 'breathy' sound from this area.

Let your arms hang loosely from your sides, then turn your hands inwards, palms upwards, without raising your arms. The tips of your index fingers should be a centimetre or two (roughly half an inch) apart in front of your genital region. Now quite slowly but firmly raise your hands, keeping the palms turned upwards and level, with fingertips close together, and as you do so breathe deeply and smoothly into the abdomen. It's as though the upward movement of the palms actively encourages the in-breath to go deep, as though there's a kind of reciprocal relationship between the palms moving upwards and the breath moving downwards. Keep the palms turned fully upwards until they reach shoulder level – so that your bent arms are parallel to the floor – at which point you turn them sharply over and they begin their slow and steady downward journey, palms level and facing down, with fingertips close, while you breathe slowly and smoothly out. Feel the out-breath coming up from deep inside you, once again moving in the opposite direction to the palms. It helps a lot for both the in-breath and the out-breath if you imagine some resistance to the movement of your palms. Throughout, this movement should feel firm and powerful. Then, when your palms reach the end of their journey downwards, having gone as far as they can go, turn them abruptly over and begin the upward movement again, accompanied by the in-breath. Leave no gap between the in-breath and the out-breath, nor between the out-breath and the in-breath. The movement of the palms should be continuous and rhythmical, and the breath should follow this movement as though it is being 'pumped'.

If you feel dizzy, stop for a short while. When you start again, try to go a little more slowly.

Lastly, you need to engage your imagination. While still keeping the focus of your breath in the back of your throat, in the oro-pharynx, imagine that you are breathing in a clear stream through the soles of your feet and breathing out white steam through all the pores of your skin. But most importantly, experience the way the movement of your arms is pulling the breath in and pushing it out.

In the second exercise you move your arms differently while imagining the breath coming in through and going out of different parts of your body.

In the same standing position, place your palms facing each other, say 4–8 cm (or 2-3 in) apart, in front of your abdomen, with your fingertips pointing horizontally away from you. For this, your arms need to be bent at the elbows in an approximate right angle, so that your elbows are right beside your waist, but not touching it. From this starting point, you move your arms directly outwards away from your sides, keeping the arms bent, until they are parallel with the ground, palms facing directly down, and as you do so you breathe in deeply, slowly and smoothly. You immediately reverse this movement (preferably with a brief moment of 'attack,' but otherwise maintaining the same tempo), returning your arms to their original position, breathing out slowly and smoothly. As in the first exercise, the movements should be slow, firm and powerful, and they work in the same way by setting up a reciprocal pump-like relationship with the flow of breath.

In this case, however, you need to add an element to your consciousness of your arm movement. Although during the upward movement of the arms that accompanies the in-breath each arm can be experienced or 'felt' as a whole, at the moment of starting the downward movement you should switch your focus to the elbows, imagining that these are leading the movement downwards and, at the same time, squeezing – even from a distance – your waist area to help expel the breath. This causes the palms to seem to 'lag behind' a little, but as the downward movement nears completion, their momentum causes the palms to follow through firmly until they almost touch. As the follow-through happens, let your focus shift from your elbows (which have largely done their work) to the palms. As your palms near each other, feel a subtle pressure growing between them – oddly similar to the way like magnetic poles repel – which slows them and prevents them actually meeting. This introduces a short pause between the out-breath and the in-breath, whereas there is no such pause in ENERGY PUMP 1. Experience it as a moment of stillness and tranquillity.

In this case, moreover, because you're putting a different kind of emphasis on the downstroke, one in which you use your elbows to squeeze the breath out, you can experience the upstroke differently too; the inward flow of air can seem to lift your arms in an almost involuntary way, so that they float upwards to shoulder height.

For the in-breath, imagine the clear stream of pure energy flowing directly into the abdomen through your navel. For the out-breath, imagine the white steam being forced out through the top of your head.

As you observe yourself carrying out these exercises, you may notice that there is an equal amount of engagement of the respiratory muscles in both the in-breath and the out-breath. The 'pump' keeps working throughout. This is not surprising, since the breathing here is intended to be energizing rather than relaxing.

If you simply tell a person 'breathe deeply,' in the way, for example, that a doctor might, and if that person focuses on what happens as they breathe deeply, they will almost certainly feel that they are using ('working') their respiratory muscles to breathe in, but that breathing out is simply a case of 'letting the air go,' without muscular 'work'.

This is also true of many deep breathing exercises that are consciously practised for relaxation. We work to draw the breath in, but we cease working – we relax – while letting the breath out. Hence most people will believe that relaxation takes place through the out-breath (as well as through the natural pause between the out-breath and the in-breath). And this is true – *for exercises of this kind.*

Re-Imagining Your Body

It is striking, and revealing, that you can reverse this. You can 'work' on the out-breath and truly relax on the in-breath!

Before I say how, I want to comment on the underlying reason why it seems 'normal' to relax on the out-breath. It's simply because we're not used to deep breathing. In our normal, everyday breathing, when we're not doing anything strenuous or vigorous, we're no more aware of 'working' on the in-breath than on the out-breath. Both come easily and effortlessly. So when someone says, 'Breathe deeply,' we immediately feel we need to make a special effort. Naturally we start with the in-breath. We could continue our special effort on the out-breath, but – again naturally – we take what is now the most efficient course of action, in effect letting gravity do the work of removing the breath from our lungs as we let our chest and ribcage 'collapse'. But such an out-breath is not good; it dispels the energy taken in through the in-breath.

EXERCISE: LETTING IT ALL IN!

So sit cross-legged on the floor, or just sit normally on a chair, with your back quite straight (not up against the back of the chair if you're using one) and your head well balanced. Breathe deeply and quite slowly in and out through the nose. 'Place' – that is, focus – the out-breath at the top of the throat (in the oro-pharynx), as you did for ENERGY PUMP 1 & 2. Make sure the out-breath and the in-breath are equal in duration. Now, as you breathe out, consciously exert some upward pressure – not too much – with your diaphragm. Keep the feeling of this pressure constant through the whole out-breath. In doing this, of course, you're engaging muscles, making them work. You only need to do this enough to get a good sense of it, a sense that it's you rather than gravity expelling the breath, so don't force anything. It helps if you focus on the noise you're making where the out-breath is focused (which should be a little forward of where it's focused for the in-breath, just behind – but not in – the nose), keeping this noise firm and steady. Now, as you keep breathing like this you should suddenly get a strong sense that you are doing nothing to achieve the in-breath! Your thorax and abdomen just seem to open like a flower, effortlessly, and the new breath just flows richly into you!

Some people are struck – I might even say *moved* – when they discover this. It transforms your relationship to the world around you. The breath of life simply flows into you, unbidden and unforced, as if it wants to, while your 'job' is just gently to expel the used air. You can also feel that it's truly energy flowing into you like this, as though energy is seeking you rather than you seeking it, while you feel a kind of 'dynamic, invigorating relaxation' as your body opens to receive it.

Just as neutrality goes beyond our usual idea of relaxation by its 'openness to the world,' so this kind of breathing promotes a sense of *relaxation as readiness*. It is the very best exercise for realizing that breath is energy.

EXERCISE: BREATHING GOOD POSTURE

Good posture is the equivalent of 'relaxed alertness' and your breathing can help with this too. So sit on an upright chair with your back straight but not rigid (not up against the chair back) and your head well balanced. Your feet should be firmly grounded, a little apart, and your thighs parallel with the floor. Rest the backs of your hands on your upper thighs, turned inwards so that the fingers of one hand overlap the fingers of the other, with your thumb tips just touching.

Breathe slowly but firmly in through your abdomen. As you do so, imagine the breath moving up through your torso as a column until it flows into your head. Make sure you don't raise the shoulders at all. Then breathe out at the same rate, again through your abdomen. As you do so, imagine the breath-column descending and disappearing.

As you breathe in, experience the ascending breath-column holding you easily upright, like a second spine. As you breathe out, feel that the upright posture that was generated by the in-breath is simply and effortlessly 'left in place'. There shouldn't be the slightest inclination to slump.

Note that in this exercise the imaginary breath-column moves in the opposite direction to the actual flow of air through the trachea. If, as an experiment, you discard the image of breathing in through the abdomen so that you can focus attention on the actual flow of air, as though the breath column goes down with the in-breath and up with the out-breath, you will find that you cannot create the sense of a posture-supporting column so vividly or so effectively.

It's a remarkable feature of the human organism that we can control our breathing, while its default mode is involuntary (or more precisely 'autonomic,' which means self-governing). Breathing is the only physiological function with two distinct (but overlapping) 'control systems'. True, you can reduce your heart rate or your blood pressure by meditation or, indeed, by deep breathing, but such an effect is indirect. You can control your breathing directly.

But why should I be emphasizing breath *control* like this in the part of the book about demoting the 'conscious controller'? The answer to this will emerge, but quite slowly. First we need to understand how complex our breath control is.

We control our breathing, in fact, both consciously, for example in practising yoga, and unconsciously, for example when we are speaking. These can both loosely be described as 'voluntary' (where this implies the opposite of autonomic) in the sense that we override the default mode of breathing in order to achieve some other purpose, where that other purpose may or may not be focused on our breathing. The default mode of involuntary breath control, then, is largely where our body (more precisely our autonomic nervous system) decides 'for us' how much oxygen we need and therefore how deep and/or rapid our breathing needs to be, though it also covers those times when we automatically use a full stopped (that is, held) breath to increase thoracic or abdominal pressure in order to carry out strenuous tasks.

There's a kind of grey area between involuntary and voluntary control of breathing. Towards the involuntary end of the spectrum, your breathing may be affected by tension and anxiety, making it shallower and 'tighter,' perhaps also accompanied by the feeling that it's not quite sufficient for your needs. Towards the voluntary end, you may well find yourself 'holding your breath' while you perform certain physical tasks, not because you need increased thoracic or abdominal pressure, but because you need concentration. Think of threading a needle. We very often 'stop' our breath in a semi-voluntary way, though it's not always clear why, or indeed *if* there is a good physiological reason. (In the case of threading a needle it's better to say that we 'still' rather than 'stop' the breath, because this action – just like shooting an arrow – requires the kind of profound internal stillness that seems to still the universe around us too.)

But why is human breathing such a complex thing?

It's probably because we speak. The human capacity for speech requires highly sophisticated breath control. It's not just that we need to be able to utter longish phrases on single out-breaths, taking rapid in-breaths only at strategically appropriate moments. It is also, equally importantly, that we need to maintain loudness and to give meaningful stress and intonation to syllables and words, in endlessly varying combinations, all of which require very subtle (though not usually conscious) control of our breathing. Even so, it's not certain whether our capacity to control our breathing evolved specifically to support human speech, or to support some other adaptive function, or whether it is a side-effect of other evolutionary developments. Interestingly, there's some relation between subtle breath control and bipedalism. The muscular control required for us to maintain balance while standing upright on two legs overlaps, at least to some extent, with that required to control our breathing voluntarily. It may even be the case that bipedalism promotes subtle breath control. So how much control over their breathing do our fellow (and part-time bipedal) great apes have? The answer to this question is unclear, but the reason it's unclear is fascinating. From what has been observed, gorillas, orang-utans, chimpanzees and bonobos show some ability to control breathing, but not to the same extent as human beings. Either this is because they are not 'hard-wired' genetically for a human-level of breath control, or because that level has not emerged among them culturally although they have the genetic potential for it (Perlman, Patterson and Cohn). By extension, we can ask: to what extent is our own ability to control our breathing related to our very complex social organization, and in what ways?

I can't answer that, of course, but I would like to stress a more specific and intriguing question that, for me, follows from it: *without the subtle breath control required for speech, would be still be able to dance?*

For the anthropologist Claude Levi-Strauss, the shift from *nature* to *culture* in human society arises on the basis of the incest taboo. To my mind, an equally good candidate for a pivotal role in this shift is dance. Dance is not like running, which is a wholly 'natural' activity, not only in the way dance generates meanings (although in modern culture, where running is no longer a simple survival skill, it too has come to generate meanings) but also – *and probably relatedly* – in the way that its rhythms cannot be mapped in any simple way onto the 'natural' rhythms of the breath. The more elaborate the dance, moreover, the more the 'natural' rhythms of the breath need to be overridden.

Is dance 'the speech of the body'?

Everything good has a downside and the physiology that underpins human breath control is no exception. Our normal breathing, at least when it's free and easy, is rhythmical. But how often throughout a normal day is that rhythm disrupted in one way or another? Sometimes such disruption becomes problematic. Breathing exercises aim, among other things, at maintaining rhythm. Rhythm is definitely good. Of course, we can use voluntary control of breathing to disrupt rhythm, as when a small child protests by holding its breath, but that's obviously not good. Less obviously, I think we need to distinguish two broad kinds of breathing exercises, or better, two ways of approaching conscious breath control. In one way, we *force* our breath to follow a prescribed pattern – so step in the Conscious Controller! In the other way, we both *partially discover* and, simultaneously, *partially impose* a pattern of breathing by tuning in to what our bodies are telling us.

It's easiest to understand this distinction by thinking about 'stopping' the breath. If you 'stop' (hold) your breath between the in-breath and the out-breath, the 'stop' cannot be other than forced (even if the in-breath was shallow). If, on the other hand, you 'stop' the breath between the out-breath and the in-breath, it can be.

EXPERIMENT 14: *To appreciate this crucial distinction, first you must stop thinking of 'stopping' the breath! Preferably lying on your back, breathe deeply and slowly into your belly and then (without any holding the breath) breathe easily out again, equally slowly. Now... just wait. Don't do anything. Wait for your body to breathe in again. Your body knows exactly when to do this, so relinquish all control of the process. Then, once you find yourself breathing in again, take only the most minimal, gentle control of the process to ensure that the in-breath is as deep and as slow as you want.... Then keep repeating the process.*

There is, I would say, a kind of pleasure in this, not so much in the relinquishing control as in the *game* you initially find yourself playing with yourself. It's like 'trying to catch yourself out' by spotting if you voluntarily launched the in-breath or delayed it just a little longer than your body wanted. But you must absolutely not play this game in a competitive spirit, because that's too close to trying to force yourself to relinquish control. No, just observe yourself. After a time, you will find that the 'game' has ceased and you have become perfectly in tune with your body. The game will have ceased because the 'observer' will have become redundant and left.

Suppose you're anxious about an upcoming interview for a job and your anxiety is affecting your performance. What do you do? Well, one option is to *breathe deeply*, as I'm sure you've heard. But maybe you also know, through experience, that that isn't always as easy as it sounds. Why not? The reason, I suggest, is this: it won't work for as long as you *force* yourself to breathe deeply. If it's going to work, it will only be because you manage to shift from 'forcing mode' to 'being in tune with your body mode'. And that's not so easy.

But here's a 'trick'. For as long as your goal is to breathe deeply, you won't manage to shift mode. Your goal should be to *find your rhythm*. Breathing deeply is just a step towards this. Notice the word 'find'. You can't impose this rhythm. It's already there, but suppressed by anxiety, so you have to let it out.

In yoga the goal of rhythmic breathing is to tune into the 'rhythm of the universe'. The profound sense in which this is true is that *you will never find a rhythm in your own ego*. Rhythms always come from beyond you, even as they infuse and traverse you, just like the mother's heartbeat in the dark all-enveloping womb.

Now, the 'amazing' thing is that breathing deeply in the right rhythmic way can help you overcome or dispel anxiety. This is 'amazing' because it seems to contradict the one-way nature of the normal cause and effect process. After all, presumably anxiety is the cause (one with its own prior causes, of course) at the psychological level, while a disrupted or disturbed breathing pattern is the effect at the physiological level. But if you can recover a smoother, more fluent breathing pattern you don't just 'treat the symptom' – you reduce or even remove its cause.

In fact this doesn't really seem amazing to me at all – at least not in the sense of surprising, although it is still wonderful. It's just that we don't fully understand the *mind-body loop* yet, so we don't know how modifying our breathing can entail or generate quite far-reaching psycho-physiological effects. When we do, it will all seem perfectly natural.

FINDING YOUR FEET

A little earlier, I noted the relationship between human breath control and bipedalism. To conclude Part Two, then, let's get back to basics – *the feet*. Your feet really are basic. They're the basis of you. So here's an exercise to help you 'find your feet,' above all to realize that they don't need the 'conscious controller'. It's not easy, though, so you'll need to spend some time exploring it.

EXERCISE: HOW CAN WE KNOW THE WALKER FROM THE WALK?

The name I've given this exercise echoes the famous line from William Butler Yeats' poem "Among School Children," *How can we*

Re-Imagining Your Body

know the dancer from the dance? Most people, I believe, probably have an intuitive sense of what Yeats meant by this, that *in the dance* the dancer and the dance somehow become one, so we cannot 'know them apart'. But a dance is a dance. Most people, I also believe, would probably respond to a similar question about the walker and the walk quite differently, that they are very knowably distinct. After all, a walk is *just* a walk, in a way that a dance can never be 'just' a dance.

But not in this exercise!

You must practise this barefoot. The surface should be reasonably level, but a certain amount of unevenness is desirable. Try it on different types of surface: rough, smooth, dusty, grainy, gritty, even stony…. The soles of your feet are extraordinarily sensitive and responsive, so you must give them plenty to 'think about'. By all means do it indoors if you don't have the choice, but it's better outdoors and great in a garden. The only proviso is that the surface must give you sufficient support, so a sandy beach may not work.

I should note here that only feet that are quite used to going barefoot are truly sensitive, for feet that spend too long in shoes tend to be oversensitive when 'let out'. If you're not used to going barefoot, try to get more used to it, especially outdoors – at least if the weather's good. Going barefoot in natural terrains from grassy hillsides to stony beaches is among the very best ways of getting back in touch with your body. For one thing, it reveals that touch is not so focused in the (manipulative) hands.

You must walk in very slow motion, as slowly as you can, but it must still be a walk. Augusto Boal has a 'slow motion race' exercise or game which encourages such reduced forward velocity (because the slowest wins) that it can no longer be counted a walk. What is the difference? At what point does a slow motion walk cease being a walk? I would say it is the point at which you lose the whole *body's involvement. In practising Boal's exercise, people commonly lift a foot and shift it slightly forwards (because you must keep moving) while the rest of the body remains statuesque. This is not a walk. In a walk, there is a continuous, rhythmical shifting of the weight of the body as a whole. You must preserve the sense of this. But you must also walk as slowly as you possibly can.*

Keep your knees slightly bent so that you experience your centre of gravity as being low. Do not lift a foot high; it should just come clear of the ground before moving forward. Move it forward no more than the length of the other foot, no less than half that length. Do not slide the foot forward. To lift and move a foot, raise the heel first, 'rolling' the foot forward until the toes come just clear of the ground, let the heel then swing forward as the rest of the foot is flexed upwards, then place the heel gently down followed by the middle part of the foot and, finally, the toes, as it were 'rolling' the foot down again. There can be something very slightly exaggerated in the way the different parts of the foot move in relation to each other, although the overall movement upwards and forwards – the displacement of the foot – is minimal.

As you make steps in this way, you will of course feel your weight shifting from one leg to the other. Be aware of the varying tensions in each leg as this happens, making sure that these are only necessary tensions. Make sure, as well, that your upper body remains completely relaxed and that your breathing is easy. No holding the breath! Maintain your sense of the slow rhythm of the shifting of weight, but also try to focus on the precise point at which your weight is transferred fully from one foot to the other. At precisely this moment, feel the foot which receives your whole body weight becoming one with the ground, fusing with it, as though it sends down a root.

Through all this, keep your primary attention focused in the soles of your feet and on what they experience. You will find you can discern the slightest variation of the surface. Not only that, you will find that your foot naturally and automatically adjusts to and takes account of the varying landscape of the surface. You just observe all the tiny adjustments your feet – in fact, different parts of your feet – are continually making. You issue no instructions or commands, for by now you should have established a kind of gently effortless, slowly rhythmical momentum which keeps you, or your walk, moving forwards, and you can safely leave it to your feet to make all the micro-decisions that your walk needs.

Now make a slight adjustment of point of view. Think of – and feel – the surface as cooperating or collaborating with you, or with your feet, or with your walk. In a way, the surface is walking you. (This will happen only when you realize that it really is a slight adjustment.)

As you continue, realize that you have now become fully free to observe and appreciate, in minute sensual detail, everything around you. To do so, you don't need to lose your primary focus in the soles of your feet – you simply add to it. Imagine that time has slowed down almost to nothing, allowing you to notice everything.

Realize: the walk walks itself – that is what sets you free.

Re-Imagining Your Body

This exercise is really a kind of walking meditation. It was originally suggested by, though it morphed into something quite different from, a *Butoh* exercise by Nakajima Natsu in which you walk extremely slowly into nothingness, then you walk back again into existence (Fraleigh and Tamah, 105-9).

PART THREE

METAMORPHOSES

PRELIMINARY THOUGHTS

What does the word *metamorphosis* mean to you? Does it make you recall your discovery, as a young child, of the wondrous process by which a caterpillar turns into a butterfly? Or does it make you think of Kafka's famous story in which a clerk, Gregor Samsa, wakes to find himself transformed into a giant cockroach? What does this word bring to mind – a miracle or a nightmare?

Metamorphosis: complete and utter transformation of the body.

The Roman poet Ovid's *Metamorphoses* (where the word is in plural form) tells of many such radical transformations, the stuff of ancient myths. A woman (Niobe) transformed into a weeping rock by the speechlessness of her grief at the deaths of all her children. A young man (Narcissus) transformed into a delicate flower by the hopelessness of his love of his own image. A young woman (Procne) transformed into a nightingale by the horror of killing her own son as revenge upon her husband, who had raped her sister....

Such transformations are deeply mysterious. True, there is a 'logic' in Niobe's metamorphosis, for grief may be immobilizing. To the Ancient Greeks, moreover, among whom the myth of Procne originated, the song of the nightingale was thought to be a song of mourning. We might even see something appropriate, though way beyond 'poetic justice,' in Narcissus's fate, for the flower named after him bends its head, as though gazing longingly in a pool, and it is delicate and short-lived. But in spite of all such rationalisation, the transformation remains shocking, arbitrary, *too much*. The metamorphosis records such an extreme of human experience that it takes the one transformed *beyond the human pale*.

I say these things to 'get you in the mood' for the exercises that follow, for they are powerful. They should be approached in the spirit of play, naturally, like all the exercises in this book, but they're also very serious. In the exercises, it's the process of transformation that matters, more than the product. As for the reason you should do them, I'll get back to it. For the moment all I'll say is: *because you can.*

Re-Imagining Your Body

Notice that some of the exercises you encountered earlier are *metamorphic*. BECOMING THE SEA and BECOMING THE WIND in Part Two (pp. 108, 109) are good examples of this type of exercise. Recall, then, the need for a kind of 'letting go' in performing those exercises. In a sense, what you're exploring in metamorphic exercises is *possession*. You are transformed when 'something else' possesses you. But of course you need to work up to this. The process matters more than the product because you need to find the moment at which the 'working up to' shifts into 'letting something else take over'. The conscious controller has no role in this.

TREES AND PLANTS

EXERCISE: BEING A TREE 1

Stand upright and centred, feet directly beneath the shoulders, preferably barefoot, with your eyes closed. Focus your consciousness in your toes. Imagine them growing, lengthening, rooting down into the ground. Let them become long and complex. After you've let your toes extend out and down as roots like this for a while, go on to imagine other roots, more like tap roots, going down deep into the earth from your heels as well. Keep the sense of both sorts of roots throughout the exercise. This means that you can't shift your weight forward onto the balls of your feet or backwards onto the heels at any point; you must remain firmly planted throughout.

It's relatively easy to get a strong sense of rootedness in this way. Even so, take plenty of time over this phase. Experience it to the full. The active process of rooting down must not cease through the whole of the exercise.

Up to now, you have only experienced your body as rooting downwards. At a certain point, however, a change occurs. Don't force the change, just let it come. Let yourself begin to feel something flowing upwards, from the roots, up into your legs, your thighs, your torso... like sap rising. As this upward flow makes you aware of your body, experience that body as being a strong, stable trunk (let it sway a little in the wind, if you like) and form an image of its outer bark (whether it's rough or smooth, thick and deeply grooved or thin and papery) – but don't lose awareness of your roots, your rooting down.

Now just wait. Trees, after all, are slow growing and you have all the time in the world. Keep the strong sense of sap rising, originating deep in the earth below you, while your roots probe deeper. After a time you should feel your

142

arms move slightly, involuntarily, away from your trunk, as though they want to grow into branches. Once you feel this, experiencing it as an effect of the upward, life-giving flow of sap, shift your focus to your shoulders. Something inside you wants to grow upward from your shoulders. But don't let this cause you to raise your shoulders more than a fraction; instead, let this new urge flow into your arms instead.

Add to this a sense of sunlight on your arms and shoulders and head. You do not need to push towards the light, for it is pulling you upwards.

Now your arms will start to move more fully away from your trunk, since they are energized both by an inner urge and an outer pull; but they do so slowly, maybe bending and twisting a little as they do so. As this happens, imagine your fingers growing longer. Don't consciously decide anything about how the branches grow – just let your arms and hands turn into branches in their own way, following the impulses from inside you. As this happens, try to imagine that you have many more than two arms, hence many branches, extending outwards and upwards to create a complete world. For that is what a tree is – a world to birds and insects.

Experience the way your branching mirrors your rooting.

As the process of growth slows, as you become that complete world for the generations of birds and insects, movement does not cease. But more and more it leaves only inner movement, which was there all along.

There is no reversing this process. To come out of 'being a tree' you must simply open your eyes. Now you can no longer be a world, for you see a world around you.

In this exercise you become a *generic* tree, not a specific one such as an oak or a larch or a willow. We seem to have a concept of a generic tree (it's what small children draw), but no such concept of a generic animal, only of specific ones. Notice also that you are not at any point required to grow leaves. The reason for both these things is that the exercise is really focused on a particular problem, such that doing the exercise successfully is solving this problem. This is the problem of 'fitting' the actual movement of your arms, as they become branches, to the inner movement that runs through the exercise. Overall, you make relatively little actual movement, but subjectively it should seem that a huge amount of movement occurs through the exercise as a whole and that this movement is *all one*.

How could you 'become a world' otherwise?

The inner movement of your imaginary growth (the rooting downwards from your toes and heels, and the lengthening of your fingers) should seem continuous and relatively smooth. In contrast, I find that the growth of the branches happens in surges or pulses. These spurts of growth lift and shape the branches, which then hold their new shape and position until the next spurt occurs. I strongly experience the *irreversibility* of this growth process. I also find that a spurt of growth typically engages not just one joint (shoulder, elbow or wrist) but all three. For me, it is as though the inner movement becomes at times strong enough to express itself in outer movement. Your own 'solution' may be subtly different, but to be a solution to the problem posed by the exercise, your inner and your outer movement must seem to you so closely connected as to be the very same thing.

EXERCISE: BEING A TREE 2

This exercise poses much the same problem. However, in this case the tree must grow from a seed, so lie on the floor, curled up in a foetal position, and... wait. Wait for the impulse to come from deep within that will split the seed case and start the process of sending out roots and shoots. Once this process begins, it's unstoppable, but it's also very, very slow. Initially, you must focus on rooting downwards, with the roots spreading out in all directions. Then, when you're ready, you begin the process of growing and branching outwards and upwards to the light. It's best to keep your eyes closed throughout.

SPOILER WARNING! As I said above, this exercise poses the same problem of connecting inner and outer movement as BEING A TREE 1. But in the way I set it up in a class (always after BEING A TREE 1), as well as in the 'minimal' way I've described it above, another, related problem arises, which most people fail to solve at first attempt. If you want to try to solve it, you first need to discover for yourself what the problem is – *so do the exercise before reading the next two paragraphs.*

Notice that in describing the exercise I did not specify any parts of your body that should send roots down into the earth. It's quite natural, in fact, to feel these roots going down from all parts of your body. As this happens, you don't just uncurl from the foetal position; you also start to roll and twist, but in slow motion. In a way, it's like a very slow process of waking up. You realize that you can take your time with it, as long as you maintain the sense of rooting down.

However, once you feel sufficiently well rooted, you know you have to start growing upwards. *But how?*

At this point, almost everyone comes to realize what the problem is: *you cannot find any way of getting on your feet which does not destroy your sense of rootedness.* It's interesting to watch students trying to solve this problem. This can go on for some time, but after a while you see that they're beginning to give up, since they've understood that it's impossible. Very few people go on to realize that it's possible to grow upwards in a different way – *feet first!* Those that do are more than halfway to solving the problem, for all that remains is to find an appropriate way to lift the pelvis and a good part of the torso off the ground, so that you get into something resembling a yoga shoulder stand (but not as 'neat' as that). An 'appropriate way' of achieving this is one that is consistent with (like an extension of) your inner movement – but this, I should admit, requires quite a high degree of physical fitness, since any 'swinging' of the lower body upwards will not feel right.

Once you're in this position you don't need to hold it very long, just long enough to appreciate its great continuing sense of rootedness.

At this point, with both BEING A TREE exercises having been completed (the second with whatever prompting is necessary), I ask: where does the 'consciousness' of a tree seem to reside, in the upper canopy of branches and leaves or in the roots? The answer I get is always "in the roots" – and this is correct, it's where most of the extraordinary hidden social and, as some would say, intelligent life of trees takes place. (See Peter Wohlleben's (controversial) *The Hidden Life of Trees* for more on this.)

What the answer "in the roots" tells us, I think, is that something has been discovered, mainly through the second of the exercises. I would put it like this: even through exercises that are intrinsically 'anthropomorphic' (that is, which produce 'human versions' of non-human beings) it is possible to go a little step *beyond the human.* And this, I think, is what *metamorphosis* implies.

EXERCISE: THE PLANT INSIDE

The following exercise is adapted from one of Grotowski's (Grotowski, 110). It too involves both inner and outer movement, but in this case they are not connected. The outer movement is simply walking. The rhythm and tempo of your walk should remain the same throughout the exercise. As you walk, imagine that there is a seed inside you. It sends out a shoot. The shoot grows, strengthens and becomes more vigorous. When the plant is fully grown inside you, filling you, it flowers. Then the flower begins to fade. The petals fall. The plant yellows. It shrivels and finally dies. Through all this, you keep on walking.

A small part of your consciousness should be given to maintaining the sameness or consistency of your walk throughout. This is to ensure that you don't 'show' or demonstrate the plant inside you in the way that you walk. Nonetheless, if someone is watching you they can 'see' the plant inside you. They can see when it is growing upwards, or flowering, or shrivelling. But you show none of this. (In Grotowski's original exercise, however, the plant is much more outwardly expressed.)

What is involved here is related to, but also different from, Zeami's adage, "What is felt in the heart is ten; what appears in movement seven" (see p. 71). In a sense, what is expressed in movement in this case is zero! But the inner life – the life, we might say, of the spirit – still shines through. It is very striking. But it is not in the least surprising. If you perform the exercise alone, with no one to 'see' the plant inside you, then – provided your inner sense of the plant is vivid to you – you will easily understand how it can be seen by others.

With students, I usually go on from this to play the following game. I ask one to choose a colour, without saying what it is, and then to *become that colour* without trying to show it in any way. The others then have to say what colour they see. Strikingly, they are right far more often than would be the case if they were randomly guessing. (Interestingly, this works best with colours. It also works, but not quite so well, with materials such as wood, metal, mud... provided an initial set of possible materials has been established. If I ask a student to be an animal without showing which, it hardly works at all. I wonder why.)

To be so transparent, the human body must be *open*. This is what Eugenio Barba calls the *dilated body*. A dilated body is a 'vividly vital' body, which is more than a body that is merely alive. It is, he says, "a glowing body", one whose particles seem more "excited" than they do in the mundane activities of everyday life (Barba & Savarese, 53). This description is metaphorical, suggestive, for it's difficult to describe this state in a more direct or technical way. What is implied is that the dilated body goes beyond mere functionality, exhibiting a kind of 'excess' that is at the same time never 'too much' or 'over the top'. It's the proverbial 110%, not manifested in extra effort, nor even in extra liveliness but in *extra life*. Barba deploys the concept in relation to performance, of course, but you can see dilated bodies in other contexts too, such as at parties among people who are really enjoying themselves – and when you see this, you realize that 'glowing' really is the right word.

ANIMALS

The next stage in the metamorphic process is for you to transform yourself into different animals. As noted above, there's no such thing as a 'generic animal;' you can only transform yourself into a specific animal – one, that is, with a precise 'energy shape'. Nevertheless we'll build on this later by creating semi-imaginary animals too.

Recall how I left animals out of the discussion of 'energy shapes' in Part Two (pp. 117-118), leaving them till later (i.e. now)? This is primarily because the 'energy shape' of an animal can only be realized *through movement*.

EXERCISE: BEING ANIMALS

There's a right way and a wrong way to 'be an animal'. Suppose a person imitates a dog by going down on all fours and panting, with his tongue hanging out. This is not 'being a dog,' it's signing a dog. (It's the equivalent of saying 'woof, woof' rather than trying to vocalize something close to the real sounds that dogs make.) When we see someone 'signing an animal' in this way, what we see is the human being doing the signing; we don't see the animal as such, we are merely made to think of it. Yet if we see a person become an animal in the right way, we see that animal 'come to life'. We still see the human being, of course, but as transformed.

A sign is external. You only need to 'hold it up,' as it were. To become an animal, very differently, you must find that animal inside yourself. It's already there, but hidden, covered over, buried.

Even so, start from observation. You need to look at and see animals, but in a certain way. You need to ask yourself, where does the vitality of this particular animal seem to be concentrated or focused? In a dog it is very much in the nose and muzzle. In a cat it is in the spine. In a horse it is in the way the neck so strongly emerges from the shoulders. In a kangaroo it is in the hind legs and tail. In an ostrich it is in the head and neck. In an eagle it is in the eyes. And so on. These are simplifications, of course. But they allow you to ask, what would it feel like if my vitality were concentrated or focused

Re-Imagining Your Body

in such a place? You must answer this question by feeling the answer, not with any thought and certainly not in words.

Finding the locus of vitality in this way is just a starting-point. Beyond this, you need to observe and incorporate in your own 'structure of somatic feeling' the variable tempo and the natural rhythms of the animal's movement. You need to find the directions of flow of that movement. And you may need to internalize how the animal breathes. All this takes time. You need to find the animal within yourself, with nothing being imposed in the whole process.

It's crucial to understand that, in these exercises, you never try to deny your human body. You are not pretending to have a non-human body; rather, you are creating a kind of non-human inner awareness and experience of your human body. For example, if, in 'being a cat,' you need to 'live more fully' in and through your spine, you will find you can do this much better while retaining your upright two-legged stance than you could if you were to go on all fours.

In this way you can try to be a cat, a mouse, an elephant, a giraffe, a hedgehog, a gazelle, a gorilla, a lizard, a dolphin... whatever you like. It is not necessary or appropriate for me to comment more on any of these since the process is one of discovery, as I've said. But it's not just that you need to discover the specific animal already within you. It's also that you need to discover which animals you can readily find within yourself and which give you difficulty. If an animal comes easily to you, it may be that it comes easily to most people; similarly, if it doesn't come easily, this may be the case for most others too. In this case you learn something about the deeper resources of the human body in a general way. If, on the other hand, you discover that certain animals come easily to you but not to most others, and vice-versa, you learn something about the deeper resources of your own particular body.

Recall Chekhov's 'Imaginary Bodies' exercise which I described in the Introduction. By taking on a character's appropriate body, the actor can become that character more easily, for the new imaginary body transforms the actor's psychology in the desired way. In the present exercise, we might say that you take on the 'imaginary body' of the animal. Your psychology is transformed by this too, not into the actual psychology of the animal concerned, but into something more radically different from your normal everyday psychology. You connect, thus, with the deeper psychophysical resources of your body.

In Part Two, when describing trees as 'energy shapes,' I briefly mentioned the *Shamanic world-view* in which everything is alive and has a spirit, not just animals and plants but rocks and hills and lakes and clouds (pp. 117-118). In this world-view everything is also *connected*. The exercises outlined above, whereby you transform yourself into a tree or into different animals, are excellent ways of appreciating this underlying connectedness, what might be called *the web of being*.

It is also appropriate, I believe, to think of 'becoming' a certain animal as a means of discovering, communing with and even taking into yourself the *spirit* of that animal. Here, 'spirit' does not mean some kind of weird substance that might glow in the dark when outside its normal fleshy habitation. It is the *structured, concentrated vitality* that is expressed in the animal, the way life *flows* in and through it.

Spirit is not separate from body, and it is only distinct from the body in an abstract way. The body *is* spirit, says the Japanese philosopher Ichikawa, when we experience our existence in a *unified* way (see Appendix 1 for some discussion of this idea). I suggest that this kind of unified experience is necessary when you are 'being an animal,' for although your focus might be on, say, your spine, it should be so in such a way that it feeds through and 'irradiates' your body as a whole.

To Shamans, human beings are far from being alone. Each of us is accompanied in different phases of our life by a *Power Animal*, a specific animal spirit – perhaps by more than one simultaneously. This is nothing like having a 'fairy godmother' who turns up occasionally to perform the odd beneficent trick. While the Power Animal is *other than us*, it is also *intrinsic* to our way of being-fully-in-the-world. If, for whatever reason, we lose our Power Animal, we suffer, perhaps becoming sick. This is simple enough to understand: the Power Animal is really a certain kind of *energy* – if we lose the animal, we lose its energy too.

With which of the animals that you managed to become through metamorphosis do you feel the greatest affinity? Could this be your (current – but perhaps long-standing) Power Animal?

There is a way to *dance your animal*, through which you can discover what your Power Animal is. To succeed, you must truly let go. You must dance down past your social body to the level of your body-as-your-unconscious, and then dance deeper. This is not easy.

Re-Imagining Your Body

The following exercise will help you prepare for it, by first 'setting free' a kind of animal that is in everyone.

WAKING KUNDALINI

In Yogic philosophy, *Kundalini* is a great serpent of spiritual energy coiled at the base of your spine. I use this term here as a powerful and appropriate metaphor for the following exercise.

EXERCISE: WRITHING SNAKE

This will help you explore and experience the fullest possible range of spinal movement. It's also excellent for discovering and tuning in to your body's impulses – for letting them live inside you. You just leave it to your body to do whatever it wants to do, by switching off your 'conscious controller'. Lastly, the exercise is great for opening up the channels that connect the lower and upper body. Above all, it's a way of *letting your body speak*. So take your time with it, because if you rush it you'll be effectively 'silencing' your own body.

HOWEVER, YOU SHOULD AVOID THIS EXERCISE IF YOU HAVE A SPINAL INJURY OR OTHER SPINAL PROBLEM.

Lie on your back (this removes the influence of gravity on the naturally upward and downward energy flows of the body), with knees raised and feet flat on the floor but with nothing under your head. Don't let your knees flop outwards, but don't hold them rigidly in position either; try to keep them easily balanced above your feet. Spread your arms, palms up, at approximately a forty-five degree angle from your torso. Relax for a few moments, eyes closed, then try to imagine your two hips, or, better, the left and right halves of the rear of your pelvis (where these contact the floor), as separate from each other, not just in space (which of course they are) but more importantly as having 'wills of their own'. Listen to what each hip or part of your pelvis wants to do. Let it move as it wants, don't decide for it. Nothing much may happen at first, but soon you'll feel definite, if faint, impulses, perhaps something like 'twitches' inside you. These impulses may not even show to an observer, but they're still movements; an impulse is always the beginning of a movement, and the beginning of a movement must be a movement. Let them just get bigger. Don't rush it. As they become externally observable, they will still be very small movements. They may be single movements or repeated ones. If the latter, they can be either rhythmical or a-rhythmical. Anything is possible. Let your hips or parts of

150

your pelvis decide which – the left or the right – moves when, as well as how it moves. Then, after a while, let the pair start to move simultaneously, but only when that's what they want. In moving together, they can move apart from each other (they really can!), or closer together, or both in the same direction – whatever they want.

After you've done this for a while, shift focus and do the same thing with your shoulders. Focus on both the shoulder joints and the shoulder blades here. Let each go where it wants and do what it wants. Then, after a while, let them start to move together. You'll probably find this a little easier, both because you've already experienced the process with your lower torso, and because the shoulders have a little more scope for movement, since they're not so firmly 'planted' on the floor.

Next, let your hips/parts of your pelvis and your shoulders start doing what they want, all at the same time. Maybe these four agents will 'move together' independently, each doing its own thing, or maybe in a coordinated way – just go with what your body wants. Before this point, your various movements will have all remained fairly small, and your back will have stayed almost entirely in full contact with the ground. If it didn't, you were probably forcing the movements, deciding on behalf of your hips or shoulders, not leaving everything up to them. But now something changes. As they work together, in the simple sense of at the same time, your hips/pelvic segments and shoulders start to engage your spine. You will probably find yourself rolling a little sideways, for example, or raising your pelvis, or perhaps slightly arching your lower back.

As this happens, and as it starts to get bigger – which will happen quite naturally – re-focus your attention on your spine. Imagine it turning into a snake. From now on, all movements originate in the snake of your spine. You simply allow the snake to do what it wants to do. Almost certainly it will start to writhe, though it may take some time before this develops to the full. Your spine will twist in different directions, undulate, stretch out, curl.... A crucial moment here may be when your knees, which have remained raised till now, are caused to 'fall' both to one side. Your legs should be fully relaxed, so this should happen very naturally. This is like a 'cue' to your body that anything goes. Your back can arch fully, your pelvis can tilt upwards, your head can start to swing from side to side on the floor, you can even roll partly over. But whatever happens, it will always seem to you like one indivisible movement, the movement of the snake of your spine. The snake will try to move as freely and as expansively as it can, in all possible directions. The rest of your body, including even your arms and your legs, just follows.

Re-Imagining Your Body

To an observer, your movements may well now seem very erotic. They will very likely seem so to you too. Enjoy this! But don't let any erotic image or idea take over your consciousness; instead, keep the image of the writhing snake – your spine – in mind. Your movements may become very big, looking like ecstatic convulsions to an observer – but only the muscles around your spine are 'convulsing,' while everything else stays very relaxed.

NOTE: Provided you have a healthy spine you don't need to worry about overdoing it in this exercise. It's true that you don't exert any conscious control over your movements, which can become very vigorous, but your body knows its own limits and will stay within them. But as I said earlier, do not do the exercise if you have any kind of spinal problem.

End when you feel like ending, letting the intensity of your movements decrease first. You will feel good, very good. And your spine will feel beautifully free.

Then, if you feel like it, go one very small (but also very big) step further. Stand up in a smooth, slow relaxed way. Feel your spine to be very long. Close your eyes, then meditate for a few moments on this sutra from the ancient Vijnana Bhairava Tantra (Reps, 162):

> Consider your essence as light rays rising from centre to centre up the vertebrae, and so rises *livingness* in you.

Next, you need to perform this exercise again, taking it further. But not straightaway – it's far too powerful to do twice in close succession, so wait a few hours or, better, until another day.

Perform the exercise in exactly the same way as before through to the last stage where the snake of your spine is writhing very vigorously. This time, however, stand up – but let the snake keep writhing as you do so. Once you are upright, let the snake continue writhing as powerfully as possible, just as it would be doing if you were on the floor. This will make you dance. Crucially, it will make you dance in a way that you could not possibly have danced without working through the floor exercise first.

This is the best method I know of taking your (free) dance to another level. It's great preparation, therefore, for DANCING YOUR ANIMAL, to which we now turn.

EXERCISE: DANCING YOUR ANIMAL

The phrase 'taking your dance to another level' would normally be interpreted as taking it to a higher level. But to DANCE YOUR ANIMAL you have to dance down past your social body to your body-as-your-unconscious and then dance deeper, as I said earlier. This is a metaphor – but it's important. Keep it in mind as you dance.

Having experienced the full potential of your dance through WRITHING SNAKE, discard the image of the snake and continue to dance – but now dancing downwards – slowly, easily, as relaxed as possible. Close your eyes, at least at times, or narrow them to restrict your awareness of the world around you. Then just let the dance grow.

"How can we know the dancer from the dance?" asked the poet Yeats. Well, we can't – and that's Yeats's point. But whereas in WRITHING SNAKE you let your body do what it wants to do (from well before it becomes a dance, of course), in DANCING YOUR ANIMAL you need to let your dance do what it wants to do. It is the dance that grows in and through you, the dance that progressively possesses you.

As you dance, naturally a part of you remains an observer of yourself. (This is true in WRITHING SNAKE too.) It's a detached and passive but curious observer. It would never dream of interfering with or influencing the dance. It is waiting for your Power Animal to appear. The idea of this exercise, you see, is that through your dance you will start to become like your Animal. This will happen when your Animal enters into you and dances through you. As a result you discover (or rather, your detached observer discovers) what your Animal is.

It may help you to achieve the necessary energy level if you find some rhythmic drumming to dance to. But be careful that any music you choose doesn't 'direct' you too much towards a certain kind of dancing that might imply a certain animal or restrict the possibilities too much.

ANIMAL 'CONTRADICTIONS'

Remember that you began the process of metamorphosis into different animals by first noting where a specific animal's vitality seemed to be concentrated and focused. You then tried to recreate this in yourself.

EXERCISE: EVOLVING LIFE-FORMS

Now you will do this again, but with the goal of turning yourself into two animals at the same time. Moreover, there should be a kind of contradiction between the two animals you choose. Of course, in reality no two animals, however different, can be called 'contradictory'. At the most they might be called 'opposite' (and that only in certain ways). But when you take two very different animal spirits into you at the same time, the effect should be like a contradiction in you. Moreover, your body must also be the resolution of this contradiction – a synthesis of the different kinds of energy that you have taken into yourself!

It's very much up to you which animals you try to combine, or synthesize, and of course you should approach this exercise in a very experimental way. Some combinations will work immediately while others will be difficult, maybe even impossible. Be adventurous! Purely for illustration, here are a few combinations that have worked well (though not necessarily immediately) with my students:

1. *A bear and a snake.*
2. *A tiger and a mouse.*
3. *A swan and a crocodile.*
4. *A fox and a donkey.*
5. *A gazelle and a jellyfish.*

In each case the 'contradiction' is between different kinds or qualities or styles of movement. That 'contradiction' is a challenge. You have to synthesize the different kinds of movement within yourself. As you do so with a given pair of animals, A and B, try starting by becoming A then adding B; then, alternatively, try starting by becoming B then adding A. Is there a difference in the synthesis in each case?

This is a very playful exercise. As you carry it out you can think of yourself as being evolution experimenting with different possible life-forms!

THE 'PSYCHOLOGICAL GESTURE'

The Psychological Gesture, or PG, is a remarkable technique developed by Michael Chekhov (See Chekhov, 63-76 and 183-215). It is not normally 'metamorphic' in itself, that is, in its more common use by actors, but even learning what is involved in such common use will help you practise the earlier metamorphic exercises in a deeper, richer way. Moreover, there is a specific use of the PG that can be called 'metamorphic,' which we will come to later.

In Chekhov's work, the Psychological Gesture has several different uses. It can be used by an actor to develop a character by finding the PG that embodies the character's underlying structure of will and desire. It can be used by an actor to find the core of the character's role at any particular moment of the play. It can even be used to determine the essence of a scene as a whole, as distinct from the scene as experienced by any particular character in it.

In all these cases, the function of the Psychological Gesture is *to capture and imprint a certain structure of feeling in one's body* – in a broad sense of 'feeling' which includes will and desire, as well as their associated emotions and moods. This is how you will use it too in a non-theatrical context. The difference is that the actor starts from (perhaps a vague idea of) the structure of feeling that constitutes or motivates a character and goes on to find the appropriate PG, thus both deepening and sharpening the sense of that structure of feeling. Somewhat differently, you will start from a PG, by letting your body spontaneously create one, and go on to discover its structure of feeling through experiencing it.

To understand the concept of the Psychological *Gesture*, we really need to begin from the idea of *posture*. If an actor is trying to build a given character, then the actor first needs to find the posture that expresses that character's underlying structure of will and desire. The *gesture*, then, will consist largely of *the movement into* that posture, followed by the way it is held (for the 'holding' must be experienced as a kind of continuation of the movement into it – yes, it's that all-important *inner movement* again). The movement out of it also matters, but not to the same extent.

Importantly, the posture which is the 'peak' or, more precisely, the 'plateau' of a Psychological Gesture is not an everyday, ordinary or naturalistic one. Rather, it is *archetypal*. Think of a highly symbolic or expressionist sculpture. The first step in creating a PG is to find this posture, which should involve the whole body. We'll see how to do this shortly. For the moment, just assume that it has been found. The second stage is to decide, by experiment, the *tempo* of the movement into the archetypal posture. This is because the movement into it is where you experience the *transformation of your psychology*, and this transformation can feel very different if done quickly or slowly. The resulting posture may be the same in each case, but its internal psychological effect will continue to feel different as you hold the posture, for as you hold the posture you should feel the inner movement into it continuing at the correct tempo.

EXERCISE: FINDING A PG POSTURE

In order to find an appropriate posture, start with a part of the body, for example one hand and arm, or even just a hand. Let this take on an appropriately expressive shape, then let it 'tell' other parts of the body how to join in. Other parts will tend either to follow or to oppose the hand and arm. Because characters are often complex and because oppositions can create much stronger, more expressive images (i.e. postures), it is a good idea to allow oppositions to arise wherever they 'seem to want to arise'. This is one reason why I introduced the ANIMAL CONTRADICTIONS exercise, in which oppositions are predominant, immediately before the Psychological Gesture. But note the crucial difference: in ANIMAL CONTRADICTIONS the oppositions arise in relation to movement, through which they also become resolved, whereas in the Psychological Gesture they arise in relation to posture, where they are not resolved. Try this a few times to get the idea and to see how it always comes out differently.

Chekhov stresses that a Psychological Gesture (in the sense mainly of its 'postural plateau') should be strong but without unnecessary tensions. It is important to keep this in mind as you go on to experiment with PGs for yourself. The key word, of course, is "unnecessary," since it is likely that somatic oppositions will generate tensions, but necessary ones.

Since his concern is with actor training, where the actor is presented with and must solve problems that are given by the play, Chekhov suggests practising the Psychological Gesture by finding PGs for characters in plays, literature and history, then for familiar living people; he also suggests creating characters in imagination and finding PGs for them. In the present context, however, there is no need to start from characters of any kind. You can start from the PG, going on to find *its* 'character'.

EXERCISE: THE HIEROGLYPHIC BODY

To clarify what it means to start from the PG and why I call this the HIEROGLYPHIC BODY, I need first to say a little bit more about the way actors use the PG. For actors, the PG is a rehearsal rather than a performance technique. While any specific Psychological Gesture is necessarily highly expressive as an image, it is never physically shown on stage. Instead, through finding and practising the PG in the rehearsal phase, the actor *internalizes* the structure of feeling that it expresses. Thus, while the PG itself could be called expressionistic, its proper use typically results in a much more convincingly naturalistic style of performance. Internalizing the structure of feeling expressed in the PG frees the actor from any need to indicate or, worse, to 'demonstrate' that structure of feeling when actually performing the role. The PG is remarkably powerful at achieving this.

But your task is not to find the 'truth' of any given character (unless, by chance, you are an actor). Rather, you are exploring and hopefully enriching your awareness of the life of the body. I like to think of the PG as revealing the 'shape of the soul,' but what matters here is that the 'shape of the soul' is expressed through the body. It is absolutely crucial in this that each and every true PG *involves the whole body*. We can see this even with those simple Psychological Gestures that arise in real life, such as the wide open arms of welcome, a gesture which is reflected in a 'forward impulse' of the lower body and a beaming face, or such as the bouncer's folded arms, spread legs and firmly planted feet, and blank stare. It is also clearly seen in Chekhov's exercises of Opening and Closing (see pp. 56-57), which we can now realize are also simple Psychological Gestures – simple because they are without somatic oppositions. In fact, Chekhov stresses that PGs should be simple, but I feel that this is open to misinterpretation. Wherever oppositions form part of a PG, it cannot be entirely simple, after all.

So let's get back to the process of creating a Psychological Gesture. As I suggested, you should start with just one part of the body. It might be the hand and arm, or the neck and head, or a foot, or a shoulder. Without thinking about it, let this part of your body take on a shape, by moving it in some way. When you are satisfied with this shape (which is just the shape of a single part of your body), enough to want to see where it leads, you retain it while allowing other parts of your body to respond to it in some way. You mustn't make any conscious decisions here. You're just an observer again, witnessing what your body decides to do. As I said above, other parts of your body can either follow or oppose the shape taken initially by the isolated body part. It's as though these other parts say either 'And another thing' or 'Yes, but...'. But although I'm referring here to 'other parts,' you shouldn't let these responses happen too much in isolation from one another. Let's say you started with just your right hand. To a certain extent, the other parts are likely to respond in a kind of sequence – first the right arm, then the shoulders, the left arm, the torso, and so on – so that the emerging posture spreads through the body. But if there's too much isolation of parts in this process, you'll be like a responding robot – a machine, which is not good. Rather than that, as the other parts of your body respond, they should also 're-discover' and 're-establish' the integrated wholeness of your body.

Once you're satisfied that your whole body is involved in the posture (don't forget your face), you can ask yourself whether it's worth developing as a Psychological Gesture. There are no 'rules' for this. It's a matter for intuition. But you can ask yourself whether your posture would be interesting to an observer. As a matter of fact, if it's appropriate for a PG, your posture should be readable by an observer, in the sense that an observer should know what it 'means'. It's in precisely this sense that you create the hieroglyphic body. But it doesn't follow that an observer could put into words precisely what your posture means – if they could, your posture would probably not be interesting enough to be a PG, in fact.

And there's no relation whatsoever between THE HIEROGLYPHIC BODY and the 'signing' that I mentioned earlier. Signing is always easily 'readable' because it's a wholly conventional token of what it refers to. The sign isn't discovered or created in the process of signing, it's merely repeated. For THE HIEROGLYPHIC BODY, each hieroglyph is new, invented for the very first time.

Up to a point, you need to adopt the viewpoint of a possible observer in this way because your posture is *not yet* a Psychological Gesture. It's true that holding this posture causes certain feelings to arise within you and that these feelings give you some idea of your posture's significance. But to let that significance truly enter your body – to become part of the life of your lived body – you need to turn the posture into a gesture by moving into it in the right way.

EXERCISE: FROM THE POSTURE TO THE GESTURE

The act of moving into the posture is not like the process of finding it. As far as possible, your whole body should move into the posture in a smooth and fully integrated way, with as little sense of your body having different parts as possible. As I also said above, the tempo of the movement into the posture also matters – you need to discover the correct tempo by experiment.

To begin, you must activate your sense of inner movement. If you feel the need, you can do this physically by walking around briskly and stopping every so often. But whenever you stop, you should feel the brisk walk continuing inside you. When you start walking again, feel that you are simply 'joining in again' with a walk that already happening inside you. (See p. 77 for the full exercise.)

When you start the actual physical movement into your posture, the movement into it should have already begun inside you. When you fully acquire the posture, the movement into it should continue inside you for as long as you hold it, which should be approximately ten seconds. Hold the posture without any excessive straining – that is, try to remain as relaxed as possible. Then come out of it by returning smoothly to your 'normal body' at a tempo which seems right for this.

In the earlier metamorphic exercises, you know in advance what you are to be transformed into, whether it is a tree, some species of animal or some combination of animals. DANCING YOUR ANIMAL is a little different, since although you know it will be an animal of some kind, you don't know which animal when you begin. But what exactly are you transformed into by means of the Psychological Gesture? The best answer is: *variations of the human soul.*

The 'soul,' traditionally, is what *animates* the body (since *anima* is the Latin word for soul). The body, in such a view, is 'inert' and in need of animation. But while we may not subscribe to this view in this form, most of us tend to think that it is our psychological (from *psyche* – the Greek word for soul) motivations in the form of our emotions and desires that *activate* us in various bodily – or necessarily embodied – ways. Michael Chekhov's Psychological Gesture, however, is based on a vitally important insight: *that body and soul form a loop.* It is not simply the case that bodily activation follows from psychological stimulus or cause, *but also the case that bodily action can give rise to psychological phenomena.*

Chekhov begins by saying that if you repeat some strong, simple gesture (well short of a PG) several times, you will notice that your will power increases as you do so, as an effect of the strength of your movement; in general, the stronger the movement, the more it increases the awareness of will. He then points out that the *kind* of movement you make in this way awakens a specific desire in you (Chekhov, 64). There is a third dimension here too, for the *quality* of a movement can arouse certain feelings in us. By the quality of a movement, he means that you can make a specific movement in, for example, a cautious or a confident way. As you do so, especially if you repeat it, you generate the psychological sensation of either caution or confidence in yourself (Chekhov, 58-9). I would add to this, however, that you must repeat the movement in the right way, with your consciousness always fully focused in it. Repetition must never be allowed to become mechanical.

You need to become as alert and sensitive as possible to the different kinds of psychological effects that a Psychological Gesture stirs in you, that is, to the way it arouses specific desires, moods and emotions.

METAMORPHOSIS AS PG

Once you feel you have acquired a strong inner sense of the power of Psychological Gestures, you should re-visit the earlier metamorphic exercises. In a way, both BEING A TREE 1 and BEING A TREE 2 *are* Psychological Gestures, each with very slow movement into the final posture, so perform these again while being as alert and sensitive as you have learned to be through practising the PG to the psychological effects that they stir in you.

As for the way you transformed yourself into various animals, including ANIMAL CONTRADICTIONS, you will need to adapt the process a little in order to experience it as a form of Psychological Gesture. Become the animal in the way that you did before, so that you are moving as that animal; then let yourself become still in a position – a posture – that seems to you to express that animal as fully as any static image can. Then stand normally and transform yourself into the animal in that posture in as smooth and as simple a way as possible, at an appropriate tempo. As you do this, observe its psychological effects on you. How does the structure of feeling that this creates differ from that which you experience in moving as the animal?

At the beginning of this discussion of the PG I briefly noted that there is one way of applying it that is 'metamorphic' in itself. This is what Chekhov calls the "Fantastic PG," which he refers to only in the Russian language version of his *On the Technique of Acting* (which was published four years later than the English version) where student actors are asked to find PGs not only for fantasy characters from myths and fairy tales but also for landscapes, buildings and plants. This shows clearly that treating the earlier metamorphic exercises as forms of the PG is perfectly consistent with Chekhov's own developed idea of the nature and value of the PG. But now let's extend the idea just a little further....

EXERCISE: STANDING STATUES

This exercise is derived from the actor training of Suzuki Tadashi (see Note in References, p. 201). For Suzuki, the trainee actor maintains a position in space, becoming different 'standing statues' in that position. In this version, quite differently, you must move around an open space freely, energetically and fairly quickly. Don't run, since this is too repetitively mechanical; vary your style of movement as much as possible as you move around the space (skipping, jogging, trotting, briskly walking… and in any other ways your body can imagine) – just make sure your energy level remains high.

Every so often, freeze. Become a STANDING STATUE. *Hold this for a few seconds, then continue moving in the same energetic, freestyle way.*

You should aim to freeze in the most precarious, unstable positions, positions that challenge gravity and are therefore difficult to hold. Be inventive and experimental. As you continue the exercise, try holding your statue-positions a little longer each time before moving on. This will be tiring!

After performing this exercise sufficiently to get a strong sense of it, compare it to the Psychological Gesture. If you've been inventive and experimental enough, you should notice that at least some, and perhaps many, of your standing statues are similar to the kinds of postures you might adopt in forming PGs. They are similar in that they are abstract, expressionistic and potentially archetypal as images. However, the postures you adopted in forming PGs were almost certainly much more stable, needing to be easier to hold. Moreover, in holding your statue-positions for as long as possible you were very probably not attentive to or aware of their psychological effects upon you. One obvious reason for this is that they presented you with the physical challenge of holding them, which became your focus. Another reason is that you adopted them suddenly; thus there was no sense of transformation.

However, it is possible to perform STANDING STATUES in exactly the same way physically, but with a different 'PG-style' psychological focus. In each of your standing statues (which should of course remain difficult), focus your entire attention of the psychological effects that it generates in you. Think of it as the product of the immediately preceding movement, so that there is movement into it, necessarily at high tempo.

Re-Imagining Your Body

Try it. Is it easier to perform with such a psychological, as against a purely physical, focus? It should be. It is generally true, in fact, that holding physically difficult positions becomes easier if we allow our psychology to harmonize with them or adapt to them. The physical difficulty of a position is at least partly the way our 'normal psychology' resists it.

At the start of Part Three I defined metamorphosis as "complete and utter transformation of the body". To this we must now add – *and with it the soul.*

For we are now fully in the world of myth.

In the old myths, of course, as in Kafka's story, it is the transformation of the soul that comes first and, in a sense, necessitates the transformation of the body. In this profoundly disturbing sense Niobe, Narcissus, Procne and Gregor Samsa all end up with *the body they deserve.* The deep wisdom contained in these stories is that the body is not a neutral 'container' for the soul. Under certain circumstances the body must reveal itself for what it truly is, the outer shape of the soul.

We will now explore another, very powerful way of becoming something other than yourself, or something other than your 'normal' self.

EMBRACING THE OTHER

EXERCISE: EMBRACE – BECOME - DANCE

This exercise is adapted from the *Butoh* dancer Takenouchi Atsushi's workshop practice "Embrace and Transform" (See Fraleigh and Nakamura, 129-133).

Sit and relax. Now recall or imagine embracing someone in a warm, loving (but non-sexual) way. What exactly do you feel in such an embrace? Provided the person you are embracing does not stiffen or hold back, but perfectly reciprocates the openness of your own embrace, do you not feel something of the essence of that person flowing into you?

It is a powerful feeling.

You are going to embrace something other than yourself, in order to take it inside yourself, in order to let it express itself through you. You will need an image of this thing. You can find the image before you stand up, or after. It can be something you see or have seen, or something you imagine. It might be the sea, a cloud, a stone, a tree, a flower, a stream, a bird, an insect... or it might be a human being, a wriggling child, a circus clown, a hunchback, a blind pianist, a frail old woman with dementia... whatever you want.

Stand in an easily upright (i.e. neither slouched nor rigid), grounded and fully centred posture. Your arms by your sides should be loose and relaxed, but also alive and alert. Close your eyes. Connect with your image, see it clearly in your 'mind's eye,' then let it go. Focus instead on the great depths inside you. Then, from your own deepest centre, begin the slow opening of your arms. Notice how your palms turn out and frontward, opening, receiving, as your arms float upwards and out to the sides. As this occurs imagine that you have many arms, all of them opening in the same way. As all your arms begin their slow sweep forward to gather something into you, let your image come vividly back into your mind. See it in front of you. As your arms reach out to it, let it grow bigger so that it seems to come towards you. It reciprocates! In front of your chest, bring your arms slowly together and towards you, gathering your image inside yourself, deep into your own being. You do not need to bring your hands into contact with your chest, for the embrace will feel complete well before this. Just let your arms relax and float downwards when you know that your image has entered into you.

Open your eyes. Feel your image inside you.

Then let the otherness inside you dance a few steps, whatever it wants – you make no choices.

I like to do this exercise several times in succession, with a different image in each case. What is crucial is that the short dance is wholly unpredictable. It should surprise you. In fact, I suggest dancing only a few steps precisely so that your 'usual self' doesn't get the chance to take over.

The 'dance of the other through you' should be surprising not just in that it is unpredictable, but also in that it is *not a mimetic representation of that other*. In the earlier metamorphic exercises it is important, of course, that you do not *simply imitate* (that is, in a purely external way) the animal or the tree. Instead, you have to find the animal or the tree inside yourself. Nonetheless, those exercises generate physical images, in the way your body is transformed, which, up to a point, correspond visually to and in that sense 'represent' what you have metamorphosed into. But in EMBRACE – BECOME – DANCE, the resulting short dance may well provide no visual clues to what the other is that is dancing through you.

This is liberating for you. You do not have to express the other – you simply let it express itself.

In the way the dance of the other surprises you, you will also be aware that the true nature of the other is there in the way it dances. There should always be, for you, a 'Yes!' – 'Yes! This is how a stone might dance,' or 'Yes! This is how a cloud might dance'. Even in the case of 'Yes! This is how a wriggling child... or a circus clown... or a frail old woman with dementia might dance,' there will be nothing *self-demonstrating* in the dance. The 'Yes!' will be your secret, unavailable to any onlooker.

I think that there is much of the spirit of *Butoh* in this exercise, as least in providing a starting-point for going beyond the more conventional types of dance to which *Butoh* is opposed. Notice above all that the procedure described is different from what we normally think of as 'improvisation'. When we improvise, in the usual sense of this word, our movements are not decided in advance (as they are when they are choreographed), but they are still self-chosen, self-decided, self-willed... (although in reality any *successful* improvisation tends to become 'autocatalytic' or self-generating). Here they come from beyond the self.

Butoh does not have the goal of promoting a 'beautiful' style of movement, at least not according to the usual sense of this term. Hence it does not need to extend or idealize the normal human body, which is the reason it does not need to impose movement patterns on the dancing body. Instead, it can let all movement emerge from within. The result can sometimes be 'ugly' – but in a way that challenges our conventional ideas of what is 'beautiful'.

Let's follow this idea a little, by going off at a tangent – in the direction of the *grotesque* – before returning to and extending the possibilities raised in EMBRACE – BECOME – DANCE.

PUTTING ON THE POUNDS – FOR FUN

The grotesque is the 'end point' of comedy. It's what comedy turns into when it takes you *beyond* laughter. It can be disturbing. And it's potentially very subversive. But it's not normally associated with the classical world. Maybe it should be.

Ancient Greece, of course, is known for many things, among them an idealization of the male body as represented in so many wonderful nude sculptures. However, starting around the year 630 BCE, a strange type of figure began to appear in the scenes painted on Greek vases, a type that continued to be depicted for a hundred years or so. These figures are male, squat, and awkwardly proportioned with protuberant buttocks and large belly. They appear to be dancing in an energetic way, with bottom slapping a common gesture. They are often associated with drinking wine and with a range of vulgar gestures or actions. Scholars refer to them as *komasts* (roughly speaking, 'revellers') or as *padded dancers* for there is evidence in a few vase paintings that the physical anti-ideal they embody was achieved by costuming. But beyond what is suggested by the images, we have little idea of what kind of ritual or other performance they were involved in. Still, these odd padded dancers almost certainly represent an important part of the pre-history of theatre in Ancient Greece, although we can only speculate about the (no doubt indirect) process that led from them to the creation of the Theatre of Dionysos in Ancient Athens around 530 BCE (Green).

What is especially interesting is the way that what they seem to represent has been rediscovered (or reinvented) in an influential branch of modern actor training, through the work of Jacques Lecoq. Among what he calls the main dramatic territories of tragedy, clowning, melodrama and Commedia dell'arte, Lecoq identifies a different one that is less well known, the dramatic territory of the *bouffon*, a strange theatrical being that seems to have much in common with the padded dancers of Ancient Greece.

In discussing Lecoq's work on this many prefer to retain the French *bouffon* because the English 'buffoon' has weakened in sense, to the point that it now suggests *idiocy* more than *jesting*. A *bouffon* is a kind of jester, not the 'court kind' who is specifically licensed to mock the king, but one of much wider social provenance and scope, able to mock anyone and everything. *Bouffons* are unfamiliar as a 'dramatic territory' because while all the other territories have remained alive and more or less 'well' in the theatre as such, true 'buffooning' has not. It seems rather to be pre-dramatic, as the Greek padded dancers were, or perhaps 'extra-dramatic' – in the sense of not containable or controllable by the institutions of the theatre.

Through his experimental work Lecoq discovered that *bouffons* are subtle, complex creatures, with many sides. Here I can only sketch in a little of their nature. Crucially, they are group or rather gang-oriented (whereas the court jester is an isolated, but dependant, individual). In this, they do not simply represent a *physical* anti-ideal, but along with it, a *social* anti-ideal. They mock society as a whole by inverting its values and trashing its rules and conventions. The key, however, lies in Lecoq's observation that the people who laugh at everything, mocking or scorning even sacred values, also generate an awareness of mystery (Lecoq, 126). For *bouffons* belong both to the society they mock and *elsewhere*. It is as though they are privy to another secret world, and this, presumably, is what lies behind the association (made by some scholars) of the Greek padded dancers with the god Dionysos, whose own haunt is often the wilder a-social places. For while the court jester is licensed to mock the king by the king himself, what is it that licenses the *bouffons* to mock society as a whole? It is not that society, but something else that lies beyond it. There is, thus, something in the *bouffon* that must be respected – as though they come from another, transcendent world. And yet... they remain wholly human, indeed 'all too human'.

Lecoq stresses that a performer cannot become a *bouffon* in her or his own body. The first and essential step in the transformation – the metamorphosis – is to acquire *a different body*. This is achieved with any kind of material inserted into one's clothes or tied on to one's given body, and it remains open to adjustment or change so that the new body never becomes 'fixed'.

The new body of the *bouffon* functions on two levels simultaneously. In the first place, it liberates the performer in a variety of ways. With a body radically other than their own, performers not only dare to do what they would not otherwise, but they also achieve what they otherwise could not (Lecoq, 125). In the second place, it makes the person being mocked more tolerant of – or more able to 'swallow' – the mockery. The *bouffon's* daring and the audience's greater tolerance are two sides of a coin, of course; only together do they explain why the *bouffon* can break all the rules.

You will surely have realized from all this that you cannot become a *bouffon* on your own, for what could you possibly do without an audience to mock? The transformation itself is fun, but the kind of fun that's far more fun when shared. Still, just thinking about all this may reveal something to you about the status of the human body. You need to ask, what is it, precisely, that needs to be *deformed*? And what is the *ideal* that must be inverted as an anti-ideal?

Another question arises at this point. In the Introduction, I introduced Chekhov's idea of 'imaginary bodies'. Is it possible, then, to become a *bouffon* by means of an imaginary body, that is, without actual padding or other physical modification? The answer is No. You can achieve this up to a point *for yourself,* but you cannot sufficiently achieve it *for others* to obtain the licence you need. Nonetheless your imagination must play an active role in the transformation. It is not enough to pad your clothes, however grotesque the result. You do not become a *bouffon* until you imagine that *the outer boundary of your padded body is your own skin.*

We have come a long way on this journey so far. Way back in the Introduction I talked about 'negative body-image' (pp. 5-8), and how to go beyond that problem. Well, here's another way to go beyond it – by accepting, even 'embracing,' the grotesque! I'm serious... well, in a way. For example, don't always feel you need to hold your belly in. Even so, the padded dancers were an anti-ideal, as I've said, which implies an ideal, and the Ancient Greeks certainly idealized the (male) body in much of their art. But what we really need to grasp here is the underlying linkage, the deep-rooted connection, between the grotesque and the beautiful. The next exercise is aimed at precisely this.

EXERCISE: BECOMING A 'BUTTERFLY'

Given the iconic status of the metamorphosis of a caterpillar into a butterfly, this, you might assume, ought to be an obvious or essential metamorphic exercise. Not at all! For one thing, it's far too easy to pretend to 'be' a butterfly in a trivial way. Why, all you have to do is imagine yourself very lightweight, up on the tips of your toes, ballerina-style, while waving your arms up and down!

To avoid such reductive absurdity, you are going to become a 'butterfly' *by becoming a human being* – a human being that emerges from a larva! (We'll skip the pupal stage.)

The reason that the metamorphosis of caterpillar into butterfly has such iconic status is that something *beautiful* emerges from something (comparatively) *grotesque.* Now, caterpillars are not truly 'grotesque' – at least, not compared to maggots. Still, we're not quite so wonder-struck by the transformation of a maggot into a bluebottle, are we? Perhaps the fly's relatively fat body 'echoes' the earlier stage too much? Perhaps what matters most is the 'dancing delicacy' of the butterfly...?

For your own transformation, the crucial thing is to become as grotesque as possible in your larval stage. So lie on the floor. Make sure your legs are together, 'joined' at the inner thighs, knees, ankles and feet. Similarly, your arms and hands are 'joined' to the sides of your torso, all the way down to your thighs. To complete your initial transformation into something like a worm, simply close your eyes. You are completely blind.

This is a kind of PG, although it's relatively difficult to achieve a 'smooth' movement into it. So notice the feelings it sets up inside you.

When you start moving, you will only be able to do so by some combination of rolling, twisting and undulating. All the while you must keep your legs joined together and your arms joined to your sides. You will be moving in search of food. You are blind, but you have a dominant sense of smell. You will simply move around, larva-like, trying to catch a whiff of something that will tell you which way to go. To do so, you will often 'rear' your head as high as possible.

Before you start moving, however, you have to complete your transformation into a larva. What I ask you to do next is the essential step.

It is also terrible to experience.

Imagine the features of your face being erased. Imagine your face becoming a kind of blank space.

(Did you know that the word 'larva' comes from the Latin for *mask?* The scientific name for the adult form is 'imago,' which means the *representative image* of a thing, that which it is truly like. A 'larva,' then, 'masks' or hides the true form. That is why I have just asked you to don a blank non-face mask in your imagination.)

Now start moving around.

At first you will feel very constricted and awkward. Keep moving, then, until your highly restricted condition comes to feel 'natural' to you. Only when you have achieved this can the metamorphosis begin.

Now lie still and begin to feel your limbs (your normal limbs, your arms and legs) 'budding' at the shoulders and hips. Imagine your limbs getting longer, growing outwards. Imagine separating them, your arms from your sides, your legs from each other, before you actually do so. Experience all this as inner movement before you let it turn into outer movement. The movement of your limbs will be small at first, but let it grow bigger, finally becoming a full stretching out.

This is the time to let your face come back. This should happen slowly and smoothly. Be as precise as possible in your imagination. In the end, open your eyes. This should recall WAKING FOR THE FIRST TIME (pp. 107-108) – but don't start to explore the new world around you. Simply let yourself be aware of it.

Now you can stand up. Once up, walk a few steps, feeling your limbs very relaxed. Finally, perform the 'archetypal gesture' (or simple PG) of OPENING (pp. 56-57).

The goal of this exercise is to discover the beauty of your developed human form by letting it emerge through metamorphosis from a grotesque kind of primal form. The 'ideal' emerges from, and was in a sense contained in, the anti-ideal. In experiencing this, you come to understand that the ideal that really matters for you as a human being is within the human form itself. It is not a particular, restricted version of that human form.

Because the emergence of the imago from the larva must be very 'easy,' the way you get up into a standing position is important. The movement needs to be economical, well-balanced and smooth.

EXPERIMENT 15: *It's a good idea to try out different ways of standing up from positions either lying or sitting on the floor. Through this, you discover that the more you can avoid any moment or phase of the process during which you need to work hard to avoid overbalancing, the more easily controlled the standing up feels and of course the better it looks. Ideally, all muscular effort should push upwards with little or none working 'sideways' (straining to keep you upright), for the latter always feels and looks awkward. Whether or not you achieve this will depend to a large extent on the precise position from which you begin to stand up, above all where your centre of gravity is in relation to your legs and feet.*

Upright posture was long regarded as distinctively human and even given theological significance in Judaeo-Christian thinking. What distinguished us from 'mere beasts' was the fact that we would naturally look towards heaven, though with our feet still on the ground. For some, upright posture was the image of God in Man. Whatever one's response to this, we should realize that the differences between quadrupedalism and bipedalism, both anatomically and functionally, are very great indeed, and that for this reason there is no simple consensus as to how and why upright posture evolved. During the 20th century, in fact, approximately thirty different hypotheses were put forward to explain it (Niemitz). Looked at in this light, it's maybe not surprising that standing up from a position on the floor can sometimes seem quite awkward! In doing it, after all, you're performing a kind of 'miracle'! (This is not as fanciful as it may seem. The main problem of explaining the evolution of fully upright posture lies in the many selective disadvantages that would arise in the transition to it. In standing up you are also 'transitioning' and thereby experiencing some of these disadvantages, such as increased stress on certain joints.)

That's merely standing on your own two feet, by the way. Actually walking on them is yet another marvel!

I said at the beginning of Part Three that I would return to the question of why you should do the metamorphic exercises (giving only the provisional answer, 'Because you can,' at that point). The reason is this: doing the metamorphic exercises helps you fully discover....

THE BODY AS POSSIBILITY

For much of western history, the body has been conceived of and experienced *as a limitation*. The 'body as possibility' is fundamentally opposed to this, but it does not imply, of course, that we can avoid weakness, incapacity, sickness and death (though we may minimize some and put others off for a time). It implies, rather, that our physical being is perfectly good enough for the expression of our spiritual being. In other words, our physical being is not some kind of brick wall against which we're always knocking our spiritual heads.

If you've explored the exercises in this book through to this point, you'll have a strong sense of the *body as possibility*, which implies the body as perfect *receptivity*. So let's go just one, final step further here, to let the body attain its full receptivity.

THE PLACE IS DANCING

In "A Note on Butoh Body," Kasai Toshiharu attributes the following insight to the German philosopher Rolf Elberfeld: "In *Butoh* dance, not the dancer as subject is dancing, the place itself is dancing and the dancer will be created by the place in which he is dancing" (Kasai (2000)).

This is an extraordinarily suggestive statement. In order to begin to understand what it means, first note the following. The last exercise introduced in Part One (immediately before the Start the Day Sequence) was Chekov's RECEIVING (p. 76). In this you let all the details of the scene before and around you enter into you, receiving them as a gift. The last exercise in Part Two was HOW CAN WE KNOW THE WALKER FROM THE WALK? (pp. 135-138). In this, you take the principle involved in RECEIVING a stage further; as you let the walk walk you, you become free to notice, observe and thus to receive everything around you. We are now at the end of Part Three. The present exercise will take this principle even further, as well as extending the core idea of EMBRACE – BECOME – DANCE above.

In fact I need to refer once again to Yeats's famous rhetorical question – *How can we know the dancer from the dance?* – as I did at the end of Part Two. Note then that there is no reference to the *place* in which the dance is danced in this question, only to the dancer and the dance. We might interpret Yeats's words metaphorically or even allegorically: the 'dancer' is the body while the 'dance' is the soul (or perhaps the mind), but it might equally be the other way round – and this, after all, is the point that Yeats is making. But although such an interpretation is valid, it is important also to see that the words *really are about dance*. They are about dance in the sense that dance is a heightened state of being in which the subject-object dichotomy is (temporarily) resolved.

Normally we would say that the dancer dances the dance, for this is the formulation that best captures our deep-rooted Western belief that voluntary action is initiated by an autonomous agent. The crucial step (which follows from Yeats's insight) is to see that *it must also be true that the dance dances the dancer*. In the first formulation, the dancer brings the dance into existence. In the second, the dance brings the dancer into existence – *as a dancing dancer*, of course.

But the latter formulation gives rise to a further question: where does the dance that dances the dancer, thereby bringing the dancer into existence, come from?

Suppose you dance to music. It's reasonable, isn't it, to see the dance as being born in the music, as flowing *from* the music and *through* you, or to see the music as taking on the form of your body. Well, then, to let the place dance through you, you must let the *place in which you dance be as music*.

But what does that mean?

Re-Imagining Your Body

When, earlier in Part Three, you were asked to metamorphose into different animals, I said that you needed to find the animal already in yourself. I also said that you needed to observe real animals, necessarily outside yourself. In other words, you needed to find the connection between something inside you and something outside you. This is, in fact, a very general principle. When, in Part Two (p. 115), I suggested that you listen to music – which, after all, originates outside you – as if it were playing inside you, I was invoking the same principle. This principle arises also, more or less obviously, at many other points in this book. But we must now see where it leads.

"We are the world that thinks itself.... The world is at the heart of our flesh" said Maurice Merleau-Ponty in his last, unfinished work, *The Visible and the Invisible* (Merleau-Ponty, 136). It is (initially) a strange idea, contrasting strongly with our received scientific wisdom. What it implies is that I am also in the things I see and touch, and the things I see and touch are also in me. But there is nothing 'mystical' in this. It is an attempt to capture a lived intuition that is profoundly obscured by our habitual use of language. To put it in other words, it is an attempt to capture, in a language hardly adequate for it, *the experience of being alive*. This experience has at its core the sense that there is a deep continuity, a oneness or equivalence, between ourselves as sentient beings and the world as it is knowable by our senses. Hence it is ultimately misguided to divide these into subject and object, as though an ontological gulf lies between them. Put differently, the 'seer' (the part of us that sees) is not *in* the body and the body is not *in* the world, although this is the usual 'Matryoshka-doll' conception. The seer *is also* the body and the body *is also* the world.

EXERCISE: BEING CREATED

("The dancer will be created by the place in which he is dancing" – remember?)

So if I say, in what is fairly conventional language, 'Go to a place, a place that means something to you... become receptive... let the place enter into you,' I can now be understood as saying, 'Go to a place... realize that the place you are in is also necessarily inside you'.

To do this, you simply have to switch off what I shall call your myth of self.

'Simply'?

Why, yes. Switching off your 'myth of self' is one of those things that you realize was very simple once you have done it, however difficult it may have appeared before you did it.

Your 'myth of self' is the sense of a self standing in opposition to the world, as against wholly within the world. This myth is the inevitable product of faith in the 'conscious controller' and of its attendant instrumental view of the body.

Nonetheless I cannot put the next steps in letting the place dance through you into words.

In this sense they are *up to you*.

In another sense they are not 'up to you' at all, but up to the place you are in...

... which is inside you.

APPENDIX 1

A SHORT HISTORY OF WESTERN DUALISM

PRELIMINARY NOTE: This and Appendix 2 are intended for those with an interest in the philosophical and scientific context of *re-imagining your body*.

If you're one of those, you will find many more related thoughts and ideas (as well as other things) at:

https://www.re-imaginingyourbody.com

APPENDIX 1: A SHORT HISTORY OF WESTERN DUALISM

Many of the ideas that our culture takes for granted and even treats as 'common sense,' have their roots in the earlier thinking of philosophers. This is especially true of ideas about what it is to be human. Strikingly, the human body has been accorded little role in this. In fact, the human body has had a raw deal philosophically; in its supposed difference from the soul or the spirit or the mind, it has found itself downgraded in many ways. It has been seen as a mere vehicle or tool, an encumbrance or burden or limitation, a temporary residence, even a prison. In the scientific age there has been too much tendency to see the body as an assemblage of (grantedly remarkable) parts. As a result, scientific questioning of vague immaterial entities like soul and spirit, even mind, has done little to undermine the tenacious assumption that the *self* is distinct and different from the (relatively mechanical) body. This assumption has deep roots, which we need to unearth. It's worth noting here, though, that our concept of self is quite recent. The idea of the self *as a private entity within* but at the same time *identical with* the person, providing both a sense of unity to that person's experience and of identity through time, only reached its fully recognizable form in the late seventeenth century. But its imagined distinction from the body rests on much that came before, so in digging up those roots we'll need to go back a lot further in time.

What I have just described is a Western view of the body and of the self's relation to it. This Western view is not static or fixed; it has evolved over time and continues to evolve. The problem is that throughout its evolution it has been *dualistic* – that is, it has set up a structure of understanding by differentiating one kind of thing from another kind of thing rather than by seeking out their unity. Here I will sketch out a simplified three-part history of this process, one in which the dualism is first expressed in terms of *body and soul*, then in terms of *body and mind*, and finally in the odd terms of *body and brain* (odd because the brain is itself a bodily organ). As will be seen, *plus ça change, plus c'est la même chose*.

1. The Fallen Body

For Medieval Christianity, the body was commonly seen as the soul's prison-house. The soul finds itself confined in the mortal body rather like a bird in a cage, until the death of the body sets the soul free. The body, of course, is also God's creation, just like the soul. But the body is not only mortal, it is also corrupted as a consequence of the Fall from Paradise, which was precipitated by eating the forbidden fruit of the Tree of Knowledge. The soul, in contrast, is immortal and although it may be *inclined* to vice and depravity as a consequence of inheriting that original sin of Adam and Eve, nonetheless it remains free to choose virtue rather than sin.[1]

The idea of the soul being imprisoned in the body originates in the pre-Christian writings of the Greek philosopher Plato (428/7 – 348/7 BCE), in particular in his *Phaedo*, and was carried over into the Middle Ages by the Neo-Platonists. In this view the soul is necessarily a *substance* (which here roughly means a 'thing' rather than an attribute or an event or a concept), since it survives the death of the body. Thus it is not merely the principle of animation of the body. Its three principal faculties (abilities or powers) are reason, consciousness and the power of deliberate moral decision. Of these, the second does not refer to our immediate apprehension of the world by means of the (bodily) senses, but to a supposed 'higher level' of consciousness at which comprehension and understanding take place.

Later, from the thirteenth century onwards, a much more sophisticated account of the body's relation to the soul was developed on the basis of the ideas of Aristotle (384 – 322 BCE), for whom the soul was not a substance at all, but something like an 'organizing principle' which gave shape and specificity to the body's potential.[2]

---

[1] There were many disputes among early Christians about the precise nature of 'original sin' (some of which resurfaced in the Reformation), which turned on the question of the respective weights to be given to free will and God's grace, including the role played in the latter by baptism. I have given a rough outline of what became the prevailing view in the Catholic Church.

[2] Since this is a relatively difficult (or at least unfamiliar) idea, I summarize Peter Hacker's very useful account of it here. The usual translation of the Aristotelian concept of the psyche [*psuchē*] is 'soul,' but this is misleading for

178

But this could not displace the Platonic account, which was far too convenient for preaching purposes. The body was usefully seen as sinful and corrupted, and in need of discipline and restriction in order to allow the soul imprisoned within it (and sometimes sorely tested by it) to commune with God. The Aristotelian view, in other words, was less conducive to social control, and best left to a few intellectuals.

Even so, it should be obvious that the Platonic idea of body and soul being radically different things (although tied together by the soul's temporary residence in the body) is a drastic oversimplification of our lived experience. While some of the things we experience such as the appetites (hunger, thirst, lust…) or kinds of physical suffering are clearly of the body, what of the passions such as hope, fear, joy or sorrow? In feeling these, is the soul engaged, or the body, or some coalition of both? Such problems were certainly raised in the late Middle Ages and early Renaissance, in ways that might have led to new insights. Unfortunately, in the early modern age the inherent dualism of the Platonic view was given a new lease of life by Descartes.

2. The Invention of 'Subjectivity'

Very few modern philosophers have been as influential as René Descartes (1596–1650). By the 'method of doubt' (which simply means doubting every proposition that can be doubted), Descartes arrived at his one certain, i.e. undoubtable, proposition: *Cogito ergo sum*: I think – or, more generally, I have mental life in the form of subjective experiences – therefore I am. We might gloss this as, *I have a mind,*

---

the English term has entirely different associations. For Aristotle, the psyche is not a theological or spiritual concept, nor even a psychological one. It is biological. All living beings have a psyche, plants as well as animals, for the psyche is that which makes the living being what it is. It is, in other words, the source of the distinctive attributes and qualities of the living being and of what might be called its specific 'life potential'. Thus the psyche of a plant is what determines its manner of growth and its specific capacities to feed and reproduce itself. The psyche of an animal includes these powers but adds to them specific capacities to move in and to perceive the world. The psyche of a human being includes all these along with the powers of rational thought and free will. Nevertheless in spite of this biological focus, in some works Aristotle argued that the human 'rational soul' was immortal, a position that Hacker describes as "not obviously coherent". (*Human Nature: The Categorial Framework*, 22-3.)

therefore I am. Notice that this serves to identify sense of self (for the modern sense of self was beginning to take shape in Descartes' time) with the (conscious) mind, since I become aware of my existence in and through my awareness of my thinking, or more generally my subjective experience. It is not far short of the claim that *I am my mind* (where 'mind' implies conscious mind). Since my mind exists (as it must, since I think), then I exist.

Descartes went on to distinguish between the *res extensa* – the material world in which objects have extension in space – and the *res cogitans* – the mental world in which 'things' such as thoughts do not have any extension in space. For Descartes, these are different domains of being. If you like, they comprise entirely different kinds of 'stuff'. The human body belongs to the *res extensa*. The human mind, by definition, belongs to the *res cogitans*. Body and mind are therefore radically different types of thing. This is *Cartesian dualism.*

Many people will either be unaware of the Latin terms *res extensa* and *res cogitans* or will think of them as abstruse and philosophically technical. Yet the vast majority of people today take for granted a distinction that is intimately related, the distinction between *objectivity* and *subjectivity* – not, however, in the secondary sense which has arisen largely in consequence of the successes of science, which is that of 'impartiality' vs. 'personal bias,' but in the original sense of 'concerning the outer world' vs. 'concerning the inner world'. In a strong sense, Descartes *invented subjectivity* when he wrote, "Thought is a word which covers everything that exists in us in such a way that we are immediately conscious of it".[3] Prior to this, thought was conceived as rational thought, something wholly distinct from the sense experience which was *of the body.* By bringing rational thought under the same umbrella not only as sense experience but also imagination, Descartes created what Richard Rorty has called an "inner arena,"[4] thus setting up not only the modern sense of 'mind' but also the basis for the modern sense of 'self'.

In other words, before Descartes, people didn't experience their 'minds' in the way we do. They didn't experience themselves as having an *inner empty space* within which thoughts, ideas, images and sensations would all keep appearing with such frequency and variety that the inner empty space was never quite experienced as empty!

---

[3] *Philosophical Works*, vol. 2, 52

[4] *Philosophy and the Mirror of Nature* (1979), p. 50

The absolute separation of domains between *res extensa* and *res cogitans* entails great difficulties, which Descartes was not unaware of. The basic problem is that these separate domains must also interact in some way. In 1643, in a letter to Descartes, Princess Elisabeth of Bohemia put the following crucial question: given that the mind (or soul, as she more quaintly expressed it) is an entirely different kind of thing than the body, being only a thinking substance without extension, how can it affect the body, for example in bringing about voluntary actions? In his initial response Descartes confesses to having left this question largely unaddressed until now, since his concern had been to stress the mind's (soul's) distinctness from the body and any discussion of their interaction might have "clouded the issue". And indeed it does, as the subsequent correspondence demonstrates. Pressed by Elisabeth (with a self-deprecating politeness that seems – today – like irony), Descartes falls back on the claim that the union of mind and body is something we 'know' by experience, but cannot properly think about, whereas the distinction between them is what is evident to rational thought. Moreover, "it seems to me," he writes, "that the human mind can't conceive the soul's distinctness from the body and its union with the body, conceiving them very clearly and at the same time. This is because this requires one to conceive them as one single thing and at the same time as two things, which is contradictory."[5]

Given these difficulties, and given the way that Descartes seems to admit here that mind and body are *not only two things but also one thing*, it is all the more striking that Cartesian dualism came to dominate intellectual life in Europe to such an extent that it has permeated deep into our structures of 'common sense'. This is largely because the dualism – the 'two different things' – that he focused and insisted on seems so much more clear-cut (provided we ignore the problem of their interaction) than the alternative 'one single thing'. Indeed, it allowed Descartes to take such a reductive view of the body that it appeared to him to be merely mechanical, as can be seen from this almost shocking passage from his Second Meditation:

> Well, the first thought to come to mind was that I had a face, hands, arms, and the whole mechanical structure of limbs which can be seen in a corpse, and which I called the body.... [B]y a body I understand whatever has determinable shape and definable location and can occupy a space in such a way as to exclude any

---

[5] Correspondence between Descartes and Princess Elisabeth.

other body; it can be perceived by touch, sight, hearing, taste or smell, and can be moved in various ways, not by itself but by whatever comes in contact with it. For, according to my judgement, the power of self-movement, like the power of sensation or thought, was quite foreign to the nature of a body; indeed, it was a source of wonder to me that certain bodies were found to contain faculties of this kind.[6]

For Descartes, thus, in his insistence on the radical distinction between body and mind, there is no fundamental difference not only between a living body and a corpse, but also between a living body and any inanimate object (other than its degree of mechanical complexity). Crucially, bodies do not even move themselves. Animals, he believed, are mere machines (presumably having been 'wound up' in advance by God), while true self-movement (involving choice) occurs only in human beings as a result of the (entirely unexplained) power of the mind over the body.

3. Grey Matter… and its 'Life Support System'

Cartesian dualism is often criticized these days on account of its implication that mind occupies a different terrain of non-physical reality (the *res cogitans*) and is therefore irreducible to body. Natural science cannot accept this: for science, everything we mean by 'mind' must be explicable at the level of the brain. Neuroscientists working on this problem – or more accurately on any of the sub-problems it is made up of – do not consider themselves as dualists, therefore, but as monists (the technical term for those who believe there is only one kind of reality). But as Peter Hacker points out, they often then go on to attribute to the *brain* all those things, such as thinking, having experiences and willing actions, that were once thought to be primary characteristics of mind, thus preserving the essence of the dualism more or less intact. Hacker stresses that it *makes no sense* to attribute thinking, reasoning, calculating, believing, fearing, hoping and such like to the brain, although this is very much the default position among neuroscientists these days, since the brain is not the person and not the human being, and only persons or human beings can be legitimately said to engage in such processes or activities.[7] At its crudest, in fact, neuroscience (or at least 'populist neuroscience')

---

[6] *The Philosophical Writings of Descartes*, vol. II, 17-18.
[7] James Harvey. "Hacker's Challenge." Interview with Peter Hacker.

promotes the grossly reductive idea that *I am my brain*.[8] With this, we arrive smack back at a dualism in which the 'body' is now so conceptually distinct from the brain as to become its 'prison house' (again)! Do I exaggerate? Well, the soul once longed to escape the body and go to heaven, presumably a very pleasant place, while the best the modern brain can aspire to is a transplant to a younger body or, failing that, long term preservation in a vat or freezer. Apart from that, no, I don't!

None of this is to say that the brain is not a most remarkable organ and that a great deal of our behaviour and our experience is strongly shaped by it. Notice, however, that I avoided the word 'determined' in the preceding sentence, opting for 'strongly shaped' instead. This is because full understanding of the determination of our behaviour and experience must surely also take account of other factors too. After all, it is well known that brain architecture is highly plastic in the sense that it restructures itself in response to sufficiently strong environmental stimuli and to physical trauma. Hence (if I may contrive the following peculiar and mixed metaphor), if and when we truly understand this complex determination we will certainly find the brain 'at the heart' of it – but not as a solo act.

There are, of course, also some good old-fashioned economic interests behind current hyping the brain. Just as during the 1980s and 1990s we were constantly informed that decoding the human genome would lead to cures for all manner of diseases, nowadays among the most strident sales pitches from scientists looking for funding for research is that neuroscience is on the point of explaining pretty much everything there is to know about being human. That's both intellectually arrogant and intellectually lazy, but even so, something a bit more insidious underlies what's going on here. It's the fact that as a culture we don't know how to think about *the body as a whole* – though there are signs that this is changing (for example in

---

[8] Still, there are some differences between the claims 'I am my (conscious) mind' and 'I am my brain'. Neuroscientists are very fond of pointing out how the brain frequently bypasses consciousness, to the extent that even free will (which is presumed a conscious process) is supposedly put in serious question. Thus the shift in equations from 'mind = self' to 'brain = self' necessarily also entails some shift in the meaning of 'self'. But the older sense of self tenaciously clings on, which often leads neuroscientists into some conceptual muddles, such as appear in a statement like 'We are not who we think we are' – where the 'we' in the middle is very problematic indeed.

conventional medicine with its growing sense of holism). Above all, we don't know how to think about the body as the kind of whole that is greater than the sum of its parts (as I stressed in the Introduction).

Only in such a context could the brain come to be mistaken for the self.

It's true that a 'self' must be located in a body. It's true that various bits of body can be removed without loss of self. But there's clearly a limit to any such amputation and/or excision process and that limit is not one in which the brain can stand alone. That is, whatever a self is, it would be lost well before everything but the brain had been removed, even given the technology to keep the brain functioning throughout. Crucially, in imagining the piecemeal removal of parts, we should see that, for a self to persist, the remaining body must continue to be a functioning whole, a totality of some sort, which is to say a viable organism (albeit one whose viability may need some technological support – a mechanized wheelchair, regular dialysis, a voice production machine...). In short, *the integrity of the body* is a precondition of the sense of self.

Still, it's easy enough to imagine an objection to this argument, along the following lines: "Sorry, but the idea of a physical brain transplant, as a way of preserving the self, is old hat. It's true (IMHO) that the brain contains the self, or the person, or the personality... whatever we choose to call it (or them?). But it does so in exactly the way that a computer contains software and data. Admittedly the brain is a vastly more complex computer than any we've built so far, but one day it will be possible to download a human mind onto a computer or even transfer it to another brain. So, you see, it's just not true that a 'self' must be located in a body, as you claimed."

Here, it seems, we have yet another dualism: hardware vs. software, or processor vs. information. But this is really a transcription of the old mind/body dualism, with 'body' now just the brain as hardware or processor. What the idea assumes is that somehow the mind (or self, or person, or personality) exists in the set of all connections among neurons in the brain, which neuroscientist Ken Hayworth has dubbed the 'connectome'. As Hayworth puts it, "[i]n the same sense that my computer is really just the ones and zeros on my hard drive, and I don't care what happens as long as those ones and zeros make it to the next computer, it should be the same thing with me".[9]

---

[9] "The Immortalist: Uploading a Mind to a Computer".

What's wrong with this? It's not the practical problem, the sheer complexity of those neural connections (86 billion neurons with 100 trillion variably-strong connections between them), brain-boggling though that complexity is. What's wrong with it is that it's a metaphor. To be more accurate, what's wrong with it is that it's a metaphor being (mis)taken for reality – for there's nothing wrong with metaphors in themselves. Still, science has a history of mistaking metaphors for reality. Nowadays, everything is seen as information-processing, a metaphor rooted in digital computing. Previously everything, from the cosmos itself to living creatures, was seen as mechanical, a metaphor rooted in the ingenious wheeled and geared machines of human invention. Before that, the dominant metaphor was that of a hydraulic system, which was used to explain human psychology and physiology, among other things. Human beings, it seems, narcissistically try to understand themselves and the world in the image of their own latest technology. Unfortunately, they often don't realize that that's all they're doing.

That the brain is a kind of computer may be an intellectually seductive idea to many, but it's just an assumption – there's no hard evidence for it. Among the neuroscientific community there is, in fact, a minority view that strongly contests this assumption. In this 'anti-representational' view, the brain is fundamentally unlike a computer in that it does not store 'representations' of the world, hence it cannot perform computations on representations that don't exist. Instead the brain *directly interacts* with the world, or more precisely with the information about the world it receives from it.[10] In this view, the brain can only directly interact with the world in its embodied state as part of the organism. Hence the title of Anthony Chemero's 2009 book, *Radically Embodied Cognitive Science*. A very clear statement of this minority view is made by Andrew D. Wilson and Sabrina Golonska in their 2013 paper "Embodied cognition is not what you think it is," where they write:

> Embodiment is the surprisingly radical hypothesis that the brain is not the sole cognitive resource we have available to us to solve problems. Our bodies and their perceptually guided motions through the world do much of the work required to achieve our goals, *replacing* the need for complex internal mental representations. This simple fact utterly changes our idea of what

---

[10] Thus the baby of information is not thrown out with the bathwater of the brain-as-computer.

"cognition" involves, and thus embodiment is not simply another factor acting on an otherwise disembodied cognitive processes [sic].[11]

On this ground, then, I repeat what I said before: 'whatever a self is, it would be lost *well before* everything but the brain had been removed, even given the technology to keep the brain functioning throughout'. It would be lost precisely as the brain's body-dependent ability to interact directly with the world became lost.[12]

Beyond dualism...

As can readily be seen from this brief history, the body has consistently been devalued within the dualisms within which it has been located. It is not that we need a 'better dualism,' however, one in which the body is no longer the inferior partner. Rather, we need to go beyond dualism, for it is dualism itself that functions to rob the body of much that is truly the body's own. In saying this, I am referring to what, in the Introduction, I called the 'body as subject'. The 'body as subject' is also called the 'lived body' or the 'I-body'. It is the body as experienced by the person whose body it is. To me, the 'body as subject,' or subject-body, is also the *true body*. This is because the alternative 'body as object' only really exists for anatomy! That is, when we see another person's body, *on the whole* we see it as their subject-body rather than as an object-body. In effect this is simply to say that we don't see another's body as we would a 'moving statue' or robot. I emphasize 'on the whole' because of course objectification also happens – but it's the exception that proves the rule.[13]

---

[11] What Wilson and Golonska are stressing here is a sense of 'embodiment' that goes way beyond the relatively commonplace idea that states of the body can affect states of mind.

[12] For a polemical rejection of the 'representational' view aimed at the lay reader, see "The Brain is Not a Computer" by Robert Epstein.

[13] Objectification may even be quite widespread, but the fact that people (especially women who suffer from it most) object to it surely proves my point. Note this also: the way we see our own body in the mirror is not quite the same as the way we see another person's body. We see the other's subject-body as a kind of 'possibility cum enigma,' insofar as the other's subjectivity, while it is evident, exists beyond us. But we see our own reflected body more as an object because our subjectivity remains in the place we are looking from and thus our reflection *cannot truly look back at us*

The intrinsic problem of dualism is the way it tends to siphon the 'subject' from the body.

In order to go beyond dualism, we first need to get as full a conception of the 'body as subject' as we can. We need to see that the subject-body itself exists along something like a spectrum. At one end of this spectrum the experience of the subject-body is strongly interfered with, maybe even distorted by, what I shall call 'intimations of the object-body'. At the other end of the spectrum no such interference takes place. Such a pure experience of the subject-body is, I believe, what Ichikawa Hiroshi means by *the body as spirit*, as this can be experienced or lived. Drawing on a very different Japanese tradition of thinking about the body, for Ichikawa the underlying reality of the body is that it is *both body and spirit*, such that 'body' and 'spirit' are mere abstractions from it, conceptual tools that we use for certain purposes in specific contexts:

> Both the concepts 'spirit' and 'body' are kinds of extremes (i.e. concepts abstracted) used as clues for understanding life. For the most part our concrete life is spent within a structure that cannot be reduced either to the spirit or the body. Hence it is wrong to see the spirit and the body as two existential principles, and to grasp reality in their intersection and separation. Rather, we should consider the unique structure as itself fundamental, and regard the spirit and the body as aspects abstracted from it.[14]

For Ichikawa, our experience of ourselves tends to the body-as-spirit (even if we don't understand it as such) the more we experience what he calls *unity*. Conversely, the lower the experience of unity, the more we tend to experience the body-as-body; this is evident, for example, when we feel pain, which draws our attention to a certain body part or area. This body-as-body, being experienced as such, remains the subject-body (pain is a subjective sensation, after all), but one which is experienced as split or divided or 'separable' or compartmentalized in some way. Thus, on the one hand, unity refers to the body as a whole (a whole which is greater than the sum of its parts, as I have stressed before), rather than an assemblage of distinct organs or

---

as the other's body can. This is why I stressed in the Introduction that the body-in-the-mirror is an object-body (p. 5).

[14] *Seishin toshite no Shintai* (*The Body as Spirit*), 1991: 4. Quoted by Chikako Ozawa-De Silva in "Beyond the Body/Mind? Japanese Contemporary Thinkers on Alternative Sociologies of the Body".

'bits,' while on the other, it echoes Descartes' idea of the *union* of body and soul as expressed in his letters to Elisabeth, which I referred to above.

Descartes' fundamental mistake, we can now say, lay in seeing soul (or mind) and body as distinctive *things* rather than as abstracted aspects of the *same thing*.

APPENDIX 2

'THE BODY WITHIN THE BODY' A POSSIBLE EXPLANATION OF HOW THE EXERCISES IN *RE-IMAGING YOUR BODY* WORK

APPENDIX 2: 'THE BODY WITHIN THE BODY' – A POSSIBLE EXPLANATION OF HOW THE EXERCISES IN *RE-IMAGINING YOUR BODY* WORK

For some people so-called 'out of body experiences' might be evidence that the self – or spirit – is distinct from the body that normally serves to 'house' it. But since out of body experiences can be produced by stimulating a certain area of the brain, it is presumably not the case that the spirit – or self – really does leave the body. Such experiences can also be induced by sensory deprivation, though not necessarily as experiences of the kind in which one seems to float above one's body looking down on it. More generally, your normal sense of self-location (both of being in a body and of that body's location in space) is tied to sensory experience, both of the external world in which your body is located (the world as it were 'around you') and of your body itself (internal somatic awareness and feeling). Astronauts experiencing weightlessness have sometimes reported the strange experience of no longer seeming to have legs, nor even occasionally arms, due to the complete relaxation of the limbs themselves and the lack of any gravity-induced pressure against an external surface. Normally, of course, we are not only aware of being inside our bodies but of being inside them in such a way that the whole of the body is experienced as being ours (even if we then conceive the self as more locally centred 'in the head'). Scientists have come to refer to this as our sense of *body ownership* – a term I dislike because of the way it implies that something other than the body (presumably the self) owns and possesses the body. Nevertheless I shall continue to use it here, scare quoted, for convenience.

Normal sense of 'body ownership' breaks down not just in out of body experiences, but also where amputees (and some others, such as paraplegics) experience 'phantom limbs,' in the strange condition known as *xenomelia* ('foreign limb syndrome' – which used to be called 'Body Integrity Identity Disorder' – in which a person strongly believes that they can only complete themselves by the amputation of a healthy limb), and in a range of 'Body Ownership Illusions' which can be induced in healthy individuals. Research in these areas has yet to produce a clear consensus as to how a normal sense of 'body ownership' arises, but it has led to some fascinating results. I will review a few of these here because of the light they throw on the complex interconnectedness of the psychological and the physiological, and thus the possible explanation they suggest of how the exercises in *Re-Imagining Your Body* work.

One debate concerns whether our normal sense of 'body ownership' arises simply as a result of the perceived synchronization of a range of sensory data or whether it rests also on a kind of internal 'map' or 'model' of the body. In one form of the 'Rubber Hand Illusion,' the subject's real hand is hidden from her view and replaced by a visible rubber hand at roughly the appropriate distance from her; one finger of her hidden real hand is then stroked while, at precisely the same time, she sees the corresponding finger of the rubber hand being stroked. As a result, it is common for the subject to experience the illusion that the rubber hand is her own hand, while, most interestingly, the brain also 'winds down' its electrical connection to the real hand. Here, the simple coincidence of visual and tactile information generates the illusion, but two other points are noteworthy; 1) the rubber hand looks just like a real hand, and 2) it is placed at roughly the same distance from the subject that her real hand would or could be. Thus the generation of the illusion might well rely on the existence of an internal map or model of the body. However, in other experiments subjects have been induced to experience non-corporeal objects such as virtual balloons and virtual squares as being extensions or parts of their own bodies, when these objects are made subject to their control in the same way that their hand is subject to their control. Nonetheless the spatial positioning of the virtual object has some effect upon the illusion; if it is placed further away from the subject than a part of the subject's real body might realistically be, the illusion is significantly less likely to arise.[15] It does not follow from this that there is no internal map or model of the body, but it may imply that any such map or model is not a simple mental duplicate of the real body and that it is transformable.

Phantom limbs have been studied for centuries, largely because they are quite commonly a source of pain (and over those centuries the battlefields have supplied enough examples). A simple 'mechanistic' view of the body would assume that such pain is

---

[15] Ke Ma and Bernhard Hommel, "Body-ownership for actively operated non-corporeal objects."

generated in the traumatized severed nerve endings of the stump, although it is mentally interpreted by the sufferer as arising within the phantom limb. However, attempts to treat the pain based on this assumption have been relatively ineffective. Notably, however, a person may temporarily relieve a cramp in a phantom hand for themselves by opening and stretching their phantom fingers. What exactly is going on here? When a patient moves a phantom limb, there is observable activity in the stump muscles and this activity varies depending on the precise movement of the phantom limb that is being made. It has also been demonstrated that movements of a phantom limb are not simply 'imagined' (that is, merely visualized), since patients are capable of doing this as well and differences between imagined and real movement of the phantom limb can be precisely measured.[16] But perhaps the most striking finding is that patients can learn to carry out 'impossible' movements of the phantom limb! In a 2009 study, some patients succeeded in learning how to carry out a movement of their phantom wrist which would not be possible with a real wrist. An entirely unexpected consequence was that some of these patients subsequently reported increased difficulty in executing certain movements of the phantom arm that had previously been quite easy.[17] One plausible interpretation of this is that any internal map or model of the body can be re-drawn or re-constructed; in this case, the transformation of the map or model required to make the impossible movement possible also made previously simple movements more difficult.

How then should we conceive this internal map or model?

One of the authors of the 'impossible movement' study, Peter Brugger, says this in a different but related context:

> [W]e often forget that everybody with a regular and intact body also has phantom limbs – we just remain unaware of their presence, because we do not separate them from the everyday flesh-and-bone experience of our limbs. We can gain glimpses of their existence during experimental procedures that separate the body-in-flesh

---

[16] Karen Reilly, "The moving phantom. Motor execution or motor imagery." I should note here that the sense of an 'imagined' movement in this context is relatively weak. It is roughly equivalent to 'thinking of' that movement. There is a stronger sense in which one can 'live' a movement by imagining it, as in 'inner movement'.

[17] Lorimer Moseley, "Amputees learn a physiologically impossible movement of their phantom limb."

from the body-in-mind, notably the rubber hand illusion, vibratory myesthetic illusions or less comfortable techniques such as pressure cuff anaesthesia.[18]

It might be more appropriate then to think not so much of an internal map or model of the body as of a 'phantom body' that we all possess. But this 'phantom body' is not neurologically fixed, as we have seen. It is not a hard-wired 'ideal body' along the lines of Leonardo's Vitruvian Man; rather, it is plastic, malleable, adaptable. (Nonetheless certain social and cultural ideals may play a part in it – see the discussion of psychoanalysis below.) It is obviously true that a person with a real wrist cannot learn to perform the impossible movement that some amputees did, and to that extent our (normal) 'phantom body' is constrained by our anatomy. Nonetheless the 'Body Ownership Illusions' of experiencing virtual balloons or virtual squares becoming parts of one's own body suggest that, within certain limits, the human brain is adept at varying the phantom body. Moreover, the 'impossible movement' study shows that variations and adaptations of the phantom body can be self-induced, via the power of imagination,[19] and hence that manipulation of sensory input and feedback is not essential.

Many of the exercises in this book can now be seen as exercises *of the normal phantom body*. The sense of making movements that extend far out into the space around you (p. 56) or movements continuing inside you when your 'real' body comes to rest ('inner movement' – see pp. 77-80) are simply the most obvious examples. Indeed the title *Re-Imagining Your Body* can now be seen as implying the stimulation and auto-development of the phantom body.

When I introduced the idea towards the end of Part One that there could be an 'inner body' serving as a bridge between the psychological mind and the physiological body, I also said that it might seem simplistic (p. 80). Two points need to be made here in order to dispel any lingering sense of oversimplification or naivety. Firstly, while the phantom body is very probably neurologically based, nonetheless it is also likely to be profoundly shaped by both psychological and sociological factors. No doubt it will take science a long time yet to understand this complex determination. Secondly, the normal phantom body is subtly interwoven with the real body, such that the phantom body tends to make its existence known only

---

[18] "Negative phantom limbs?"

[19] In the simple sense of 'thinking about' or visualizing. See note 16.

when something goes wrong. This is the simple reason why we are not normally aware of our phantom bodies.

Things can go wrong, of course, as we've seen already. Therefore I cannot leave this subject without at least acknowledging a significant overlap with psychoanalysis, which concerns itself with a different but related kind of 'going wrong'. It may seem that psychoanalysis is fundamentally at odds with a neurological approach, but, if so, there is no reason to suppose it must remain so in the future. Psychoanalysis is based on one powerful insight: the human being – including the human body – is enmeshed in a *world of meanings*. The body itself – or rather its correlate the phantom body – is at least partly constructed from these meanings, not solely through connections between neurons.

For the psychoanalyst Jacques Lacan, the ego is formed via the 'mirror stage' in which the infant internalizes an imaginary image of its own corporeal unity, a unity that exceeds what is actually the case at that point in the child's development. This provides the basis for an "imaginary anatomy," as Lacan called it, which is not a simple reflection of real anatomy but subject to psychological, social and cultural influence.[20] The internalized body, thus, follows different 'laws' than the organic body, at least up to a point, and this helps to explain the somatic symptoms, such as paralysis of a healthy limb, suffered by Freud's early hysterical patients.[21] Elizabeth Grosz goes further, arguing that it also helps explain historical shifts in the specific forms that hysteria takes. Such forms are historically and culturally determined, like 'fashions'. In the nineteenth century, she argues, hysterical symptoms tended to be focused on the breath and

---

[20] For the mirror stage, see Lacan's seminal essay, "The Mirror Stage as Formative of the *I* Function as Revealed in Psychoanalytic Experience". Hysterical symptoms, says Lacan in "Some Reflections on the Ego" (13), "follow the pattern of a certain imaginary anatomy which has typical forms of its own.... I would emphasize that the imaginary anatomy referred to here varies with the ideas (clear or confused) which are prevalent in a given culture. It all happens as if the body-image has an autonomous existence of its own, and by autonomous I mean here independent of objective structure."

[21] This can be seen as the other side of the coin of a point made earlier concerning 'impossible movements'. A real wrist may not be able make the 'impossible movement' that an amputee's phantom wrist can make, and the normal phantom body will accept this constraint. However where a non-amputee's phantom arm cannot move, their real arm will be paralyzed in a way that is 'impossible' to explain physiologically.

difficulties with breathing in particular. In the twentieth century, however, eating disorders such as bulimia and anorexia nervosa became the main focus.[22] Strictly speaking, it is very questionable whether such eating disorders should be classified as forms of hysteria, or 'conversion disorder' as it's often called today (because a psychological cause is converted into a somatic symptom),[23] although they tended to be seen as such in the nineteenth century. In anorexia and bulimia the 'symptom' is chosen, after all (in a way that paralysis or breathlessness are not). The broader point here, however, is that historical and cultural shifts affect the way the *meaning* of the 'imaginary body' or 'body image' is experienced, though crucially it is always experienced *as the real body*. Thus the symptoms of disorders that are related in some way to the 'imaginary body' vary with those shifts. This is not surprising given that such symptoms are really 'messages' and thus meanings themselves, although inscrutably so to the sufferer.

Hysteria and other such disorders are 'mere' neuroses, however. It is among psychotics that the strangest and most disturbing deformations of the 'phantom body' can occur (although not in this case as 'messages'). The psychoanalyst Darian Leader stresses that for the psychotic the body is not a 'given' in the way that it (mostly) is for the rest of us. He cites an example of a patient who continually needed to touch the inside of her mouth with her tongue to reassure herself that she had a body. Other patients experienced their bodies as being in pieces, in a state of disintegration. Schizophrenics can feel that their bodies, including the physical sensations they experience, do not belong to them but to someone else.[24] Thus, in psychosis, the existence, the unity, the location and the identity of the body can all be put in question.

Psychosis is delusional and a common sense view of delusions is that they exist 'in the mind' – which implies *only* in the mind, of course. Relatedly, some might maintain that I should have entitled this Appendix not 'The Body Within the Body' but 'The Body in the Mind,' and indeed in the literature on phantom limbs and related

---

[22] *Volatile Bodies*, 40

[23] I'm not sure that DSM 5's fairly recent renaming of 'conversion disorder' as 'functional neurological symptom disorder' will catch on among the wider public. But it certainly rules out anorexia! (The DSM is the *Diagnostic and Statistical Manual of Mental Disorders* published by the American Psychiatric Association.)

[24] *What is Madness?* 45

phenomena it is common enough to see the distinction made between 'the body in mind' and 'the body' (where the simple term is assumed to be enough to denote the 'real thing') or, as Brugger puts it (somewhat more satisfactorily) in the earlier quotation, 'the body in flesh'. But this is a fairly direct route back to dualism. It is far more appropriate to see the 'phantom body' (or whatever, in the end, we decide to call it) being entirely enmeshed and interwoven with the 'real body' (the real subject-body, that is), such that without the 'phantom body' the 'real body' simply could not exist.

Now we can plausibly say why *imagination* is so powerful in the exercises given in this book. It is because these exercises work *directly* on what can be called (among other possibilities) the 'imaginary body,' where that is truly an aspect of the real body.

REFERENCES

Barba, Eugenio and Nicola Savarese. *A Dictionary of Theatre Anthropology: The Secret Art of the Performer*. New York: Routledge, 2006.

Brugger, Peter. "Negative phantom limbs?" Online at **http://www.bodyinmind.org/negative-phantom-limbs/**

Callery, Dymphna. *Through the Body: A Practical Guide to Physical Theatre*. London: Nick Hern Books, 2001.

Chekhov, Michael. *To The Actor: On the Technique of Acting*. London and New York: Routledge, 2002.

Descartes, René. *Philosophical Works*, volume 2. Translated by Elizabeth S. Haldane and G.R.T. Ross. Cambridge: Cambridge University Press, 1911.

Descartes, R. "Correspondence between Descartes and Princess Elisabeth." Online at **http://www.earlymoderntexts.com/assets/pdfs/descartes1643_1.pdf**

Descartes, R. *The Philosophical Writings of Descartes*, volume II. Translated by John Cottingham, Robert Stoothoff and Dugald Murdoch. Cambridge: Cambridge University Press, 1984.

Epstein, Robert. "The Brain is Not a Computer." Online at **https://aeon.co/essays/your-brain-does-not-process-information-and-it-is-not-a-computer**

Fraleigh, Sondra and Tamah Nakamura. *Hijikata Tatsumi and Ohno Kazuo*. New York: Routledge, 2006

Garvey, James. "Hacker's Challenge." Interview with Peter Hacker. Online at **https://jamesgarveyactually.files.wordpress.com/2011/03/hackers-challenge.pdf**

Green, J. Richard. "Let's Hear it for the Fat Man: Padded Dancers and the Prehistory of Drama." In Eric Csapo and Margaret C.Miller (eds), *The Origins of Theater in Ancient Greece and Beyond: From Ritual to Drama*, 96-107. Cambridge: Cambridge University Press, 2009.

Grosz, Elisabeth. *Volatile Bodies: Towards a Corporeal Feminism*. Bloomington: Indiana University Press, 1994.

Grotowski, Jerzy. *Towards a Poor Theatre*. London: Methuen, 1975.

Gupt, Bharat. *Dramatic Concepts: Greek and Indian*. New Delhi: DK Printworld, 1994.

Hacker, P.M.S. *Human Nature: The Categorial Framework*. Oxford: Wiley-Blackwell, 2010.

Kasai, Toshiharu "A Butoh Dance Method for Psychosomatic Exploration." *Memoirs of the Hokkaido Institute of Technology*, No 27 (1999), pp. 309-316. Online at **http://www.ne.jp/asahi/butoh/itto/method/butoh-method.pdf**

Kasai, Toshiharu. "A Note on Butoh Body." *Memoir of Hokkaido Institute of Technology*, Vol. 28 (2000), pp. 353-360. Online at **http://www.ne.jp/asahi/butoh/itto/method/butoh-body.pdf**

Kuriyama, Shigehisa. *The Expressiveness of the Body and the Divergence of Greek and Chinese Medicine*. New York: Zone Books, 1999.

Lacan, Jacques. "The Mirror Stage as Formative of the *I* Function as Revealed in Psychoanalytic Experience." In *Ecrits: The First Complete Translation in English* (75-81). Translated by Bruce Fink. New York: Norton, 2006.

Lacan, Jacques. "Some Reflections on the Ego." *International Journal of Psychoanalysis* 34 (1951), 11-17. Online at **http://lacantoronto.ca/wp-content/uploads/2012/05/Some-Reflections-on-the-Ego1.pdf**

Leader, Darian. *What is Madness?* London: Hamish Hamilton, 2001.

Linklater, Kristin. *Freeing the Natural Voice: Imagery and Art in the Practice of Voice and Language*. London: Nick Hern Books, 2006.

Ma, Ke and Bernhard Hommel, "Body-ownership for actively operated non-corporeal objects." *Consciousness and Cognition* 36 (2015), 75-86. Online at **http://bernhard-hommel.eu/Body-ownership%20for%20actively%20operated%20non-corporeal%20objects.pdf**

Marshall, Lorna. *The Body Speaks: Performance and Physical Expression*. London: Bloomsbury, 2008.

Merleau-Ponty, Maurice. *The Visible and the Invisible*. Edited by Claude Lefort. Translated by Alphonso Lingis. Evanston: Northwestern University Press, 1968.

Moseley, Lorrimer. "Amputees learn a physiologically impossible movement of their phantom limb." Online at **http://www.bodyinmind.org/amputees-learn-a-physiologically-impossible-movement-of-their-phantom-limb/**

Newlove, Jean & John Dalby. *Laban For All*. London: Nick Hern Books, 2004.

Niemitz, Carsten. "The evolution of upright posture and gait – a review and a new synthesis." *Natturwissenschaften* 2010 March, 97 (3) 241-263. Online at **https://www.ncbi.nlm.nih.gov/pmc/articles/PMC2819487/**

Nietzche, Friedrich. *Thus Spoke Zarathustra*. Translated by R.J. Hollingdale. London: Penguin Books, 1974.

Noguchi, Hiroyuki. "The Idea of the Body in Japanese Culture and Its Dismantlement." *International Journal of Sport and Health* Science Vol 2 8-24, 2004. Online at **http://wwwsoc.nii.ac.jp/jspe3/index.htm**

Oida, Yoshi and Lorna Marshall. *The Invisible Actor*. London: Bloomsbury, 2002.

Ozawa-De Silva, Chikako. "Beyond the Body/Mind? Japanese Contemporary Thinkers on Alternative Sociologies of the Body." *Body & Society* 2002 8:21. Sage Publications. Online at **http://bod.sagepub.com/content/8/2/21**

Perlman, Marcus, Francine G. Patterson and Ronald H. Cohn. "The Human-Fostered Gorilla Koko Shows Breath Control in Play with Wind Instruments." *Biolinguistics* 6.3–4: 433–444 (2012). Online at **http://www.biolinguistics.eu/index.php/biolinguistics/article/view/243**

Reilly, Karen. "The moving phantom. Motor execution or motor imagery." Online at **http://www.bodyinmind.org/imagined-and-actual-movement-of-phantom-limb/**

Reps, Paul (compiler). *Zen Flesh Zen Bones: A Collection of Zen and Pre-Zen Writings*. New York: Anchor Doubleday, 1989.

Rodenburg, Patsy. *The Right to Speak: Working With the Voice*. London: Bloomsbury, 1992.

Rorty, Richard. *Philosophy and the Mirror of Nature*. Princeton: Princeton University Press, 1979.

Suzuki, Tadashi. *The Way of Acting: The Theatre Writings of Tadashi Suzuki*. Translated by J. Thomas Rimer. New York: Theatre Communications Group, 1986. (Note: this text, though important, only hints at the practical application of Suzuki's ideas. For a useful online source of elementary training in the Suzuki Method, see **https://prezi.com/edqccdhhrtnm/tadashi-suzukis-actor-training-technique/**)

Wilson, Andrew D. and Sabrina Golonska, "Embodied Cognition is not what you think it is." *Frontiers in Psychology*. 12 Feb 2013. Online at **http://journal.frontiersin.org/article/10.3389/fpsyg.2013.00058/full**

Wright, John. *Why Is That So Funny? A Practical Exploration of Physical Comedy*. London: Nick Hern Books, 2006.

Zeami. *On the Art of Nō Drama: The Major Treatises of Zeami*. Translated by J. Thomas Rimer and Yamazaki Masakazu. Princeton: Princeton University Press, 1984.

"The Immortalist: Uploading a Mind to a Computer." Online at **http://www.bbc.com/news/magazine-35786771**

INDEX OF EXERCISES